THE MIND OF THUCYDIDES

A VOLUME IN THE SERIES
Cornell Studies in Classical Philology

Edited by Frederick M. Ahl, Theodore R. Brennan, Charles F. Brittain, Kevin M. Clinton, Gail J. Fine, Michael S. Fontaine, David P. Mankin, Sturt W. Manning, Alan J. Nussbaum, Hayden N. Pelliccia, Verity J. Platt, Pietro Pucci, Hunter R. Rawlings III, Éric Rebillard, Jeffrey S. Rusten, Barry S. Strauss

A list of titles in this series is available at www.cornellpress.cornell.edu.

The Mind of Thucydides

Jacqueline de Romilly

Translated by Elizabeth Trapnell Rawlings

Edited and with an introduction by
Hunter R. Rawlings III and
Jeffrey S. Rusten

Cornell University Press
Ithaca and London

Original French edition, *Histoire et raison chez Thucydide*. Copyright ©
Les Belles Lettres, 1967.

Copyright © 2012 by Cornell University

First published 2012 by Cornell University Press
Printed in the United States of America

Library of Congress Cataloging-in-Publication Data

Romilly, Jacqueline de.
   [Histoire et raison chez Thucydide. English]
The mind of Thucydides / Jacqueline de Romilly; translated by
Elizabeth Trapnell Rawlings; edited and with an introduction
by Hunter R. Rawlings III and Jeffrey S. Rusten.
     p. cm. — (Cornell studies in classical philology)
   Includes bibliographical references and index.
   ISBN 978-0-8014-5063-1 (cloth : alk. paper)
   1. Thucydides. History of the Peloponnesian War. 2. Greece—
History—Peloponnesian War, 431–404 B.C.—Historiography.
I. Rawlings, Elizabeth. II. Rawlings, Hunter R. III. Rusten,
Jeffrey S. IV. Title. V. Series: Cornell studies in classical philology.
   DF229.T6R613   2012
   938'.05—dc23   2012019948

Cornell University Press strives to use environmentally responsible
suppliers and materials to the fullest extent possible in the publishing
of its books. Such materials include vegetable-based, low-VOC inks and
acid-free papers that are recycled, totally chlorine-free, or partly composed
of nonwood fibers. For further information, visit our website at www.
cornellpress.cornell.edu.

Cloth printing   10 9 8 7 6 5 4 3 2 1

CONTENTS

Editors' and Translator's Preface

Jacqueline de Romilly's *Histoire et raison chez Thucydide* turned the modern study of Greece's most admired historian upside down, focusing not on *what* he thought but *how* he thought, and particularly on the unique consistency and rigor with which he set forth the account of his war. This work, published to great acclaim in 1956, marked the start of a career of expounding the greatness of ancient Greek thought that took Romilly to the Sorbonne in 1957, the Collège de France in 1973, and the Académie Française in 1989.

Histoire et raison remains in print more than fifty years later, and we are certainly not the first to wonder why it has never been translated into English to make its insights available to readers of Thucydides at every level. It seemed particularly appropriate that the initiative be taken by Cornell University, where Romilly delivered the Messenger Lectures in 1967 (*Time in Greek Tragedy* [Ithaca, NY: Cornell University Press, 1968]) and was A. D. White Professor-at-Large in 1974–80. The editors and translator conceived this project together, with the enthusiastic support of Peter

Potter, editor in chief of Cornell University Press, and Charles Brittain and Hayden Pelliccia, chairs of the Classics Department at Cornell.

All three of us have worked together from the start. Elizabeth Rawlings prepared the translation of the French in consultation with Hunter Rawlings, Jeffrey Rusten added and translated the Greek and provided fuller references to ancient texts and a bibliography, and both Hunter and Jeffrey revised the translation extensively with the Hellenist reader in mind. We were pleased that Pietro Pucci and Jeannine Routier-Pucci, longtime friends of the author, could advise us on some remaining uncertainties. Cynthia King and Marian Hartman Rogers made numerous corrections to the final manuscript. Jake Nabel prepared the indexes.

We have not attempted to update the bibliography or notes, since the book's sense of discovery and its cogency seemed to us in no way dated or altered by subsequent work. Readers interested in later scholarship on any part of Thucydides are urged to consult Simon Hornblower, *A Commentary on Thucydides*, 3 vols. (New York: Oxford University Press, 1991–2009), or the systematic bibliography in Jeffrey Rusten, ed., *Thucydides*, Oxford Readings in Classical Studies (Oxford and New York: Oxford University Press, 2009). Romilly's many subsequent writings on Thucydides, building on and extending the method presented here, have been helpfully collected with a preface by Monique Trédé in *L'invention de l'histoire politique chez Thucydide* (Paris: Rue d'Ulm Presses de l'École Normale Supérieure, 2005).

Elizabeth Trapnell Rawlings
Hunter R. Rawlings III
Jeffrey S. Rusten

Editors' Introduction

Thucydides was the first prose author in the West to compose a work consciously designed for close reading. He makes this intent clear in his preface, 1.21–22, where he criticizes his predecessors for their superficial appeal to immediate listening pleasure and proclaims his own history a permanent image of reality that requires and repays active and repeated scrutiny: "It is possible that for reading, the lack of traditional stories in my narrative will seem rather unappealing; but if those who will want to study the truth of what happened and is going to happen again in similar or related form according to the human condition judge my account useful, I shall be content. For it has been composed as a permanent acquisition to be read repeatedly, rather than as a popular piece to be read just once." Jacqueline de Romilly heeded Thucydides' explicit call for close reading and first uncovered the principles of his historiographical composition. This was the contribution made by the publication in 1956 of her *Histoire et raison chez Thucydides*, a book that set Thucydidean scholarship on a new and productive path still followed today, over a half century later.

Romilly's achievement is especially striking when one considers the entrenched position of the two schools of thought then dominating Thucydidean studies. When she published *Histoire et raison,* "Die Kompositionsfrage" had absorbed German scholarship on Thucydides for over a century. In the tradition of the "higher criticism" that began with the Bible and moved to Homer in the eighteenth century, F. W. Ullrich introduced the separatist analysis of Thucydides' text in 1846, with the publication of his *Beiträge zur Erklärung des Thukydides.* From that point on, German scholars employed the analytical tools developed in biblical and Homeric criticism to deconstruct the text of Thucydides—that is, to "uncover" the different stages in which Thucydides was supposed to have composed discrete sections of his work. British scholars followed, and by the early decades of the twentieth century almost every classicist working on Thucydides had to declare whether he was a separatist or unitarian: is the work a pastiche of passages that reveals the author's changing points of view over the course of a long war, or is it a text unified by a single vision and plan?

The other major school of Thucydidean studies, centered at Oxford, was almost exclusively historical. This approach correctly saw Thucydides' *History* as the major source of eyewitness and documentary evidence for the Peloponnesian War and for Athenian political and military conduct in the second half of the fifth century B.C.E. Oxford historians made great progress in unveiling the inner workings of the Athenian Empire, partly through close investigation of Thucydides' narrative, partly through expert study of Athenian public inscriptions. Their work culminated in a major epigraphical achievement, *The Athenian Tribute Lists* (four volumes published between 1939 and 1953), and in a superb work of scholarship, *A Historical Commentary on Thucydides,* whose first volume was published in 1945. This commentary, eventually extending to three authors and five volumes, the last of which did not appear until 1981, became the principal aid for all scholars of Thucydides to consult, no matter what their interest in the historian might be. The work has numerous virtues, but, as the title suggests, it neglects the power and sophistication of Thucydides' rhetoric and, for the most part, ignores his literary artistry. As an indication of how the two dominant approaches to Thucydidean studies merged, the final volume of *A Historical Commentary* contains a sixty-page appendix titled "Strata of Composition."

Enter Madame de Romilly. In her earlier book on Thucydides (Romilly 1963, 7; originally published in 1947), she gave "Die Kompositionsfrage" a fitting epitaph: "Exhausting by the immense bibliography which it offers, completely negative in its results, the question of the composition of the work can at present be considered as the perfect example of a vain and insoluble problem." Rather than mining the text for clues to its layers of composition, or for its disclosure of historical data, she treated *The Peloponnesian War* as a work of art deserving rhetorical and aesthetic analysis, confident that a literary approach to Thucydides offered a more productive and nuanced way to study the text.

It is telling that Romilly begins the introduction to *Histoire et raison* with the words "La lecture de l'oeuvre de Thucydide revèle immediatement des particularitès de forme assez remarquables," and then proceeds to speak of the work's "exceptional art." Form and art are the subjects of this book, and like the historian himself, Romilly never strays from her focus on her subject, nor does she relax the rigor with which she examines it. This is why she is, in a sense, the first person fully to carry out the project Thucydides asked his readers to conduct, though she benefited from the findings of two other scholars in particular, J. H. Finley and Louis Bodin. In a well-argued paper entitled "The Unity of Thucydides' History," first published in 1940 (*HSCP* Suppl. 1) and later reprinted in his *Three Essays on Thucydides* (Cambridge, MA: Harvard University Press, 1967), Finley made the case that the work evinces a unified artistic conception replete with major and minor themes and a consistent literary structure. Romilly dedicated *Histoire et raison* to the memory of Bodin, her collaborator on Thucydidean studies who so inspired this book that she calls him "to some extent its author." Bodin had conceived a major analysis of Thucydides' compositional method but did not live to publish it. He left his preparatory notes to Romilly, and she warmly acknowledges her debt to his ideas and to his collegiality.

Romilly accepts that readers will benefit from Thucydides' account because they will learn permanent lessons from it. But, she argues, these lessons are implicit in Thucydides' account, not explicit. Like many other ancient Greek authors, Thucydides generally does not signal his meaning overtly but lets it emerge from clues in the text, in particular, from repeated words and phrases and from the "nearly mathematical rigor" of the relationships he draws between separate events. This is the coherence or unity Romilly identifies as the principal characteristic of Thucydides' text, the product of Thucydides' *raison*. Such implicit methods require attentive and sophisticated readers to appreciate them, and Romilly identifies precisely these qualities in the audiences of sophists and Attic drama, and particularly in readers of Pindar's intentionally complex odes and Plato's refined literary parodies. Such readers were accustomed to detecting allusions to earlier passages and to following subtle threads and larger chains of argument through a performance or a text (pp. 20–23, 49–59). It is these readers whom Thucydides addresses in 1.22.4 when he refers to "those who will want to study the truth of what happened," and when he calls his work "a permanent acquisition to be read repeatedly."

Romilly demonstrates that "Thucydides' War" proceeds according to a commanding logic that reflects its author's total control over the stuff of history, from his rigid principles of selection to his contrived juxtapositions, from his artificially opposed speeches to the systematic relationships he draws between plans and outcomes, from his insistence on the constant battle between intellect and chance to the meaning that he imposes on even the smallest event. Thucydides' mind found (or created) unity and coherence everywhere in history: this is the *raison* that Romilly nowhere defines but associates with the reasoning mind, with logic, with argument, with dialectic: the Greek term for all of these concepts is *logos*, that all-encompassing word that constitutes the crucial instrument of the fifth-century enlightenment of which Thucydides is an outstanding exemplar. Romilly's great achievement is to have proven that Thucydides imposed this reasoning intellect on the history of his time and thereby discovered the governing principles of human motivation, which, as he says, will continue to drive human action "as long as the nature of mankind remains the same."

Romilly's first chapter shows that even the apparently most factual of battle narratives, the seemingly simple chapters describing the arrival of Gylippus in Syracuse and his thwarting of the nearly complete Athenian encircling walls, is shaped with consummate control in three ways. The first is Thucydides' extreme selectivity of detail (p. 15):

> Thucydides starts with the disorder of raw facts . . . revealing different points of view. One might say that he covers this disorder with a screen; this screen blocks out everything that he considers extraneous, so that the only visible elements are those that have an internal relationship to each other: at

this point, like a message where all the letters that are not important are hidden, the whole becomes readable, acquires meaning.

The second is his constant repetition of the concepts selected for emphasis, for which Romilly uses the metaphor of the "guiding thread" that leads the reader through the labyrinth of detail. The third, especially active in these battle accounts, is his interruption of the narrative at points calculated to demarcate units with a specific meaning that can be juxtaposed to other such meaningful units (p. 32): "The effects of each are related. They are not related for those involved, but for the readers."

The next chapter moves from the simplest battle narratives to the most complex ones and first brought to scholarly attention as a masterpiece of Thucydidean composition the successive sea battles narrated in book 2. The first battle is controlled by tactical experience and knowledge of local conditions, factors set forth in advance and constantly foregrounded by the narrator. But the next battle takes these factors as already played out and introduces new controlling factors: the number of troops and ships on each side, and the morale of each side based on the previous outcome and the changed numbers. These two factors are analyzed in opposite ways in paired speeches by each of the commanders in advance of the battle. But one more factor is held back, namely chance and the way different combatants react to its intervention. Other complex battle descriptions play out similarly, most of all the great battle in the harbor at Syracuse, where Thucydides, along with great selectivity in framing the issues he has reasoned out, employs masses of detail to express the pathos of the final catastrophe.

Chapter 3 uses the opposed speeches to investigate the instruments of Thucydidean thought, which Romilly identifies as the logical reasoning and dialectical argument invented by Protagoras and developed by Gorgias, Antiphon, and other Greek thinkers. Particularly compelling is her demonstration of how many Thucydidean speakers are adept at taking the premises of their opponents, without any alteration of their factual basis, and giving them a different perspective to "invert" them to support the opposite view. She identifies further the uniquely Thucydidean tendency to reduce traditional factors like "courage" to quantifiable abstract elements that can be presented as quasi-arithmetical terms and manipulated for different results. Thucydides extends these logical and rhetorical methods to the domain of history, whose "truth" he discovered in recurrent patterns lurking beneath the surface of events.

Chapter 4 sets the keystone on Romilly's argument by considering the opening chapters of the so-called Archaeology, since here the historian she has shown controlling the narrative to "let the facts speak for themselves" audaciously undertakes "history without facts," an argument about a largely unknowable Greek past based entirely on reasoning from resistant evidence and conceptual frameworks derived from the present. It amounts to a "rationalist manifesto" such as was never attempted again in ancient historiography but pioneered innovative methodologies that are still in use today (and, Romilly points out, are implicitly used even by those who seek to disprove Thucydides' actual deductions).

Like Thucydides himself, Romilly is patient but relentless in tracing step by step the inevitability of the techniques she has discerned and the results they produce. One of her favorite words is "rigor," and the thinker she sets before us is nothing if not austere and disciplined. But she does not press the results too far (as have some subsequent interpreters): not only does she not say, but she expressly denies, that Thucydides' techniques manipulate or alter the truth, or that he is a writer of fiction rather than history. "Actions and words are the material of tragedy, but also of scientific observation. And the subtlety of literary means may, as a result, be used in the service of truth" (p. 47).

Most especially, she resists the romantic temptation to construct an intellectual biography of her subject, or the enthusiastic reader's compulsion to make grand pronouncements on Thucydides' political or moral views; this is not a book about *what* Thucydides thinks, but about *how* he thinks, and the techniques with which he communicates his views to his readers, and the resulting effect on the latter.

The success of Romilly's analysis became clear in the decades following the publication of *Histoire et raison*: a spate of books and articles emulated her approach, employed her methods, and furthered her findings, while separatist arguments about the composition of the text waned, and historians began to recognize that Thucydides' account must be used not as a repository of data, but as a singular interpretation of what one man saw. The following are just a few of the scholars who, although they differ greatly in their conclusions, implicitly accept Thucydides' powerful control of his narrative, and the call of Romilly's pathbreaking book for a close and painstaking reading of his text: H.-P. Stahl, *Thukydides: Die Stellung des Menschens im geschichtlichen Prozess* (1966); V. Hunter, *Thucydides the Artful Reporter* (1973); C. Schneider, *Information und Absicht bei Thukydides* (1974); L. Edmunds, *Chance and Intelligence in Thucydides* (1975); H. Rawlings, *The Structure of Thucydides' History* (1981); W. R. Connor, *Thucydides* (1987); T. Rood, *Thucydides: Narrative and Explanation* (1998). N. Loraux also wrote a series of penetrating articles that continue in one way or another Romilly's style of close interpretation of Thucydides' text.

Author's Dedication

This book is dedicated to the memory of Louis Bodin, though such a tribute is inadequate for the substantial debt of gratitude I owe him. Louis Bodin is, in no small part, the book's author.

Throughout his life, Bodin studied the composition of Thucydides' work, revealed its distinctive qualities, analyzed the structure of each episode, accumulated notes and outlines. The work that he had planned to write, and that would have been his doctoral thesis, was never finished; ideas for it were indicated in detailed studies produced for conferences or various articles; his preliminary notes were left to me. Thus the collaboration we had begun for a book on Thucydides continued after his death. His earlier discoveries have confirmed for me certain conclusions and stimulated new research; the questions he asked were questions I was asking myself. I am no longer able to distinguish his experience from my own: much of what I find in his notes had already struck me as well; much of what I discovered later also appeared in his notes.

In any case, it is true that the distinctive details that form the basis of this study and inspired these reflections are, in most cases, ones he noted. Yet I have not presumed to attribute to him in any way authorship of the whole: I was reluctant to make him responsible for an undertaking whose stated principle he could not know and about which he might have had reservations. Yet it is important to make clear that for me his efforts furnished numerous elements and these are, without doubt, among the very best.

Jacqueline de Romilly

THE MIND OF THUCYDIDES

INTRODUCTION

Readers of Thucydides' work are immediately struck by several exceptional stylistic qualities. Not only in the interlaced formulations and dense brevity of the speeches, but in the narrative itself, in its austere rigidity and its theoretical brilliance, there are clear indications of a remarkable artistry. It is to the elucidation of this singular style and artistry that I would like to make a contribution in the present work.

And yet in fact my concern is not solely a matter of style and expression. Expression is only a sign, and its originality reveals something more personal: it forms the author's investment in his narrative, indicating his way of thinking about the facts, the aspects he wants to expose there, the personal form he means to give them. To attempt to define the characteristics that the exposition takes in Thucydides is thus to inquire how, starting with a variety of facts derived from his research, he manages to develop the highly coherent and personalized discourse that is his narrative, and the formal characteristics of the work ultimately define even his relationship to history. In a time when history in general finds itself to be the object of extraordinary attention, such a study may thus take on added interest. Following on the many works treating history itself, history as human endeavor, or the knowledge that can be gained from it and its limits, an analysis of the procedures actually used by a historian like Thucydides might be presented, in some manner, as both a theoretical model and its application.

The example provided by Thucydides is indeed exceptional. This is not simply because it involves one of the first historians worthy of the name, nor because he is one of the greatest; it is, rather, that through the characteristics mentioned above readers are made acutely aware of the active and creative role of the historian in developing the history.

Naturally, the historian is expected to be self-effacing, to stand apart and be "objective." Yet in practice, what will that mean? Certainly it will mean that he is scrupulous in research and honest in setting forth factual information. It will also mean that in writing the account he will refrain from offering, in the form of commentary, personal opinions. But will all these virtuous efforts suffice to ensure objectivity? That would be too simplistic.

The historian is constantly making choices. Defining the field, limiting the scope, doing the research—all of these require selectivity. Furthermore, from the data collected, necessarily an incomplete selection, and from the documents seen and retained, also a limited selection, he must make further choices. After first establishing the sequence of events, once he writes a sentence linking two events, he is introducing an interpretation. We could entertain ourselves in this way by describing, in an apparently objective fashion, an event chosen at random—for example, the fall of a government—by recounting the facts exactly, in the exact order in which they occurred, but applying a bias to emphasize one explanation of events or another; one series will set forth the negligence of a minister, another the economic difficulties, a third foreign involvements, a fourth some ideological development, and so forth. The historian is like a photographer, from whom perfect rigor is demanded but who is asked to photograph an object that is a thousand times wider than the field of his lens and that is constantly shifting. In such a case, it becomes essential to seek out the most characteristic aspects and then, after snapping the picture, to make from them a careful montage. According to which criteria? Surely here again one will demand that the historian prove both honest and scrupulous. Yet once again he will have to make choices. And even if one concedes from the outset a scope of interest that is always more or less a function of the times in which he lives, even within that scope he still has to apply all the qualities of his mind, choosing and organizing according to his own thought process. To return to the point, his work is, by necessity, creative.

It is precisely in this that Thucydides' history is so original and why it provides an exceptional example.

This history brings together, from the point of view of objectivity, unusually favorable conditions. Thucydides is relating contemporary events, minute details of which were readily available to him; and as it happens, he researched these with a care and an impartiality that are universally acknowledged. He chose a limited subject—the history of a war—enabling him to do exhaustive research. In addition, in the presentation of the history, he so assiduously sought objectivity that he shunned almost all personal analysis, consistently allowing his characters uncompromising severity in speech and action. This objectivity is not surprising when we remember that, while he had himself been involved in the events he is reporting, he refers to himself in the third person, without explanation or commentary of any kind, doing what amounts to the opposite of Xenophon's practice. As for his interpretation, his montage (to return to the example of the photographer), it is so difficult to see in it the reflection of either personal taste or *a priori* ideas that different critics have reproached him for favoring one side or else the other, judging him as too severe or too indulgent.

And yet this history, which offers such lofty assurances and strives so impressively for perfect scholarly objectivity, is actually one in which the author's intervention is most profound. Everything in it is the product of his construction and his will. Every word and phrase, every silence and remark, serves to present a meaning made distinctive and imposed by him.

He has made it distinctive with his lucidity and clairvoyance; nothing has been his guide save his own intellect, nothing his criterion except his own reasoning. Ultimately, he has chosen, constructed, and revised the history. While he removed himself from the work as an individual, he did so in order to assert his role as interpreter and creator. No history could give more respect to the documentation, and yet no history could be further from a simple series of documents. In short, he achieved that paradox of putting the strictest objectivity in the service of a creation that was completely personal.

Indeed, this is what gives his work that expressive force that never fails to impress readers; this is why the procedures that enabled Thucydides to achieve it should themselves be closely analyzed. But at the same time, to the extent that these procedures imply an original approach—audaciously systematic and yet unassailable—they suggest the multiplicity of solutions the historian may adopt, and in particular the difficulty of the problem confronting him once he undertakes the work of a creator.

In this respect, the more precise the study of the procedures, even the more technical, the more convincing it will be and the more lasting. The originality is seen only upon close examination. Obviously, all historians must organize their research data and intervene through a series of choices and constructions in order to make their accounts clear. The manner of intervention, in itself, may be instructive. The strong fusion in Thucydides' work of what is strictly speaking narration with interpretation demands even more minute examination.

This is the reason it will be necessary, in each of the following studies, to consider quite detailed examples and why they are analyzed not only in their structure but word by word. Obviously I do not claim to have explored all the problems presented by the text, or to have considered all aspects of each passage, nor resolved all the difficulties—far from it. Nor can I claim to have dealt with the methodology of the entire work: the task to which L. Bodin committed himself has not been realized here. In any case I have tried, by selecting certain characteristic episodes, to expose the most obvious qualities, and thus to delineate, little by little, the most remarkable aspects of the methodology Thucydides adopted. Moreover, whenever possible, I have tried to place these procedures in the context of the movement of the thought of his contemporaries, to see how Thucydides distinguished himself from his predecessors in order to develop methods similar to our own, and also to see how faithful he remained to ancient customs, enduring or temporary, which today we find confusing precisely because they correspond to something in the classical Greek heritage that has been lost or abandoned.

Such a project obviously involves difficulties of presentation. Passages studied too closely are apt to become tiresome; on the other hand, comparative studies can seem discursive. In particular, there is a risk of repetition in the conclusions from one example to the next. In an attempt to overcome these obstacles to some extent, these analyses have been organized according to a logical sequence. Taking advantage of the fact that this study was never intended to be exhaustive, in characterizing Thucydides' methodology I have deliberately tried to adhere to four successive aspects of it able to offer close-ups of its movement and to mark the stages, as it were, as increasingly the power of his intelligence becomes more visibly active.

Because the task is to determine the scope of Thucydides' personal intervention and interpretation in the development of his account, it seems necessary to begin with the simplest examples. Hence, we consider first how he comes to grips with the historian's problem in its most ordinary form, and examine a part of the work that seems one of the most objective, by isolating a purely narrative episode, which includes no speeches or analysis but describes a brief series of military operations that are certainly important in their consequences, but strictly limited in time and space. The example chosen is that of the Athenians' attempt to blockade Syracuse. Even in a passage of this type it seems to be possible to identify a whole series of choices, intentions, very subtle means intended to pack the account with meaning, to conceive, organize, and transform it into intelligible discourse.

This taste for reasoned analysis, combined with the taste for external objectivity, would lead Thucydides to unfold before readers the reasoning process of his characters also. This is why the speeches in Thucydides' work play so essential a role and one that is so easy to grasp. Indeed, it is on them that the whole interpretative system that appears in different episodes depends. Superimposed on the plan of intelligence, they are the perfect place for analysis; the connection established between the speeches and the narrative therefore constitutes the framework of the account. In order to study this principle it is necessary, once again, to start with simple and clearly defined examples. So I have avoided a consideration of a causal relationship (often at long distances) between the political speeches and the action that they foresee and prepare. Instead I have chosen for this purpose the case of the military speech and have studied the role that it plays in the account, considering it within the context of battle accounts generally. The originality that Thucydides shows in the material, and what distinguishes these accounts from those of all his predecessors, lie squarely in the role that preliminary analysis plays, that it should be put into indirect discourse, or better, into a speech, or better yet, into two antithetical speeches, whose opposing processes of reasoning are placed in confrontation.

Yet if this is the direction in which Thucydides' narrative is moving, it seems natural to study next the procedures of this confrontation in a pure state, in other words to follow the dialectical plan into which Thucydides leads his readers when, prefatory to some action, whether political or military, he offers a system of antithetical speeches. In the dryness of their tone these speeches respond to each other, exchange their arguments and words, with a precision that betrays technical learning. To a great extent this fashion is traceable to the customary style of his time; but Thucydides' use of the method is so pronounced, so subtle, so precise, that it attests, more than any other quality, the effort he made in the service of reasoning.

So starting with this presumed "object," which, in its most extreme form, would amount to exhaustive yet inorganic documentation, we observe it being penetrated ever more deeply and more freely by rational interpretation. We progress from facts reconsidered to facts subjected to analysis to pure analysis. Thus it would seem that this dialectic would establish a sort of limit and conclusion of the method and consequently provide its content at the conclusion of our studies.

The role of rational interpretation can, however, be taken even further; this is the case when a historian does not settle for simply organizing, by means of rational interpretation, the data that he knows from eyewitnesses to be accurate and clear, but rather calls on reason to furnish the data themselves. Owing to the nature of his subject and to the features of his method, such an occurrence within Thucydides' work can only be an exception. It does, however, occur. And while unique, it is nonetheless typical. For when Thucydides prefaces his work with an account showing how, in his view, the evolution of Greece should be represented, from earliest times up to the Peloponnesian War, he can be seen deliberately to take up a poorly understood history, about which there was almost no valid, firsthand documentation. That he was able to do so is solely based on his confidence in reasoning. He could do it only because reasoning seemed to him competent not only to organize the factual data, but also to bring them to life and to supply, even in their absence, both the fabric and the very substance of history. And just as he organized the results of his research with more force and intellect than anyone else, he devoted himself to this different task with a keen consciousness of the intellectual innovations it implied and which he possessed in more abundance than anyone else.

Such an undertaking is found only in Thucydides; since this ultimate triumph of reasoning was entirely committed to confronting the problems of history, it attained its limit: reason can go no further without corrupting history. But this limit is exactly what could have been predicted from the tendency itself of the rest of the work; and this exception is exactly the one that best proves the rule.

In any case, obviously such a distinction and such a difference in intensity, established in this way between various points of view where the intervention of reasoning betrays itself, correspond only to a purely theoretical classification and are justified only by the convenience of the analysis. In the development of the work there are no stages of progression; the constructive intellect exercises total and absolute control over the historical data throughout. The way in which it is notable varies only according to circumstances. In this respect, the four studies that follow are not linked in a simple sequence: rather, they all lead to a common conclusion, each one a confirmation of the other.[1]

---

1. A few of these analyses first appeared in talks or as earlier essays. In particular the subject of the first analysis was the theme of a talk given at Cambridge in August 1951 at the Triennial Congress of the Federation of English Associations of Classical Studies; and the fourth, on the Archaeology, incorporates in detail remarks from my *thèse secondaire*; in addition, their conclusions have been outlined in various talks in Paris, Copenhagen, and Ghent.

1

Narrative Methods

Most striking to readers of Thucydides' work are the speeches and their content. Speeches represent the element of the history that most clearly differentiates it from the norms of modern practice and that, in its reasoning as well as in its implicit freedom, makes it most suited to personal analysis. Yet, despite the conspicuous presence of these speeches and their density, the entire interpretative function is not exclusive to them, nor is the rest of the account, by contrast, a simple reproduction of facts. The fact that there are few sweeping statements does not suggest that historical reconstruction is less real or less personal. There is no such thing as simple reproduction of the facts, and least of all in Thucydides' work, and so it seems most appropriate to begin the study of narrative methods by considering an account in which there are no speeches.

For this purpose, one could select any chapter in the work. The best example, however, would involve an episode to which Thucydides gives a great deal of attention, such as the set of chapters that describe, without speeches but still with great force, the Athenian attempt to invest Syracuse with a circle of walls and the failure that ensued following the arrival in Syracuse of the Lacedaemonian Gylippus (6.96–7.9).

If there were other accounts written by contemporary historians, it would be instructive to compare them with Thucydides' reporting, but, since these events have been recorded only by historians for whom Thucydides is the principal source, the usefulness of such comparisons is quite limited. What is clear, however, is that this episode, so fraught with consequence, merited the author's full attention. The narrative that he makes of them may therefore show such distinctive characteristics as to provide all by itself a particularly clear and complete idea of his methodology. In this case, it can show how Thucydides selects and expresses certain facts that he wishes to retain, as well as how he organizes his narrative of them, in one particular order in preference to any other.

Unity

Choice of Elements and Guiding Threads

From the same series of facts, known from a single source, two different historians will obviously select different elements.

According to Plutarch, Euripides says that the Athenians won eight victories between the time of their arrival in Sicily and their first defeats, a number that Plutarch considers too low (*Life of Nicias* 17). On the basis of Thucydides' account, it is difficult, if not impossible, to reconstruct what these eight victories could have been. We might recognize some of them (five, probably) within the group of chapters considered here. But the very difficulty of identifying them shows that Thucydides, less concerned with extolling the merits of the troops than with clarifying the chain of actions, did not think he had to single them out as events. They are, for him, contained and nested in the unifying element of the text, namely in the attempt to surround Syracuse with fortifications and its failure.

Will Athens succeed? Will its fortifications manage in time to isolate Syracuse? This is the sole question that is asked and that dominates the whole account. An Athenian victory depends entirely on the possibility of undertaking and achieving the construction of a wall; a Syracusan victory becomes simply a matter of delaying or preventing it. And this opposition gives to the text a corresponding continuity and unity and allows readers to follow step by step, in detail, the narrative progression, the unfolding of a single enterprise, a single project.

The passage opens with the Athenian landing in the region of Syracuse. The Syracusans had wanted to defend the plateau at Epipolae in order to make it difficult for the Athenians to surround them, even if they won the battle. In fact, however, the Athenians took Epipolae as soon as they landed, and constructed their first fort: the effort to surround the city, the primary concern of these two opposing sides, has begun.

Thucydides describes all the work that followed and refers to its progress in detail. It begins with the construction of the circular wall (6.98.2: ἐτείχισαν τὸν κύκλον, "They walled the circle"), they proceed first, building the northern wall (6.99.1: ἐτείχιζον . . . τὸ πρὸς βορέαν τοῦ κύκλου τεῖχος, "They walled the northern wall of the circle"), then beginning the southern wall (6.101.1: ἀπὸ τοῦ κύκλου ἐτείχιζον οἱ Ἀθηναῖοι τὸν κρημνὸν τὸν ὑπὲρ τοῦ ἕλους, "From the circle the Athenians started to wall the cliff above the swamp"), then completing it (6.103.1: ἀπὸ τῶν Ἐπιπολῶν καὶ τοῦ κρημνώδους ἀρξάμενοι ἀπετείχιζον μέχρι τῆς θαλάσσης . . . , "Beginning from Epipolae and the sheer area they started to wall up to the sea . . .").

Corresponding to each of these moves is the Syracusan defensive effort to construct transverse walls. First comes the countermove of 6.100.1 (ὑποτείχισμα, "cross-wall"), undertaken beneath the Athenian encircling wall.[1] This is a response to the Athenian construction of the north wall; it leads to a military intervention by the Athenians and the subsequent demolition of the construction (6.100. 3: τήν . . . ὑποτείχισιν καθεῖλον, "They destroyed the cross-wall"). The second wall, a response to the first southern fortifications, is undertaken further south, across the swamp (6.101.3). This one consists of a ditch and a palisade. The Syracusans then despair of ever preventing investment (6.102.4).

At this point, the Athenians have almost succeeded; references to the various constructions are sufficient evidence. This is what gives the interruption that follows its dramatic force: the Lacedaemonian Gylippus, who was sailing to the aid of Syracuse, hears about the status of the fortification

---

1. On the exact interpretation of these indications, see the topographical appendix to Thucydides books 6 and 7 in Romilly et al. 1953–72, 78–79.

(7.1.1) and moves quickly; he soon reaches Epipolae. When does he arrive? In case we were not paying close attention to the progress of the work so clearly indicated by Thucydides, he specifies the exact state of the works: "His arrival happened to coincide with the critical moment (7.2.4: ἔτυχε δὲ κατὰ τοῦτο τοῦ καιροῦ ἐλθὼν . . .) when the Athenians had completed, with the exception of a small portion next to the sea that they were still working on, a double wall to the Great Harbor; as for the remainder of the wall, above the circle wall and extending to the sea by way of Trogilus, stones had been brought in for the greater part of the distance; some sections had been left half-built, others were entirely completed. The danger to Syracuse had indeed been great." In this passage both the precise technical summary and then the comment, which does not lack emphasis, are remarkable; just as each separate detail is linked to the progress of the siege walls, the reversal itself is portrayed in terms of that progress. Only the intensity is greater to the extent that this progress will be more altered by it.

What can Gylippus actually do? Under his direction, the Syracusans, while attacking a weak point in the south wall, begin to build on a plateau, to the north, a new transverse wall (7.4.1): just in time, he manages to intercept the Athenian wall (7.6.4). The Syracusans accomplish their goal; even in the event of an Athenian victory, the investment of Syracuse is now impossible.

All of these chapters, by returning to a single problem and to the struggle between two opposing aims, are ultimately presented as a minidrama, entirely coherent, in which a perfect unity of action prevails. This outcome will appear all the more remarkable when one considers that even such authors as Plutarch and Diodorus, who followed Thucydides and found his material fully organized, are still not able to preserve this clarity because they had other interests. Plutarch in particular, wishing to show the worthiness of his hero Nicias, claims that one of his exploits was to have "surrounded Syracuse with fortifications"; it is only later that he says he "almost entirely" succeeded, and it is not until help has arrived that he indicates what the situation actually was. Neither brevity nor the effort to concern himself with Nicias alone can purport to explain this, since we find details in Plutarch that are not in Thucydides and that have nothing to do with Nicias.[2] Instead, the truth is that Thucydides, by relating everything

---

2. As in the single combat between Callicratus and Lamachus (Plutarch, *Life of Nicias* 18.3) or the initial mockery of Gylippus by the Athenians (*Nicias* 19.4).

to a single idea, wished to clarify a particular sequence of events, whereas Plutarch was driven by a different concern.

One might suppose that if Thucydides chooses to center everything around the story of the siege in this way, it is because the siege itself interests him. As a historian of war, of strategy itself, he would naturally bring to military details the interest of a technician, and the pages that concern us would transmit, in a more precise manner, his sense of siegecraft. Such an interpretation should be dismissed. Evidence against this view is readily furnished by the account itself. No technical detail is given, neither the nature nor the exact placement of the various constructions is provided, and the operations are so incompletely described that we even find, several chapters later (7.43.4), three camps that had never been mentioned.

Consequently, while all the events are related only as a function of the progress of the siege, this is not because the siege is of interest to Thucydides in itself; it is because the siege creates the unity and order of these events.

Some combatants are fighting, others are at sea; some are good tacticians, others fight bravely, or are zealous on behalf of their allies. But paramount to their individual intentions and isolated motives is a general motive in view of which, ultimately, every action is accomplished: one side wishes to invest, and the other to prevent the investment. And Thucydides focuses on that matter alone. He pays no attention to the detail of motives, of actions, of circumstances; what interests him is the ultimate goal that embraces everything. And, if everything in the account holds together, it is because everything is linked to this ultimate goal.

But this very characteristic involves another one. Thucydides chooses to link his entire account to the broadest intention (γνώμη) because it gives unity to this whole group of events. In this case, of course, that tendency could not be limited to this set of chapters alone; it permeates a larger group as well, and the intention (γνώμη), which creates the unity, is only the expression of another, even larger unity.

One example is provided by the Syracusan idea of setting a union of Sicilian forces against the Athenians. The Syracusan Hermocrates mentions the notion of hegemony at the beginning of book 4 (4.59–65). In book 6 Nicias worries about it (6.21.1), Alcibiades discusses the possibility (6.17.4), and both Hermocrates and Athenagoras predict it (6.33.4–5, 6.37.2). Additionally, Hermocrates at Camarina speaks of the urgency of hegemony

(6.77.1), while the Athenian Euphemus attempts to alarm his audience by referring to the threat of it (6.85.3). It is obvious Thucydides is taking great care to frame the episode under study here by two references connecting it fully to the theme. Before the arrival of Gylippus, in fact, it is Nicias who receives the Sicilian forces: a contingent meets the Athenians in 6.98.1 at the moment when the Athenians have just set foot on Epipolae. Just prior to Gylippus's arrival, in the midst of the Athenian success, Thucydides again signals the arrival of new reinforcements (6.103.2). But Gylippus himself arrives with Sicilian troops (7.1.3–5), and soon, having halted the investment, he leaves Syracuse to recruit new troops elsewhere in Sicily (7.7.2). Then the Syracusan idea begins to take shape. And Nicias's letter emphasizes this circumstance, repeating as many as four times that Gylippus has raised troops, is raising them, and will raise more (7.11.2, 7.12.1, 7.15.1, 7.15.2). The episode's conclusion is thus revealed through this idea. It is the same through all of book 7; each battle throughout the book is framed between the arrival of the Sicilian reinforcements and the departure of Gylippus, who leaves in search of new alliances. Each departure (7.7.2, 7.25.9, 7.46.1) and each return (7.21.1, 7.32–33, 7.50.1)—in other words, any movement in the coalition of forces—is stated with precision. So precisely, in fact, that we track the progress of this plan just as we tracked the progress of the investment in the episode involving Gylippus. And as in that episode, just before the reversal, which is here the arrival of Demosthenes, Thucydides makes his point on this subject (7.33.2: "Indeed almost the whole of Sicily, except the Agrigentines, who were neutral, ceased merely watching events as it had previously done, and now actively joined Syracuse against the Athenians"). Thucydides places Demosthenes' arrival in the context of the coalition of forces just as he had placed Gylippus's arrival in the context of the progress of walls. Only this time, Demosthenes' arrival does not change the face of things, for new reinforcements will not stop arriving until the end (7.50.1). Thus the notion of Sicilian unity constitutes a new intention (γνώμη), a new guiding thread, one more far-reaching but with a similar effect. Like the effort to invest Syracuse, a Sicilian coalition is a unifying element, and for this very reason Thucydides will trace its progress.

One could, in books 6 and 7, find many other such examples. If the incident involving Gylippus is situated along the path leading to Sicilian unification, it is situated on another path as well, this one no less obvious, one that leads to Spartan intervention and consequently to the waging of a double war against Athens, in Sicily and in Greece. This is not the place to consider all the steps by which this result was gradually attained;[3] however, it may be of interest to point out that, even in the episode involving Gylippus, Thucydides is careful, simply by remaining silent, to put aside all adventitious details that would cloud the picture and cause one to lose sight of the guiding thread. Specifically, Thucydides says simply "Gylippus the Lacedaemonian" (6.104.1), without further introduction of the person, without even giving his father's name;[4] this discretion[5] makes clearer the relationship between these events and Alcibiades' speech advising the Lacedaemonians to send to Sicily "a Spartiate as commanding officer" (6.91.4). Yet a historian driven by other concerns might have drawn some lesson from the identity of this Spartiate.[6] Thucydides prefers a clear theme to richness of detail.

Alongside these two ideas, both relating to the intervention of the states in the conflict, there are others one might trace. Militarily, for example, Thucydides neglects anything episodic or anecdotal (for example, the single combat between Lamachus and Callicratus) but is attentive to the tactical intention. Thus it is that battles conducted in the same theater can be linked together; here too we see Gylippus personally drawing a lesson from his first defeat and adapting to the circumstances of the battle. Everything follows. The technique is perfected, corrected. Even the series of battles later fought in the harbor of Syracuse also seems to be the realization of a similar adaptation; their particularities are left aside, but the common strategy that directs them is made very clear.[7]

The same episode may sometimes be situated in relation to different ideas, of more or less general applicability. Ultimately, they all lead to the

---

3. I have had occasion to analyze in this respect the structure of the two books in the "Notice" to Romilly et al. 1953–72, books 6–7, pp. xii–xxv; I have already had to repeat too often ideas contained there and hope to be excused, where statements of fact are concerned, from repeating information that can be found elsewhere.

4. The name appears at 6.93.2 but without any detail or explanation of the naming.

5. This point was addressed in Bodin 1939.

6. Beloch (1914, 202) mentions very early the role played by Gylippus's father at Thurii (this role is taken from what Thucydides says in the passage when, at 6.104.2, Gylippus claims the "right of citizenship previously enjoyed by his father"; the anecdotal details are found only in other works: Diodorus 12.106; Polyaenus 2.10).

7. See the next chapter, pp. 87–95.

conflict pitting Athenian imperialism against its enemies. If Thucydides has highlighted so starkly, throughout the work, the nature of this imperialism, it is because his thought process leads him to recognize in every event the features that relate any one event to the greatest possible number of other events. Inclined to the broadest possible unity, he also inclines to the deepest possible interpretation. Moreover, it is remarkable to notice that this tendency leads him to consider ever larger series of events, to go deeper into the past in order better to explain the present. He goes back at first to the Persian Wars—in the Pentekontaetia—and then to the very origins of Greece—in the Archaeology:[8] in thrall to his desire for unity, Thucydides is barely able to stay within the confines dictated by his subject.

This unity that gradually ties events together is never directly expressed; there is seemingly no interpretation added to the strict reporting of facts. It is the historian's selectivity that creates the unity: the facts he relates are only those that bear witness to it. Thucydides starts with the disorder of raw facts, or more exactly—because it is difficult to involve such a dubious notion of objectivity—the disorder that might appear when the historian is confronted with a variety of linkages, all of them partial ones, revealing different points of view. One might say that he covers this disorder with a screen; this screen blocks out everything that he considers extraneous, so that the only visible elements are those that have an internal relationship to each other: at this point, like a message where all the letters that are not important are hidden, the whole becomes readable, acquires meaning.

A different historian might have imposed a different screen and allowed us to read a different meaning in the facts. But in doing so, he would have been borrowing Thucydides' method, one that consists of retaining only what is most continuous, and allowing that continuity alone to evoke connections the readers will then be able to perceive.

Verbal Correspondences

The style makes these connections still more apparent. If the consistent principle of showing connections and linkages might seem to betray above

---

8. The latter is not intended solely to clarify the exceptional importance of the Peloponnesian War; it furnishes a general interpretation of Greek history; see. chapter 4.

all the intervention of reasoning, the formal method itself that Thucydides uses in this intervention is his own.

He is not content with noting a summary relationship between events, attaching them, for the most part, to a common idea; he is careful, in the very choice of words and phrases, to give to these relationships an almost mathematical rigor. Similar elements assume a similar form; the conclusions match the plans. Whatever succeeds or fails, repeated or changed, stands out self-evidently without needing to be expressed.

What Syracuse wanted to do first of all was to make it impossible for the Athenians to invest even if they won (6.96.1: οὐκ ἂν ῥᾳδίως σφᾶς, οὐδ' εἰ κρατοῖντο μάχῃ, ἀποτειχισθῆναι, "that even if they [the Athenians] won in a battle they [the Syracusans] would not easily be walled-off"), and the conclusion of this episode corresponds textually with this vow (7.6.4: ἀπεστερηκέναι, εἰ καὶ κρατοῖεν, μὴ ἂν ἔτι σφᾶς ἀποτειχίσαι, "[so that] they had deprived them of ever walling them off in future, even if they won in a battle"). Clearly, Thucydides was not striving for a precise identity that would have needlessly robbed his work of its natural character. It suffices for him to use the same two words, κρατεῖν and ἀποτειχίζειν, in the same connection, to make the rigor of the correspondence felt, without making his intrusion in any way presumptuous.

One might say that these two words and their relationship are an indispensable element of thought, as much at their introduction as at the conclusion. When we observe the development that separates that introduction from that conclusion, we notice that such a reencounter is not at all unusual.

In this account, as I have said, the construction of two walls by the Athenians, one in the north and the other in the south, is the key element. In cases where the systematic nature of the effort might escape attention, Thucydides expresses the two attempts in very similar terms. The consequence of the first Athenian victory is the first construction (6.99.1): "The next day the Athenians began building the wall to the north of the circle." Where did they build it exactly? "Along the shortest line for their wall to go from the great harbor to the sea on the other side" (6.99.1: ᾗπερ βραχύτατον ἐγίγνετο αὐτοῖς . . . τὸ ἀποτείχισμα). Similarly, the second victory led to the construction of the second wall (6.101.1): "The next day the Athenians from the circle proceeded to fortify . . .". And where did they build? "The heights above the marsh which on this side of Epipolae looks toward the great harbor, and where the shortest line was for their wall as they went down across the flats and the marsh to the harbor" (6.101.1: ἧπερ αὐτοῖς βραχύτατον ἐγίγνετο . . . τὸ περιτείχισμα). The Syracusan attempts were no less similar in nature. During the construction of the wall to the north, they "accordingly sallied forth and began to build, starting from their city" (6.99.3: ἐτείχιζον οὖν ἐξελθόντες ἀπὸ τῆς σφετέρας πόλεως ἀρξάμενοι). During the construction of the southern wall, they did the same thing (6.101.2: ἐξελθόντες καὶ αὐτοὶ ἀπεσταύρουν αὖθις ἀρξάμενοι ἀπὸ τῆς πόλεως, "Sallying forth they too began to fence it off, starting from the city").

Naturally the facts are similar, and, once Thucydides commits to following the details, he could hardly have expressed himself very differently. It is obvious, however, that, without exaggeration or artifice, he was able to give this repetition a particularly striking precision. The very permanence of intentions, on both sides, acquires a more systematic character, just as the presentation of facts acquires the appearance of necessity. Thucydides could, for example, very well have described the geographical location of the Athenian construction; the information would have been more precise, but the continuity of the enterprise would have been less clearly traced. He could also have expressed more quickly the Syracusan reaction. Gustave Glotz's *Histoire grecque* (1931, 693), obviously drawing on Thucydides' account, speaks of the circumvallation generally as of two counterapproaches, without distinguishing between the north and south walls, thus removing from the mechanics of the events the rigor they have in Thucydides' account.

This rigor also reveals, with the help of the formal similarities, the role played by the differences; the very difficulty the Syracusans have in lining up for battle (6.98.3: ὡς ἑώρων . . . καὶ οὐ ῥαδίως ξυντασσόμενον, "when they saw . . . it was not staying in formation readily"; 7.3.3: ὁρῶν. . . οὐ ῥαδίως ξυντασσομένους, "seeing . . . they were not staying in formation readily") leads the Syracusan leaders to retire but leads Gylippus to change his station.[9]

---

9. Similarly, at the end of book 7, the ill will of the Athenian and Syracusan soldiers was the same (7.72.4: οὐκ ἤθελον, "They were unwilling"; 7.73.2: οὐ δοκεῖν ἂν ῥαδίως ἐθελῆσαι, "They thought they would not be readily willing"), which underlines the efficacy of the ruse adopted by Hermocrates.

From this report we could say that each fact, each idea, acquires a definite, even definitive, quality, the features of which we recognize even when they are separated by several pages.

In fact, this process is no more limited to the immediate context than are the connecting threads Thucydides is tracking. The same words are used throughout all the books and the entire work to characterize the same concepts; they draw attention to the linkages among the relevant passages.

Thus, in the episode that concerns us, the arrival of Gylippus has the effect of reaffirming Syracusan morale (7.2.2: ἐπερρώσθησαν, "They were reinvigorated"). The same word, or other forms of the same word, ῥώμη ("vigor"), stress, from one end of book 7 to the other, the development of this "morale." This, when the episode concludes, has been greatly strengthened (7.7.4: πολὺ <u>ἐπέρρωντο, "They were very invigorated"</u>) among the Syracusans; and the same effect occurs among the Corinthians when they learn of it (7.17.3: πολλῷ μᾶλλον ἐπέρρωντο, "They were much more invigorated") and especially among the Lacedaemonians (7.18.2: μάλιστα δὲ τοῖς Λακεδαιμονίοις ἐγεγένητό τις ῥώμη, "The Lacedaemonians had especially acquired a sort of vigor"). When Demosthenes arrived, it was the Athenians' turn to be encouraged (7.42.2: ῥώμη τις ἐγεγένητο, "They acquired a sort of vigor"). But, as his arrival itself changed nothing, the Syracusans were comforted (7.46: πάλιν αὖ ἀναρρωσθέντες, "They were reinvigorated once again in turn"). This time the affair was decisive, and Thucydides falls back on the rare word ἀναρρώννυμι, one he uses nowhere else. It is curious, in any case, that the series is presented so completely and that no compound of the word θάρσος, for example, intrudes to break the homogeneity. If we add to this fact that the first of these compounds is presented, before this episode, in order to mark the renewed confidence that Alcibiades' advice gives the Lacedaemonians (6.93.1: πολλῷ μᾶλλον ἐπερρώσθησαν, "They were much more invigorated"), we must conclude that this homogeneity is meaningful. To a great extent it renders sensible the progression leading, step by step, to the Athenian collapse, and also to the reversal that could, during that progression, momentarily cast doubt on the outcome.

Moreover, this last example also shows that the parallelisms in expression do not simply mark the unity of guiding threads, and that they can be applied to something besides the principal ideas; the improved Syracusan morale is not one of the major themes of the book. In each case, however, morale marks the importance of the progress made. In this case, the parallelism reveals the common result of two different events. It no longer marks one theme, but a junction in the historical account.

As a result a vast field is opened for the subtlety of the author. The verbal comparisons may not suggest important words or important ideas, but they always establish connections, they unify. They bring together grammatical phrases of any kind, marking parallelisms and suggesting interpretations.

Thus right after the episode described, we find the same δὲ καὶ. . . ὅπως ("and also . . . in order that . . .") moving from offensive to defensive efforts, as much on the Athenian side as on the Peloponnesian (7.17.2 = 7.18.1). The parallelism brings out the mechanism by which these two intentions (γνῶμαι) match perfectly.

Similarly, for the Peloponnesians, the effort concludes with the occupation of Decelea. Thucydides does not shy away at this point from a word of commentary, writing that "it greatly harmed the Athenians . . . and first and foremost ruined their situation" (7.27.3: πολλὰ ἔβλαπτε τοὺς Ἀθηναίους, καὶ ἐν τοῖς πρῶτον . . . ἐκάκωσε τὰ πράγματα). This formulation, containing an unusual phrase (ἐν τοῖς πρῶτον), oddly echoes another very similar one that Thucydides uses in commenting on the taking of Plemmyrion by Gylippus, which "first and foremost ruined the Athenian army" (7.24.3: ἐν τοῖς πρῶτον ἐκάκωσε). The sending of Gylippus was as troublesome for the expeditionary force as the occupation of Decelea was for the situation of Attica. The similarity of the commentaries makes readers aware that the two realizations of Alcibiades' advice were closely related;[10] and these two blows were of the utmost importance, tracking the progress of the disaster every bit as much as the rise in the enemy's "morale." The effect is all the more remarkable in that we are no longer dealing with terms necessitated by the context. The affiliation exists only in the mind of Thucydides. While it is perhaps not deliberate, it is his doing; and so, despite contenting himself with conveying the bare facts directly, it becomes in a sense still more personal.

In any case, from adjacent elements of a simple account to widely separated junctions of a very complex one, one may say that Thucydides' work is completely filled with echoes, reminders, and correspondences.

---

10. The connection was noted and commented on by Louis Bodin (1939, 89).

J.H. Finley Jr. revealed these connections in his effort to establish the unity of the work from the point of view of its genesis.[11] He was determined to follow several of the guiding threads that lead through all the work, and was successful in exposing many subtle relationships. He described the "recurrent and interwoven complex of ideas," the "progressive, interrelated statements," affirming that "the unity of the work is revealed not only in the coherence of its analyses but in the more subtle coherence of style and manner." He wrote: "One might almost say that there is practically no page that does not contain a phrase suggesting, in form or content, another phrase found elsewhere." This quality, which to his mind, implies a temporal affiliation, would seem to me rather to be the result of a methodology—one that tends to seek unity above all, and to make it known through increasingly distant verbal similarities.[12] The characteristics noted at the outset of this analysis show well that Thucydides never, to any extent or at any point, considers relating a fact without proceeding in this way.

The Technique of Verbal Correspondences in Greece

One could certainly accept the idea that somehow this process happened without his full knowledge. Such may, no doubt, frequently be the case. It is in his mind that the affiliations between facts are established; it is therefore natural that he would give expression to ideas closely related to these relationships, and, given the rigor of his style, we should not be surprised to find that he expressed in similar form whatever he considered to be closely related. In this case, he may have perceived the unity as he showed it to his readers, but he may have been no more aware of the verbal similitude than are the readers. In fact, it was necessary to wait for the analyses of Louis Bodin or J. H. Finley to become alert to these curious connections, combinations, and repetitions.

If this interpretation is true—and to a great extent it certainly is—then one must consider these details as involuntary. Thus they are all the more

---

11. Finley 1940. The quotes are taken from pp. 267 and 284 (=pp. 132 and 153 of the 1967 reprint).

12. While Thucydides' development led him not to contradict himself but to refine and strengthen his thoughts, he was able to use that method without writing everything at once, but simply by keeping in mind what he had written previously. The most tightly composed works are not always those that are so composed at a single time.

characteristic of Thucydides' thinking. In fact, when the unity of thought is so strong that the expressions themselves are stamped with the same mark, when the framework of the work is so rigorously present in the mind of the author that the words order themselves involuntarily in systems and mark their junctions with the same trait, it is a clear sign that no one ever thought more of detail as a function of the whole, and of a whole almost mathematical in its precision, than he.

But given the extreme to which this tendency is stretched, one might also imagine that there is, at least in certain cases, a deliberate and intentional method.

The Greeks were subtle. Greeks loved to employ learned techniques with an eye to a particular effect. The proportions of the Parthenon show us that they were capable of making unequal something that was meant to appear to be equal. If we can believe M. J. Bousquet (1952), they were even capable of wanting to introduce intellectual innovations from mathematical research into architecture. In the literary domain, the teaching of the sophists implies that they were equally aware of the means at their disposal. And it should be added that the very process of comparisons and correspondences would find them to be alert and discerning listeners—without which literary parodies, sometimes created from a single or a few words, would not have achieved the success that the works of Aristophanes and Plato imply.

One might go even further: when we consider Greek authors who, for one reason or another, refrained from expressing directly the totality of their thought,[13] we can see that repetition and verbal correspondences are precisely the characteristics of their method.

It is this observation that has been at the root of a recent renewal of interest in Pindar, among others. G. Norwood explains the odes by attributing a symbolic meaning to them; this meaning is brought out in particular by verbal connections, or repeated imagery. The symbol in the first *Pythian* is the lyre, sung from the beginning; the notion of harmony returns in the σύμφωνος ἡσυχία ("concordant calm") in line 70, as in the evocation of the barbarians' ἀλαλατὸς ("battle yell") immediately afterward; and the darkness of Phalaris is finally recognized as ending with something with which his name was not associated . . . the lyre! This is not the place to enter

---

13. See below, pp. 49–59.

into the detail of these interpretations, at times a bit bold, but often seductive; it suffices to show that, even in the details, the verbal correspondences provide the key to understanding. *Pythian* 2, for example, first recounts the myth of Ixion, who, punished for his love for Hera, was duped by Zeus and raped a cloud mirage; and, at the end, the ode contains the eulogy of Rhadamanthys. Norwood writes: "A parallelism of phrasing that cannot be accidental links the passages that describe Ixion's delusion and the delusion escaped by Rhadamanthys; in each there occur words that are not perfectly natural but are suited to recall the other description."[14] According to Norwood, if the cloud that Zeus offers Ixion is called a "lie" (ψεῦδος), it is due to the comparison with the case of Rhadamanthys, who is apt to detect calumnies; inversely, Rhadamanthys's scorn for trickery is rendered by the verb οὐ τέρπεται, which instead is a reminder of Ixion's love for the cloud. In fact, besides this type of exchange, there exists a rather nice parallelism in the words: one finds on one side the "hands of Zeus," and on the other "the hands of man, peddler of lies" (40 and 75: παλάμαι). And contrasted to the ἄϊδρις ἀνήρ ("unknowing man") who is Ixion (37), to his μαινομέναις φρασίν ("maddened mind," 26), is the wisdom of Rhadamanthys, who φρενῶν ἔλαχε καρπὸν ἀμώμητον ("was allotted the blameless fruit of mind," 73–74). One might add that on one side is the ruse (δόλον) of Zeus; on the other the deceitful (δόλιον) citizen. To the beautiful phantom that Ixion caresses (40: καλὸν πῆμα, beautiful bane") is the response of the monkey that he is "beautiful to children" (71–72: καλός τοι πίθων παρὰ παισίν, αἰεί καλός, "Beautiful is the monkey among children, always beautiful"). This is, then, the echo between the words that furnishes the key to the meaning.[15]

The same echo conspicuously reappears, though for a different effect, in Plato; and with what subtle irony the repetitions there accent each step of a demonstration! Most familiar is the example of *Gorgias*.

---

14. Norwood 1945, 190.

15. In the same ode I believe that the obscure advice given to Hieron in line 72 (γένοι', οἷος ἐσσὶ μαθών, "Learn what sort you are, and become that") may similarly be explained by the contrast between that μαθών and the ἔμαθε δὲ σαφές ("he learned clearly") of line 25, relative to the lesson that Ixion learns at their expense: Hieron has only to be himself faithful to the lesson (whether, depending on the interpretation one accepts, that is the lesson of Pindar or of life or of self-knowledge).

There Socrates contrasts, using the same words, the supreme judgment where he intends to triumph, and the earthly judgment where Callicles hopes to prevail; thus he uses against Callicles all the arguments that were used against himself: "I blame you for being incapable of defending yourself when your turn in this trial comes; you will be speechless and confused"; "You will be exposed and see yourself totally defeated, insulted."[16] Furthermore, Socrates seems to recall the very words Callicles used to condemn moral concepts: "Everything else," he had said, "all those phantasms that rely on human conventions contrary to nature, they are nothing but foolishness and vanity" (οὐδενὸς ἄξια, 492c). The last sentence of the *Gorgias* is a short, very simple statement; it concerns Callicles' ideas, which Socrates challenges him to abandon: "for they, Callicles, are vanity" (ἔστι γὰρ οὐδενὸς ἄξιος, ὦ Καλλίκλεις 527e7). Put with the others, the connection hardly appears to be an accident; it marks with perfidious humor the reversal of positions. But as such it also gives us proof of something more,[17] and attests to the subtlety with which, for different purposes, Greeks in the classical period enjoyed using verbal comparisons that are not at all obvious to us in order to bring out similarities and to mark the closest articulations of an analysis.

It is therefore not surprising that Thucydides should use this process to mark connections between facts. It is all the more consistent in the work because the effort to show linkages between facts seems to be Thucydides' primary preoccupation. When the action itself, through repetition, conveys the unity of intention, he reports it in similar terms. When there is no repetition, as in the case of the taking of Plemmyrium and the occupation of Decelea, a casual detail in phrasing, a similarity of the effect produced by the wording, helps one follow the guiding thread. Always, the unity is preserved, and strongly expressed.

Intelligibility and Generality

The penchant for unity is clearly what gives Thucydides' account the quality of intelligibility. The moment Thucydides identifies an intention, one common to different actions, and methodically picks out anything that

---

16. 526e–527a = 486b–c: all the meaningful words are the same from one passage to the next.
17. Tragedy also felt the effects of this genre; see pp. 53–54 below.

could be an indication of the sequence of its success or failure, that intention on the one hand provides sufficient explanation of the action, and on the other the reason for success or failure is isolated and made somehow readable. The simple chronological juxtaposition then establishes a coherent and comprehensible sequence.

Thucydides makes the sequence clearer still by emphasizing unity. The sequence becomes even more obvious through the resolute removal of everything that does not relate to it directly, in other words any particular, extra, or concrete detail.

We have seen how Plutarch, in a few pages, managed to give details omitted by Thucydides, something Plutarch does consistently. Consider the many proper names, the many individuals, one can extract from Plutarch and Diodorus! Thucydides was unwilling to burden his account with this; he was relentless about removing all unnecessary details.[18]

Of course there are some concrete details in the work; they are, however, almost always[19] intended either to explain directly a technical procedure or some aspects of a situation,[20] or, alternatively, to give a fuller picture of an incident.[21] In the latter case, color, scenery, or pathos serves to better draw our attention to the elements deemed important and thus to help us discern, indirectly, the author's analysis.[22]

As a result, the narrative, by returning to its essential themes, becomes not only clearer but even more rigorous.

Since Thucydides eliminates the peripheral and random and retains only what helps to advance the action, and since conversely when he takes up an action he neglects not a single detail, it seems that his account is

---

18. An example of this occurs in the account of the third battle in the harbor at Syracuse: Diodorus (13.13) provides the proper names of six leaders of different wings on both sides; he specifies that Eurymedon lost seven ships and that it was Sicanus who tried to burn the Athenian ships.

19. Perhaps it would be best to separate certain geographical notes (e.g., 2.80, on the Chaonians) in which the wish to correct errors or omissions seems to stand out. See. Finley 1942, 108; and Pearson 1939. Yet I think that, overall, examples for which there is no other justification are extremely rare (in particular, 2.96–97, on the Odrysians, is justified not only by personal experience, but by the importance of Sitalces himself and the attempted expedition).

20. On their role in the battle accounts, see below, pp. 95–102.

21. See below, p. 30.

22. G. F. Abbott (1925, 202) believes that in the account of the Sicilian expedition there are two exceptions to the author's usual restraint: the departure of the fleet and the account of the last battle; obviously, the two exceptions correspond to the two decisive moments, not only of the expedition, but of the war itself.

constructed as a demonstration. The conditions he has retained are, in terms of the outcome, both necessary and sufficient. One cannot remove or change anything. Moreover, the coherence that the narrative assumes—from premise to conclusion—takes on an appearance of necessity.

In addition, from the fact that these conclusions are linked to the simplest premises, and to the most complex circumstances, it would seem that one is tending toward a sort of inherent verisimilitude, more or less apparent depending on the cases.

The tendency in Thucydides to consider each situation in terms of what is most general and to explain it in reference to other cases is indicated in the current passage in a modest, but characteristic, way. When Nicias based his actions on the small number of ships accompanying Gylippus, Thucydides adds, as a note of explanation: "just as had happened to the Thurians" (6.104.3: ὅπερ καὶ οἱ Θούριοι ἔπαθον). Now, another explanatory comment of this type appears already in the preceding chapter. In that case, however, he moved from a simple repetition to a rule of probability: the discussions took place in Syracuse "as was natural when people are confused (οἷα δὲ εἰκὸς ἀνθρώπων ἀπορούντων) and more closely besieged than ever before" (6.103.4). This reference to what is normal, human, and probable is the explanation to which history always returns. It is expressed directly in a certain number of parentheses, bearing on the habitual or regular behavior of men, as in the gnomic statements of the speeches; but it always underlies the narratives as well as the speeches. The linkages that his history extracts are the least subject to chance.

The same is true for the "intentions" that the history brings to light, as these take on a life of their own, independent of individual cases.

Clearly, they first appeared to us as representing true intentions shaping the events. And it follows from this that history is, in some measure, psychological. Perfectly suited to the political and military realms that are the subject of this work—a subject that involves action, events, motivations of the antagonists, and that does not require a deep inquiry into economic, social, demographic conditions—Thucydides' method primarily reveals motives and reflections; events are shown initially as the individuals involved might have seen them.

But Thucydides does not, cannot, confine himself to this level; even in the episode given here as an example, we can see that the notion of "intention" gradually changes meaning.

Clearly in the case of completing the wall surrounding Syracuse, we may speak of intention and attribute that intention to an individual. But it was already clear that this individual counts little in the whole affair; neither Nicias nor Lamachus plays any part in it; as for the personality of the enemy Gylippus, Thucydides studiously avoids mentioning him. The intentions are strictly those of the Athenians, or those of the enemies of Athens.

Even these are seen from a distance. When the question concerns uniting the cities of Sicily against Athens, everyone, in both Athens and Syracuse, argues about the possibility: Alcibiades as well as Hermocrates, Athenagoras as well as Nicias. The effort is not a personal one, and the psychology and spirit of the people are no more mentioned than are those of the individuals. Once Syracuse has decided to resist the Athenians, and once Sparta has decided to help, they must, logically, act in a certain way. Led as the Athenians were to new conquests, Athens' blindness is read in the facts more clearly than the Athenians themselves can see; the relationship between the taking of Plemmyrium and the occupation of Decelea is felt by readers more clearly, obviously, than it is by the parties involved. To the extent that it grew and deepened, the intention (γνώμη) that gives unity to the events takes on a more general significance. It ceases to be an intention and becomes the principle behind a series of acts; it ceases to refer to a psychology, of any type, and constructs, beyond the actors and their motivations, deep connections between the facts. The extreme clairvoyance of the speakers that Thucydides puts on stage can surely be explained, to a large extent, by a stylistic invention, by virtue of which he attributes to these speakers, in advance, the clear awareness of all the possibilities that, often, he had to discover alone during the uncertain course of events.

The individual being thus disappears into a system that transcends him and brings together conditions, factors, forces, and makes room for each; the explanation not only seeks to clarify τί βουλόμενος ("with what in view") an individual acts, but πῶς εἰκός ("as a result of what normal sequence of events") he is led to act in such a way and to experience some success.

Therefore the sense of plausibility and rigor that the work presents is explained, doubly, by the bias for unity that animates it from beginning to end. This bias gives to specific sequences an unfailing mechanical rigor. Moreover, it allows us to discover, beneath individual acts, the existence of trends, motives, and sequences that are increasingly profound and widespread. Their plausibility appears more and more abstract, and more independent of circumstance and of individuals; these sequences seem all the more likely to repeat themselves as they are increasingly reduced to what is essential.

Of course, the event described is a particular one, but its significance tends to become general. Similarly, a line might depict a mathematical formula, have a universal value, and be necessary in all its points, without ever ceasing to be a given design, or even to define the shape of a given object. Thucydides proceeds to do the opposite: he sketches an object and reduces it to its essence so well that his draft seems more like a blueprint; Thibaudet (1990) has expressed this repeatedly.

This important truth is both truth and clarity: it is what Thucydides calls τὸ σαφές.[23]

"Clarity" here is the fruit of an active and discerning intellect. Yet Cardinal de Retz also treated historical facts in an intelligent way; Tacitus as well. Thucydides' way was entirely different; for him it was less one of intelligence than one of reasoning.

Arrangement

Rigorous Chronological Order and Division

Facts, chosen and expressed in a particular way, organize themselves, and a description of their chronological development should suffice to reveal their meaning. This is precisely what Thucydides does. Yet if we look at the arrangement adopted in the episode we have chosen as an example, we quickly notice that things are not, and cannot be, quite so simple: Thucydides' role in this domain is felt no less keenly than in the other, and no less subtly.

Naturally, there are cases in the account when we find a simple chronological sequence. In such cases, Thucydides relates events without additional commentary.

---

23. On the mental process that this expression implies, see Weidauer 1954, 50–52.

Nevertheless, when the junction between one event and the next occurs in the mind of the actors and translates their group intention, there are times when this junction needs to be specified. Then we find a sort of normal balancing of the domains of fact and of judgment, the domains to which causes and results belong. If the connection is causal, it is expressed by a form of subordination such as "considering that . . . , thinking that . . . , seeing that . . .";[24] if it expresses purpose, the subordinate element becomes "with the desire to . . . , in order to . . .";[25] often the two are joined, and it is as though the fact is bracketed by judgment: the individual then, "learning that . . . , does this or that, in order to . . .".[26]

This type of sentence, so characteristic of Thucydides' style, clearly shows how facts, once clarified by selection, can be used in a completely systematic exposition, in which everything is ordered to reproduce a dialogue between two intentions in mutual opposition.[27]

The rigor of this dialogue is pushed so far that many phrases, going even further with this method, incorporate, in the statement about the goals pursued, another statement about causes that the other side will have thought about (or vice versa); thus there is a subordinate clause of the type "in order that the other, thinking that . . .".[28]

In any form, whether implied or expressed, simple or complex, the psychological connections are always apparent. And, as these generally express the contrast between two objectives, it is not unusual, in addition to balancing all these phrases taken separately, in which thought and act are shown to alternate, for there to be a further, and weightier, balancing of the two camps: "the Athenians on one side . . . , the Syracusans on

---

24. Thus, in the first chapters of the episode: 6.96.1 (ὡς ἐπύθοντο, "when they learned"; νομίσαντες, "having considered"); 6.98.3 (ὡς ἑώρων, "when they saw"); 6.100.1 (ἐπειδὴ . . . ἐδόκει, "since they thought"; φοβούμενοι μή, "fearing that"); 6.101.5 (δείσαντες δέ, "and fearing"); 6.101.6 (ἰδὼν δέ, "and seeing"); 6.102.1 (ὡς ἑώρων, "when they saw"); 6.102.2 (ὡς ἔγνω, "since he knew"); 6.102.4 (ὁρῶντες, "seeing"; νομίσαντες, "having considered"); 6.104.3 (πυθόμενος, "having learned").

25. Thus, in the first chapters of the episode: 6.96.1 (ὅπως μή); 6.96.3 (ὅπως); 6.97.5 (ὅπως); 6.101.2 (ὅπως μή).

26. Thus 6.96.1, 6.97.5.

27. The continuity that is elicited may even serve as a link between two episodes: Thucydides moves from the events at Corcyra to those at Potidaea by making a connection in the minds of the Athenians (1.56.2: "The Athenians, guessing their [the Corinthians'] hostility . . ."); the specific reasons and the situation at Potidaea do not appear until later.

28. See 1.52.3; 2.90.2; 3.22.8, etc.

the other." The episode under consideration provides many such examples:[29] they correspond even to the dueling walls and counterwalls. In the work, the same is true of all the passages recounting a battle fought at close range: the siege of Plataea, in two pages of the Oxford edition, changes subject six times, regularly passing from the Plataeans to the Peloponnesians and back again. Thucydides' history is an example of antilogy at work.

To be sure, this method, consisting of following the development, respectively and reciprocally, of the objectives of individuals may, in cases of this type, seem quite natural; but it appears that Thucydides has pushed it to an exceptional degree, preferring these rigorously alternating sequences to all other structural forms.

Even in the episode of Gylippus, it is quite clear that the action of the Athenians on one side and of the Syracusans on the other can be grouped together more than Thucydides does (the résumé of the episode given at the start of this chapter suggests as much).[30] But we should add that Thucydides remains faithful to this method in circumstances where its benefit is less obvious. Two such categories can be cited: cases of information that is timeless, and cases of parallel actions. The Gylippus incident allows us to judge in each case.

By timeless information, we mean general facts—for example, geographical facts. Faced with the task of describing the siege of Syracuse, most historians would no doubt hesitate between two possibilities: either give this information, briefly, at the beginning of the account, or assume it to be known. Thucydides does neither. The name Epipolae appears for the first time in 6.75.1, with no clarification; then, in 6.96.2, in order to explain the thinking of the Syracusans and their desire to protect access to the plateau, Thucydides enters into a detailed description: "Indeed, the rest of the plateau is precipitous at this point and forms a cliff . . .": thus geography is inserted by way of this "indeed," and based on a rationale. It becomes part of a psychological sequence, to further strengthen the unity of action. Yet no matter how many specific details later historians would have loved to know, the fact remains: if the details had no role in explaining a decision, they could be skipped.[31]

---

29. See 6.96.3–97.1, 6.99.1–2, 6.101.1–2, 6.101.2–3, 6.101.4–6.

30. See p. 10 above.

31. Just as we regret that those involved never thought about the possibilities of access to Euryelus, or about the size of the Lysimeleia marsh! For the rest, the same principle applies to repetitions, as well as to the introduction of certain characters twice.

The second case arises when Thucydides must follow an action that takes place on several fields at once. Here the solution he adopts seems, at first, to operate on the opposing principle. One might expect to see Thucydides, faithful to the unity of psychology, follow one of the two γνῶμαι as far as possible, even if that means going back in time later in order to follow the other one. He does the opposite. And it is obvious that, even when the two actions have no effect on each other, he never tries to conclude the account of one before taking up the next; he knits the two together, with a tight chronological correspondence. The incident under consideration may provide both the proof and the explanation, thus helping to resolve any apparent contradiction.

In this episode it might seem that the most natural way to proceed was to set forth the events at Syracuse, including the battles, the effort to surround the city and all the defensive works, right up to the arrival of Gylippus, or until the moment when Syracuse received news of his imminent arrival; then, having reached this turning point, the account would go back in time to explain the arrival by reporting Gylippus's trip itself. This is the method chosen by the classical historian Diodorus (13.7.6), as well as by the modern Beloch.[32] Thucydides rejects such a layout. Even before the episode, he has described the preparations for Gylippus's departure (6.93.2–3). Then, in the episode itself, after having taken his account of the works to an almost successful completion, he interrupts himself to tell his readers about the voyage of Gylippus (6.104.1: "Yet Gylippus . . ."). Gylippus, at this time, is not thinking about saving Syracuse: he does not even believe that is possible, since he believes the city to be entirely surrounded. Will he learn the truth in time? We see him delayed, caught in a storm. For readers who, thanks to the preceding account, know very well the importance of the passage of time, the significance and meaning of each of these delays are quite clear; they require readers to assess the circumstances on which the result depends. On this occasion, when everything rests on chance, Thucydides, for once, gives all the concrete details; the historian who loves generalities provides multiple details: "Caught opposite the Terinaean Gulf by the consistently heavy wind that blows out of the north in that area,[33] he

---

32. Beloch 1914, 364: "Da im letzten Augenblick kam der bedrängten Stadt Rettung. Schon während des Winters . . .". (Beloch even goes as far back as the request for help.)

33. Even in these concrete circumstances, Thucydides was fond of bringing up the foreseeable laws and conditions.

was carried out to sea. Then another, very violent storm, drove him back to Tarentum. There, hauling out of the water the ships that had been most damaged by the sea, he set about repairing them." These details keep the readers knowledgeable about the situation at Syracuse in suspense; they make them impatient with worry; they provide some adventure to the story; given after the result, they would have been meaningless.

Thus, despite appearances, the principle is the same in the two cases: Thucydides insists always on showing, with great chronological clarity, action as it is happening. He provides only such information as the action demands, just where it is needed; inversely, however, he does not fail to restore all the elements, in the order necessary, in such a way that readers see nothing incongruous about the combination. As a historian of war he is not tracing the carrying out of an intention (γνώμη), but rather the conflict between two of them. Between Gylippus's departure, Nicias's progress, Gylippus's progress, Nicias's inaction, Gylippus's arrival, the readers' attention is sought on two fronts, but by a single action; and only the passage from one front to the other can account for the result in a way that is both dramatic and exhaustive. Thanks to this, Thucydides exposes connections in the action that escape the actors themselves—as in a play, newly arrived characters are ignorant of the action in the preceding scene; this action, known to the audience, explains the character's future fate.

The text is full of examples testifying to the fact that efforts like these were both systematic and intentional for Thucydides.

Book 7, for example, contains another case in which the problem consisted of knowing if reinforcements were going to arrive in time.[34] Yet this time the situation is reversed: the Athenian expeditionary force is waiting for reinforcements under the leadership of Demosthenes. Things happened just as they had for the arrival of Gylippus. Here too the natural way of proceeding would have been to put together as a whole the story of Demosthenes' trip; nothing prevented that, not even Thucydides' usual composition, since the trip took place, with all its various corresponding events, in the space of a single season, from April to July. Once Demosthenes arrived at Syracuse, the account could have gone back to relate the different battles that had happened in the meantime in the harbor. This

---

34. The word φθάνειν ("anticipate"), framing the account of the trip, is used in 7.25.9 and 7.36.1 exactly as it had been used in the episode of Gylippus (6.97.2 and 6.99.2; 7.1.2 and 7.6.4).

is the method adopted by J.H. Finley, for example, in his summary of Thucydides' account.[35] One might also, in a similar fashion, have followed all the events at Syracuse up to Demosthenes' arrival, and then gone back to relate the voyage. This is roughly what Diodorus did. Nothing is less natural than chopping up events, the voyage, the season, into a whole series of interrelated episodes, as Thucydides does. In his narrative, Demosthenes' voyage is interrupted by four passages, three of which concern the situation in Sicily.[36] Why all these interruptions? The events on the two fronts certainly have no reciprocal effects; and Thucydides could have, without harming in any way either of the two actions, followed each, respectively, from beginning to end. And yet the effects of each are related. They are not related for those involved, but for the readers. For them, the clear knowledge of all the conditions is a useful element, one that allows them to gauge the urgency of the situation, the hazards and the risks. They follow the progress, independently, of each of the two forces whose confrontation will be decisive. And no aspect of the reality is arbitrarily sacrificed to the other, with one explanation being made anticlimactic after the outcome is known.

No less remarkable is the example shown at the beginning of the Sicilian expedition itself. The expedition, after having been debated in Athens, put to sea in 6.32; Thucydides then transports readers to Syracuse, where one continues to doubt the Athenians' ability to sustain such a project; after that, we return to the progress of the expedition (6.42), but not without quickly encountering a new interruption, devoted to the progress in the preparations being made by Syracuse (6.45). Obviously Thucydides could have saved his analysis of the Syracusans' intentions. But would that have had the same impact? Hermocrates' bold plan and Athenagoras's doubt bring out valuable information about Athenian imprudence; they serve to more accurately assess the risks; they relate to the specific situation created

---

35. Finley 1942, 238: "By the time that Demosthenes reached Syracuse with his reinforcements in the early summer of 413, Nicias had already met two more defeats."

36. The transitions he uses are characteristic of this balance. We return to Demosthenes in the following phrases: 7.25.9–26.1: καὶ οἱ μὲν ἐν τῇ Σικελίᾳ ταῦτα ἔπρασσον. ὁ δὲ Δημοσθένης . . . , "This is what those in Sicily did on the one hand, but Demosthenes . . ."; 7.33.3: καὶ οἱ μὲν Συρακόσιοι . . . ὁ δὲ Δημοσθένης, "And the Syracusans on the one hand . . . but Demosthenes . . ."; 7.35.1: καὶ ἡ μὲν ναυμαχία οὕτως ἐτελεύτα, ὁ δὲ Δημοσθένης . . . , "And that is how the sea battle ended, but Demosthenes . . ."; 7.42.1: καὶ οἱ μὲν . . . ἐν τούτῳ δὲ Δημοσθένης . . . , "They on the one hand . . . but meanwhile Demosthenes . . .".

by early reports, which were surpassed as quickly as they could be confirmed; the information contained in the reports was valuable only at the time when the speeches were given. Moreover, by exposing this aspect of conditions at this particular point in the account, Thucydides gives everything that follows greater dramatic force, as when poets present tragic irony on the stage: even the actors are unaware that their confidence has taken on a menacing quality.

There are numerous such examples. The beginning of the Peloponnesian War would demonstrate the impact of passive resistance, a plan imposed by Pericles that thwarted the Peloponnesians' expectations. The connection is based on a story that passed from Sparta (2.10–12, 18–20) to Athens (2.13–18, 21–23), according to the same practices as elsewhere. A. W. Gomme, in his very fine book *The Greek Attitude to Poetry and History* (1954), has brought out the same subtlety in Thucydides' way of blending, in book 4, Brasidas's progress in Thrace and the Athenians' plans in Boeotia: Gomme has shown, by means of this astute comparison, Athens' blindness, when the Athenians should have been concerned with defending Amphipolis. In order to explain this, Gomme resorts to a concrete interpretation, supposing that Thucydides reports the facts in the same order in which the Athenians actually learned of them. This explanation is worthwhile only if the psychological aspects are removed; in fact, Thucydides reports the facts in the order the Athenians could or should have received them, just as he reports all facts, that is, in the same strict order in which they might come to a perfectly informed judge, so that contrasting or interfering information may become apparent.[37]

So it is not enough to say that Thucydides composed his history according to seasons, grouping within each season everything that concerned each theater of operations: whenever a single action occurs in several theaters, and also whenever a connection is made between actions happening here and there, Thucydides carves up and fragments the account, to whatever extent necessary for the different forces at play to have a specific place of their own, and for the different relationships to have their full impact.

---

37. Gomme 1954, 134–37. All the analyses given in that chapter are completely consistent with my remarks. The reservation expressed below has already been indicated in my review of this work, Romilly 1955.

Thus the segmentation has, in all these varied cases, the effect of giving the factual account even greater significance.

We may ask ourselves if the same is true of the seasonal segmentation that Thucydides uses throughout. This split seems more rigid and more external, and it is often perplexing. Dionysus of Halicarnassus may have been the first to be bothered by it,[38] but he was not the last. Even J. H. Finley, without actually complaining about it, sees in it a side of Thucydides' mind "which was concerned not with judgment but with fact alone."[39] In fact, quite often the seasonal split interrupts an account in a somewhat artificial manner, and Thucydides hardly seems to have tried to remedy it. It seems he could not, without risking some confusion and obscurity, follow the tactics of the siege of Plataea, spread out over three years, and then go back in time. But he could perhaps have grouped more tightly the events relative to Mytilene that were, in the history, interrupted on several occasions (3.7, 3.19–25, 3.26, 3.29–36);[40] he certainly could not cut the account of the Acarnanian campaign by the brief references in 3.103–4, nor the account of Pylos by the two short chapters on Sicily (4.24–25).[41] These criticisms would seem to call for different responses.

First, the cases where the break is not justified are extremely rare: almost everywhere, we quickly notice that the complexity of the facts almost demands such an arrangement.[42] Consequently, the exceptions also need less justification; for, if the principle of a split composition is explained, as a general rule, by the desire to follow the network of acts that are interdependent, then it was legitimate for Thucydides to remain faithful to this principle throughout his work: he had to be consistent in respecting the strict framework he created. Lastly, to the extent that these breaks come to segment the action into a series of episodes, they lead us to consider events from a different angle, and to recognize in the arrangement Thucydides adopts a supplemental organization. This organization quite deliberately

---

38. *On Thucydides* 9; see Gomme 1954.

39. Finley 1942, 108.

40. Yet for the most part these interruptions are fully justified by the very complexity of the facts; the Mytileneans demanded action from the Lacedaemonians in Attica (3.15) and counted on it (3.18.1), thus linking the two theaters of the war. Also, everything that concerned Alcidas was necessarily linked to the business of Mytilene, for which he had set out.

41. The matter is raised by Abbott (1925, 177), who believes that a revision would have led to a regrouping.

42. See n. 40 above.

divides and breaks up the action. It is superimposed on the chronological rigor without negating it; it completes it, by giving it an internal structure, using procedures that in themselves deserve study.

Internal Organization, Pauses, and Juxtapositions

It is in the context of such an organization that the term "episode," as used throughout this chapter, is to be understood. Within chronological series, Thucydides essentially isolates tightly linked groups that have a beginning and an end; the splitting of the account itself helps him do so.

The events that extend from Nicias's arrival at Epipolae to the sending of a letter relating his failures (6.96–7.8) are contemporary with other events, which take place in Greece and to which Thucydides devotes a total of three chapters. These Greek events appear in strict chronological order: the first "the same spring" (6.95.1), the second "about the same time in this summer" (6.105.1), the third "at the close of the same summer" (7.9.1). These expressions themselves indicate sufficiently that the concurrence remains fairly vague; Thucydides could have inserted these three chapters almost anywhere, together or separately, within the main account or in the margins. Yet by placing one before the group of chapters and the other after it, he achieved the effect that the group 6.96–7.8 was isolated from the others, amounting to an independent whole, an episode. The choice of facts to report and the form used to express them lend to this episode its dramatic unity; the break that marks its beginning and its end completes this unity and makes it stronger.

The choice of a beginning and an end is not, in fact, that simple: it suggests both analytical and compositional effort.

The truth of this statement is demonstrated when we find a single fact referred to twice, as happens frequently in Thucydides' history: in one place as conclusion and elsewhere as prelude. Even the case of Nicias's letter offers evidence of this: that letter is mentioned right after the Athenian failure as the result of this failure ("Moreover, as he saw his own difficulties increase, day by day, along with the enemy forces, he too sent messengers rushing to Athens"). But after a chapter about Thrace, which makes a break and marks a change of episode, we move to Athens, to the beginning of winter, when that same letter arrived, and this time the text of the letter is given. It plays a new and primary role: it convinces the Athenians to send Demosthenes with reinforcements. As such, it becomes part of a different group, one in which, in a parallel manner, the different preparations made during the winter in each of the two camps are revealed. Clearly, from beginning to end of the two books, there is continuity: Alcibiades' speech leads to Gylippus's departure, Gylippus's success leads to Nicias's letter, and Nicias's letter leads to Demosthenes' departure. Yet this continuity is quite strongly marked by those narrative threads identified earlier; these make the continuity apparent despite clear junctions that interrupt the succession of events. The double role played, in this instance, by a single event is meant specifically to create bridges between these succeeding moments that accommodate the dual demands of unity and analysis.

This becomes quite obvious when we consider another example, when the Syracusan embassies set off to request reinforcements elsewhere in Sicily; throughout book 7, their departure marks the conclusion of each victory, their return prefaces each new battle.[43] Hence we never lose sight of either the continuity in Gylippus's diplomatic activity or the connection between this and the military action; the battles form small, clearly defined dramas, which are nevertheless framed by causes and consequences of a diplomatic nature.[44]

It is owing to this same concern for organization that the project to fortify Decelea is mentioned first, somewhat uncertainly, as a consequence of Alcibiades' speech, then, more specifically, as part of the preparations for winter, in 7.18.1. The first reference is one of the vaguest (6.93.2: "They then embarked on the project to fortify Decelea") and is not followed up with any practical measures; we might wonder if there is not something a little premature about this, Thucydides having put together all of Alcibiades' interventions in a single statement and then having had to put together their consequences as well.[45] Conversely, the actual decision is held until the analysis of the preparations for winter, when it should have been

---

43. Departure and return at 7.7.2 and 7.21.1, 7.25.9 and 7.32–33, 7.46.1 and 7.50.1. See above, p. 13.

44. Plutarch, by contrast, having an army of reinforcements appear by surprise at the end of the *Life of Nicias* 22, develops neither continuity nor connection between battles and embassies.

45. See the note in Romilly et al. 1953–72, books 6–7, pp. xxxiv–xxxv.

taken up in the interim, if we are to believe Thucydides himself.[46] This being the case, the absolute demand for structure that required Thucydides to mention the decision first with its causes and then with its consequences would become an effort to achieve perfect accuracy.

In any case, the result is that through the deft management of pauses Thucydides uses the splitting up of the narrative to introduce logical breaks. We saw above that the account of the Mytilene affair may have been more scattered than was necessary; however, it is clear that, because of that fragmentation, the business fell into a pattern like that of a five-act play; first, there was "revolt and Athens" (3.2–6): preparation for war; then, "revolt and Sparta" (3.8–19): a Mytilenean embassy secures the help of Sparta, which leads to battles between Sparta and Athens; then, "Sparta encourages Mytilene" (3.25); next, "Mytilene capitulates" (3.27–29): Sparta delays too long; finally, "the fate of Mytilene" (3.36–50), with the debate in Athens. The breaks, which are presented to us as the inevitable consequence of a rich counterpoint of meaning, thus have in themselves a positive value and contribute directly to the discovery of their significance, to the extent that the breaks define combinations that are easily grasped, and whose importance emerges clearly. We might add that the dramatic value grows along with it: what we actually find in Thucydides' account resembles that which is spoken by the messenger in the *Persians*, and which the dialogue comes to split into successive sections.

This process seems consistent enough to be explained in the same way as the seemingly surprising breaks, such as the one in book 7 that interrupts Demosthenes' voyage to relate the battle of Erineus, begun "at about the same time" (7.34.1) and having no direct connection to Demosthenes' trip. Its placement is surprising,[47] but it actually serves to prolong Demosthenes' voyage by isolating each of his stops, and especially the one when he delays, imprudently perhaps: "They remained in the country in order to resolve these questions."[48]

---

46. See 7.18 and the role attributed there to the events of 6.105.

47. He must, however, relate it in any case, if only for the famous "fortified catheads," literally "ear-timbers," ἐπωτίδες (7.34.5), whose use will be decisive at Syracuse (7.36.2)

48. This is also at the moment when Demosthenes has just completed the crossing that the ships at Erineus were supposed to help his enemies to make. Finally, this arrangement recalls the voyage of Demosthenes every time, before and after each event: see above, pp. 31–32.

Thus we can say that the length of the episodes, their beginnings, their ends, seem to have been chosen for the benefit of the composition and, without in any way threatening chronological accuracy, in order to organize it by following the rhythm of entirely personal analyses.

Yet this type of composition is not limited to division into episodes.

I have spoken of beginnings and endings within each episode. It is actually quite clear that in each episode there are elements that are more general than narrative, and these elements in turn serve as pauses between episodes, determining, in addition to the beginning and the end, the parts themselves.

In the Gylippus episode these parts are given in a way that is very clear from the nature of the facts themselves. There are actually two groups, separated by Gylippus's journey: these are, first, Nicias's arrival and victory; then, Gylippus's arrival and victory. Yet it is also obvious that Thucydides does everything in his power to make us aware of the existence of these two adversaries and of a parallelism between them.

First, he marks this parallelism in his choice of facts and expressions, according to a process already analyzed. Thus Gylippus repeats the arrival via the Euryelus (7.2.4 = 6.97.2) and the fort at Labdalon (7.3.4 = 6.97.4); Thucydides even notes these similarities, specifying (7.2.4): "exactly like the Athenians at the beginning." Gylippus's success corresponds to that of Nicias; his speech contrasts with the awkwardness of the former Syracusan chiefs;[49] his constructions may thus reach the Athenian constructions, as before. But additionally, in the arrangement itself, it seems that each part has its conclusion and that these two conclusions are in opposition. The part relative to the success of Nicias ends, in effect, with a two-paneled painting presenting, in contrast, the Athenian success and the Syracusan discouragement (6.103). Athens' success is mainly expressed by the arrival of numerous competitors in Sicily from Italy or Sicily; the Syracusans' discouragement is principally based on their having been deserted. The part relating to Gylippus's success also ended with a twofold conclusion, presenting the contrast between the Syracusan victory and the Athenian discouragement (7.7): Syracuse's victory is expressed particularly by the arrival of reinforcements from Greece and the request for reinforcements

---

49. See above, p. 18.

elsewhere in Sicily;[50] Athens' discouragement[51] is marked by the fact that assistance appeared to be necessary. The two passages thus balance each other too well for readers, even inattentive ones, to miss the unity of this grouping, and the reversal that has occurred.

Naturally, this internal composition is all the more readily and power-fully marked as the role of analysis becomes greater, and that of the narra-tive proper is reduced. Thus the description of the preparations for winter following the episode of Gylippus offers an example of a particularly de-veloped composition. Specifically, this includes the offensive and defensive projects of the Athenians first, and then of the Peloponnesians; and even the terminology underlines the parallel construction.[52] Yet this group of projects is followed by a discussion of the measures effectively taken, by the Peloponnesians first, then by the Athenians. The chiasmus completes the parallelism; and a particularly formal order thereby presides over the entire exposition.

Even if the pattern cannot always be implemented, and if the methodi-cal organization does not always predominate, we can say that, whether sovereign or subordinate, it is always present, always felt.

So it may be surprising that in the Gylippus episode Thucydides does not use the third independent chapter (6.105) to indicate sharply the break between these two parts. The events reported in that chap-ter are situated simply as "at about the same time of summer," and they are completely independent of operations before Syracuse. Thucydides could therefore describe them wherever he wished; a historian like Be-loch (1914, 307) did not hesitate to refer them back to a time just before the conquest of Plemmyrium. Why then report them at a point that does not mark beginning, middle, or end of the episode? Doesn't this oddity ruin the conclusions that the use of the other two independent chapters would suggest?

---

50. Even in their details, the two groups are parallel; see the final enlargement of the success in 6.103.2 (καὶ πάντα προυχώρει αὐτοῖς ἐς ἐλπίδας, "And everything was making progress as they [the Athenians] hoped") and 7.7.4 (καὶ ἐς τἆλλα πολὺ ἐπέρρωντο, "And in others also they (Syracusans) were much invigorated").

51. The Syracusans' difficulties (6.103.4: ἀνθρώπων ἀπορούντων, "when people are con-fused") correlate exactly with those of the Athenians (7.8.1: τὴν σφετέραν ἀπορίαν, "their own confusion").

52. See above, p. 19.

In fact, quite the opposite: neither of these two chapters is used with that much meaning or utility. It is quite enough to consider at what point 6.105 makes a break, and where it directs the minds of the readers. The break occurs not where an organic division would be placed—that is, between the two large parts—but in the episode itself. It occurs, in fact, just before Gylippus finally learns the truth and is able to rush to Syracuse, just at the moment when readers are left in suspense, knowing exactly what the situation in Syracuse is, and that Gylippus is coming, and that Nicias does not expect him, just at the moment when the Athenian success is going to end. And, to some extent, the pause that comes corresponds well to the organic division, for, between the two groups of chapters regarding Nicias's victories and those of Gylippus, there is a kind of no-man's-land: Gylippus's voyage. This no longer belongs to the Athenians' successes, but it does not yet belong to the others, for Gylippus knows nothing yet, doesn't count, isn't involved; the second part can only really begin when the contact is made between Gylippus and Syracuse—in other words, after our chapter 105.

That is what causes this strange situation: Thucydides begins an account of the voyage, tracing Gylippus's progress, and suddenly, in the middle of the trip, he interrupts the account, drops it, and moves on to something else. How could we not, at this point, feel that we are entering a new phase? The shift in perspective is abrupt. The pause, more subtle than others, but also more dramatic, is so important that Thucydides puts the separation of the two books at that point, in the middle of the year, of the season, of the event.[53] In fact, it prepares for the flashback to the arrival of Gylippus. The break requires him to wait and reappear. Becoming the hinge between two parts, representing first Athenian and then Syracusan victories at Syracuse, it is also a hinge for the contrast between Athenian ambitions in book 6 and the Athenian disaster in book 7.

It must be added that by indicating a stop at this location, the pause also makes us consider the responsibility of Nicias, who, as the last words say,

---

53. Books 2, 3, 4, and 5 begin at the start of a year. As the Sicilian expedition was a very distinct episode, book 6 encroaches on the preceding winter with regard to some of the preparations, and book 8 begins with the consequences of the expedition and the end of summer. Yet no break is as remarkable or as "affecting" as that between books 6 and 7.

"took no measures for defense." The emphasis given to the reversal of the situation highlights everything about it.

And lastly, if this interruption is so decisive, it is worth considering its contents, in which case one perceives then that it might have, in Thucydides' eyes, a further justification. Obviously, this chapter is about events that are independent of the siege of Syracuse, because they occur in Greece itself. Yet this independence is only provisional, or rather, is simply an illusion. There are only events that seem independent but that will, at the first opportunity, come together. Athens will find itself facing a war on two fronts. In cases where this foreshadowing goes unnoticed by hasty readers, Thucydides allows himself, for once, a bit of commentary, implying a reversal: "And it was these ships," he writes (6.105.1–2), "that were most clearly violating the treaty with Sparta. Previously, the Athenians. . . . But this time, under orders from Pythodorus, Laispodias, and Demaratus, they sailed to Epidaurus Limera, to Prasiae, and to a few other points of the territory, which they sacked, giving the Lacedaemonians a chance in the future to invoke good arguments for defending themselves against Athens." The notion of a dual war, in Sicily and in Greece, so strongly indicated here, is exactly what Nicias and the Syracusans foresaw (6.10.1, 6.34.3, 6.36.4); its fulfillment would come in the course of the following winter; but, at the very moment when Sicilian affairs are going to do an about-face, Thucydides has seen fit to give us a glimpse of its imminence: 6.105 connects the episode to a guiding thread. It seems to be about something else, but, actually, at the time of the event, it connects the action to a more general realm of ideas, exactly as a chorus would at the same point in a tragedy.[54]

In other words, this unique and brief episode reveals, alongside chronological accuracy and in addition to it, a whole series of interventions, by which Thucydides, playing with the freedom that this gives him, manages to sketch not only the episodes, but the back-and-forth, capped by conclusions and separated by pauses, the whole suggesting parallelisms or contrasts, and therefore gaining importance by the location itself assigned to each element.

Henceforth, all connections can become rich with meaning. This happens even between episodes. The catalog of allies assumes a dramatic

---

54. Meaningful pauses are also found in philosophical dialogues: see pp. 55–56 below.

quality just before the final battle; it sets up the importance of the battle, first by evoking the scale of the fight, but also by seeming, by being placed at this spot, to warn readers that now the die is cast and the final climax has come.[55] The dialogue at Melos might also seem to have been composed as a function of the Sicilian expedition, inasmuch as just before that Thucydides analyzes very sharply the imperialist chain of events and its risks.[56] The account of the plague too may strike some as a cruel counterpoint to the Funeral Oration.[57] And finally, at times the digressions, considering their context, assume the quality of a warning, a suggestion, an explanation.[58]

At the very least, even if the placement of these episodes seems necessarily and inevitably tied to the demands of chronology, Thucydides is nevertheless a master at giving them the appropriate scale. Nicias sent many messages to Athens (8.1): Thucydides cites only one, but that one *in extenso*. Similarly, the episode at Melos derives its importance only from the dialogue that Thucydides attributes to it.[59] The historian is free to develop whatever he deems important in itself or significant in relation to other things.

This option is among those at Thucydides' disposal for placing events within a chronological order; it facilitates and strengthens them. It also allows him to emphasize certain relationships. Thus it helps insert into a simple exposition of facts, absolutely objective and rigorous, thinking that is analyzed, reconstructed, that actually amounts to an interpretation of everything.

Intention and Meaning

That interpretation is clear, dominant, and complex. Proof of this can be found in the episode under consideration.

I have happened to refer to it quickly as the "Gylippus episode." Actually, the decisive role played by that individual is sharply illuminated by

---

55. See 7.59.1: "From this moment, each of them had all his troops with him; neither one could receive further reinforcements."

56. Wassermann (1947, 30) finds, with almost excessive subtlety, tragic irony in the manner in which the Athenians treat their confidence in fortune just before the expedition in which their general, Nicias, is no longer going to count on that same fortune (7.61.3, 7.77.2).

57. See Gomme 1954, 144; he calls the dramatic effect "overwhelming."

58. On the digressions, see, among others, Münch (1935, 84).

59. The fullness given to the account of the plague seems to me more than justified by the immediate importance of the epidemic; see Schmid and von Christ 1929, 76 n. 3.

the composition of the account itself. First, the rigor with which the work of investment is traced gives readers a better measure of the exact degree of danger and, in concentrating their attention on a single action, makes them more aware both of this very danger and the crisis that concludes it.[60] On the other hand the creation of two parallel groups, with symmetrical conclusions, brings out the reversal of the situation; and the presence of a pause, just before the moment when Gylippus is warned about the situation, suggests that this was the cause of the reversal. So it is certain that the attention is on Gylippus's role. Moreover, in the very detail of the account, analogous processes have the effect of drawing out the full import of his merits: between his experience and the inexperience of the Syracusan leaders, the similarity of situations, rigorously indicated in the text,[61] provides a comparison that is entirely to his advantage; between the two engagements of the battle that he joins at 7.5, the comparison, clearly formulated in an indirect speech,[62] reveals the progress; and in the same stroke we see that the outcome of the battle was really a function of his talents.

Why, then, under the circumstances, should it be surprising that Plutarch read the account of this episode as a judgment? He writes: "That all the credit goes to Gylippus is not only what Thucydides said, but also Philistus . . ."[63] Thucydides actually said nothing of the sort; not a word, not a remark from him. But Plutarch was not wrong: the historian's judgment can be read as clearly in this account as if he had stated it in his own name; and the objectivity of the report gives to it an even stronger evidentiary force.[64]

Gylippus's arrival, however, could have been prevented either by Nicias or by chance. Thucydides, by the arrangement of his account, brings out, with equal sharpness, the role played by both. Nicias, who had conducted

---

60. Thucydides, it is true, emphasizes this crisis in a brief commentary (see above, p. 11); however, that commentary retains a strictly objective quality and expects readers to take the time to appreciate it; he says simply: "That was how great the danger had been."

61. See p. 17 above.

62. 7.5.3: Gylippus will say to them "that the failure was not theirs, but his: because of where he had positioned them . . ."

63. *Nicias* 19: κἀκείνου τὸ πᾶν ἔργον γεγονέναι φησὶν οὐ Θουκυδίδης μόνον, ἀλλὰ καὶ Φίλιστος.

64. Moreover, there is no need to say, like Glotz and Cohen (1931, 695): "Alors, la fortune change de camp" (Then fortune switches sides); the account says it even more strongly.

so favorably the building of the wall, commits an error here, one that is perfectly excusable:[65] he is not concerned about Gylippus. And Thucydides says this; he says it right after the pause, just before the reversal, thus giving full play to this unique negligence. On the other hand, by recounting Gylippus's voyage in a detailed way, at a moment when readers recognize the urgency of it without needing to know the outcome, Thucydides accords even more importance to everything that delays Gylippus. In the drama playing out before Syracuse Thucydides thus not only establishes a unity of action that shows the cost of the reversal; the clarity of the reversal's emergence illuminates the role that the different characters play in relation to it. There are three involved: Gylippus, Nicias, and chance. The narrative indicates with consummate artistry the precise responsibility of each.

The facts alone might have sufficed to show this, but less clearly, less plainly. Here a simplification moves aside all the other aspects (psychological or purely military, economic or topographic) that could have distracted our attention: the episode becomes a blueprint, containing only simple and necessary lines, allowing for no misunderstanding.

If it is true that, by the arrangement of the narrative, Thucydides is able to show clearly the responsibility devolving on each actor, the procedure by which he reveals, from one episode to another, the guiding threads makes this blueprint part of another one. After the immediate action, the blueprint also provides a model for the overall strategy.

And first, because Gylippus, despite his importance, is only presented as the man who comes from Sparta, everything has been cut back in such a way that he should appear, quite literally, as the application of Alcibiades' advice incarnate. The parallelism later established between the loss of Plemmyrium and the occupation of Decelea will further reinforce this framework. That framework reveals a strategic system whose principle is introduced in Alcibiades' speech. At the same time, it shows a dual responsibility: that of Alcibiades, adviser to Sparta, and that of the Athenian politicians, responsible for his exile. So even the account of this brief military episode is not without a role in the system of explanation that Thucydides himself lays out in 2.65, when he blames internal struggles for the defeat of Athens.

---

65. The remark in 6.104.3 ("just as had happened to the Thurians") reveals a potential excuse for Nicias: obviously, Thucydides does not want to blame him.

Finally, the episode returns, as we have seen, to two other guiding threads: to the extent that Gylippus is introduced as the man from Sparta and his departure linked to the occupation of Decelea, the account is tied to that theme of a "double war"; to the extent that it marks the early progress toward a collection of Sicilian forces, it is tied to the theme of "the union in Sicily." These two aspects are indicated in the episode with restraint and discretion: what is important is that they are handled in the same way in all episodes. Since, at every turn, Thucydides takes care to underline anything about these two ideas, foreseen in earlier speeches, one can say that every episode helps to reveal the mechanism of their realization and that Thucydides systematically imposes on his readers such an explanation of events. From now on, as Athens watches threatened peoples and its rival taking action ever more against it, there emerge inexorably the risks run by its imperialism, and the process of destruction that awaits Athens.

Just as the role of Gylippus seemed to Plutarch to be expressed very clearly in the account of his arrival, so too in the account of the Sicilian expedition, many readers feel keenly the rigorous logic that led Athens to its fall. G. F. Abbott (1925, 204–5) has written the following about book 7: "From the very first everything contributes, we know not how, to create a vague feeling of uneasiness—a shadow which hangs over and pervades all, gradually deepening and preparing our minds for the inevitable doom."

The reasoning behind this expression emerges clearly. It is explained by a series of procedures in the selection, arrangement, and expression of the facts; these, more or less consciously perceived by readers, guide them authoritatively in a world set in order, rethought and remade. This world has the deceptive appearance of objectivity; but the smallest details are revelatory of an intention, or at least a style of thought, that belongs to its creator.

That is why it does not seem to me easy to distinguish, as some have done,[66] between pure narrative in Thucydides and sections of interpretation. The latter already include, along with the speeches, an entire series of analyses, commentaries, and digressions. But in fact we are soon forced to add, with J. H. Finley, a certain number of narrative threads; as he writes, "A large number of recurrent themes great and small illuminate and bind

---

66. Finley 1942, 296–97: "Though predominantly factual, the narrative itself often rises to the level of interpretation. . . . All these passages perform an essentially different function from the ordinary factual narrative, a function, namely, of direction and interpretation."

together the advancing narrative."[67] Next, looking more closely, one notices that, little by little, there is no part of the account that is not arranged with a view toward producing a certain effect and to revealing particular connections. The simplest narrative leads directly to highly personal interpretations; but, conversely, one cannot reconstruct an interpretation without immediately applying to it every word of the account, in such a way that there does not remain the least residue, the least obscurity, the least unprocessed material.

This is only possible because of that quite remarkable characteristic of Thucydides' history that wants interpretation and judgment to be expressed by means of narrative by itself, without any apparent intervention by the author.

This principle operates in two ways. First, it requires of the author greater subtlety in the development of the account, forcing him to load every detail with meaning in order for his judgment to be understood. But it also widens, to the same extent, the field of possibilities: he may express in his own voice opinions or isolated theories, but not an infinite number of them; once those opinions and theories proceed from the facts themselves, however, their number is no longer limited; they can intertwine, merge, combine, as far as the author stretches his thinking and his interest in detail. The account of the Sicilian expedition is undoubtedly one of those where this elaboration has been pushed the furthest: book 8, on the other hand, is one of those with the least elaboration; while those events may seem more obscure than they do elsewhere, the personal commentaries are also more numerous.[68] But elaboration makes commentary superfluous.

---

67. Among these, Finley cites the slowness of Sparta, the false notion that the Spartans would easily emerge victorious, the surprising revelation of the Athenian troops, the desire of the Athenian people for conquests, the importance of the battle. But in the article already cited (1940), Finley himself identifies a number of other narrative threads whose link to the narrative is a tight one.

68. See in particular 8.24.4 (the moderation of Chios); 8.27.5 (the intelligence of Phrynichus); 8.64.5 (the urban sentiment); 8.86.4 (the assistance given by Alcibiades); 8.87.4 (Alcibiades' true intentions); 8.96.5 (differences between Athenian and Lacedaemonian leadership); 8.97.2 (value of the government of the 5000). It seems unlikely that a revision could easily have eliminated these remarks (other books contain them occasionally); but they may correspond to a more complex period, in which Thucydides did not manage to reconstitute a coherent system making each detail obvious. If that is the case, Thucydides' method would suit not only his personal inclination but also his clearly delimited subject.

Thucydides' history tends to let the facts speak for themselves as much as possible. It rejects analyses, explanations. If it becomes necessary to shift to thinking or reasoning, even then it still hides behind speeches. And when the historian does explain something about his method, in 1.22, he specifically considers only actions and words.[69] His own role consists entirely of arranging them, putting them on stage. This is one of the reasons why the work has often been compared to tragedy.

Both have this principle in common. They also share certain methods that result from it. Based on the unity of action, they practice equally a kind of thorough simplification to support that unity: as J. H. Finley (1942, 323) has shrewdly observed, we know about Pericles only those acts and those words that relate to the conflict, just as we know nothing of Antigone or of Oedipus beyond the conflicts in which they are engaged. In the same way, in order to allow readers or spectators to follow, simultaneously with the actors, the actions being played out, to indicate the times, the events, the ultimate causes, both Thucydides' history and tragedy depend on procedures of placement, contrast, and allusion that are often similar. And the result is the same level of interest in the unfolding action.

But if there is a principle in common, and often similar methods justifying a comparison that can be found in no other form of history, it should not be forgotten that this principle, prohibiting the historian from involving himself in any way in the actions or words, conforms also to that principle of the strictest objectivity. Actions and words are the material of tragedy, but also of scientific observation. And the subtlety of literary means may, as a result, be used in the service of truth.

F. M. Cornford is credited with pointing out convincingly the qualities that link Thucydides' history with tragedy and that distinguish it from other histories; but that led him to forget that this quality might serve exactitude and a concern for truth. Lamb, Finley,[70] and Gomme are among those who have made an effort to remember this. The first was thus led to speak of an artistic history able to transmit the truth in a way just as sure as a proposition of Euclid;[71] in addition, very recently A. W. Gomme,

---

69. See Cornford 1907, 52–53; also Wassermann 1947, 24.

70. Finley 1942, 324–25: "It would be incorrect, as some have done, to press this element of tragedy in the History too far.... The substance of that pattern is the substance of history, not of drama."

71. Lamb 1914, 65.

after having spoken of the union between science and art, considers that in Thucydides' work there is not exactly a union, but two aspects of a single reality.[72] Actually, an analysis of these methods, like the one I attempted at the beginning with a specific example, leads to conclusions that are on the same path. They merely show that one can travel farther. Between Thucydides' "tragic" methods and his historical objectivity there is more than equivalence and even more than an intimate cohesion: there is, if we may say so, a link of cause and effect. The desire to withdraw from his history, to be simply the organizer, to let the facts speak with totally scientific rigor, demands that Thucydides rely on such methods. His judgments, opinions, theories, pervade the entire account, but only because Thucydides does not doubt that they are inherent in the facts and refuses to speak of them if one is not supposed to see them.

The result is that the history can be read in two ways. A cursory reading brings out general impressions, clear and strong, but whose justification does not always appear right away. A more attentive reading reveals a series of echoes, repetitions, contrasts, suggestions, relationships, that allow more precise and complex interpretations to emerge. The work is charged with intentionality and authorial intervention.

Moreover, that fact should not be surprising, because, in the eyes of many specialists, it seems to be the very character of his style. Lamb (1914, 104–11), studying certain phrases in Thucydides' work, expressed himself as we would do in studying an episode. Thus, on 5.16.1 (104–5): "From all the talk and speculation aroused thereby he has abstracted this essence, as most important for us to know: he has determined that it shall be grasped as one organic whole; he has endeavored to express it accordingly, in compendious shape." He writes as well (110) that "Thucydides . . . is . . . anxious to place the two pairs of men . . . together, and to bring out, at one and the same instant, a group of significant contrasts." The analysis of the phrases often marks the failure of such attempts from the purely formal point of view and the harshness that they introduce into the style. It is evidence at least that the desire to organize, to reveal, to signify, defined Thucydides' work in a consistent, profound, and sometimes disorienting way.

---

72. Gomme 1954, 144.

For more attentive readers, those who really try to have a clear view into events (1.22.4: ὅσοι δὲ βουλήσονται τῶν τε γενομένων τὸ σαφὲς σκοπεῖν καὶ τῶν μελλόντων ποτὲ αὖθις, "those wishing to study the clarity of what happened and what is going to happen once again"), this aspect of the work allows for a deeper comprehension of the facts, their connections, and their links to each other. To the extent that these relationships and linkages are placed there by Thucydides, it also allows the critics to retrace their thinking. One has simply to determine what is intentional or not, personal or not.

In the matter of intentions, one can never be positive, but this case resembles that of verbal similarities: pauses, breaks, correspondences, indicate in all cases the way Thucydides perceives reality. The subtlety of the relationships expresses the subtlety of his thinking; their sharpness reveals its power.

What they cannot convey is his originality. There are, here again, some facts that Thucydides juxtaposes simply because they follow each other in time. There are elements that provide comparison, because they oppose each other in reality, and because this opposition is inescapable. In all these cases, there is no reason to reject the comparison, the contrast, the similarity. But we must avoid drawing conclusions about Thucydides. That is the one difficulty, for the reserve that has led him to express his views only under the cover of facts also means that readers who are committed to this path may not be able to tell where the facts end or Thucydides' own views begin. Thucydides' work mixes the historian into the history so well that personal interpretation looks like evidence, and sometimes, contrariwise, critics make the mistake of taking the most necessary facts to be personal.

This error itself, while it may be understandable, is but further confirmation of our conclusions. Thucydides calls for subtlety, and subtlety includes risks.

The Art of Implied Meaning in Greece

This respect for external objectivity, and this dexterity in adding to it supplementary meanings for more attentive readers, are two traits by which Thucydides' method of presentation approximates a certain number of Greek works of the sixth or fifth century. This similarity itself is a further reason for acknowledging its presence in his work.

The tendency to represent facts by putting on stage individuals engaged in some action is the very foundation of tragedy; tragedy was the literary work *par excellence* for the Greeks. We should add that the epic form itself, though a narrative, includes more or less mimetic and expressive speeches that bring it close to tragedy.[73] Finally, it is notable that in the fourth century, when these art forms ceased to be the main ones, most works expressing political, moral, or philosophical ideas were offered in the form of so-called historical accounts or in dialogues between individuals in a scene, as shown by Xenophon and Plato. For the same reason, praise of great men of the past is the best medium for projects of reform. Personal opinions are content to wrap themselves in seeming reticence.

Among a certain number of writers this tendency is wedded with another, no less important, that consists in suggesting, in some seemingly objective format, relationships and meanings that are understood only by those most attentive. I stated earlier, in connection with the first of the procedures of Thucydides, one means of doing this, specifically the use of verbal similarities. But this method is not, among those authors mentioned, the only one, any more than it is the sole method in Thucydides' work. Actually, in both, multiple resources of composition and of arrangement join to complete it. These different qualities are explained by the obligations that all authors impose on themselves, for different reasons, to fold into their work a meaning that has not been formulated anywhere else.

The subtlety of Thucydides' methods, glimpsed through these verbal parallels, is thus even greater than it seems. More importantly, it calls for an equally subtle understanding by readers who are responsible for retracing the steps leading to the author's intention.

The most striking examples of this subtlety are almost always literary in nature. And of these, perhaps the most remarkable is the subtle intentionality found in Pindar's lyric.

Pindar, moreover, did not disguise the fact that it required a subtle and attentive mind to understand his odes. The famous passage of the second *Olympian* (82–85) leaves no doubt about this: "I have in reserve, in my quiver, a great many quick shafts: quick minds can understand them

---

73. See Plato, *Ion* 535e; and Eustathius, *Commentary on the Iliad*, vol. 1, p. 9: ὑπεκρίνοντο δραματικώτερον ("They performed it more like drama").

(φωναέντα συνετοῖσιν, literally "they are speaking to the wise"); to be understood by the mob, interpreters are needed."

The first of these "shafts" to which the "quick minds" should pay attention is no doubt the composition. At first glance, this composition seems strange. It unites themes of circumstance, of fairly remote myths, of moral lessons: the unity is to be found only deeply, by one able to discern in each element the general, shared intention. A. Croiset demonstrates this in his analysis of several odes. In *Olympian* 1, the myth of Pelops echoes a lesson about moderation that Pindar addresses to Hieron, where he contrasts the glory of moderate and pious kings with the fate of the imprudent Tantalus: "Thus, in the first *Olympian*, the lyric idea, the generative idea of the poem, returns easily to a lesson that may be expressed by this proposition: 'Unite with your glory, o Hieron, a pious moderation.' I hasten to add that Pindar's thought does not take such abstract form."[74] Also, in *Pythian* 1, for example, both the story of Coronis and that of Aesculapius are used to suggest to a sick man that he must practice resignation.

Sometimes, however, the leading idea is still more difficult to discern: it is expressed only in abstract terms and is a symbol that unifies the ode. A. Croiset clearly recognizes this in *Pythian* 1, in which the unity, according to Rauchenstein, is attributed to the symbol of harmony and to music.[75] This is the same type of explication that G. Norwood has now applied generally. It is, of course, a troubling mode of explication, difficult to apply; but it is a fact that, without it, the interconnection of themes is often quite obscure. It is clarified, on the contrary, if one allows that, for very different reasons, the guiding thought emerges, in Pindar's work, in the encounter of different lyric themes, just as the historical judgment emerges, in Thucydides' work, from the encounter of different narratives.[76] As A. Croiset writes about *Pythian* 1, the general idea resides in the combination of themes: "This idea is nowhere and it is everywhere; nowhere is it formulated in an abstract way, and hardly could be; but it inspires the entire poem, for it consists essentially in that parallelism, so deeply felt and conveyed,

---

74. Croiset 1886, 338.

75. See above, p. 21.

76. Pindar and Thucydides are related in other ways, among others that tendency to see in the particular an illustration of general laws (Croiset 1886, 425), or to adorn their writing with abstract words (396–97). However, there is nothing less rational than the work of Pindar nor more rational than that of Thucydides.

between the sensitive harmony of the music and the superior harmony of the moral life: or rather, it is by layering this one over that one and in the ease with which Pindar moves from the glory of the visible feast to the invisible beauty of virtue . . ."[77] It is precisely these methods—juxtaposition, parallelism, and contrast—that convey the profound meaning of the work.

This is how we get to the idea of the subtlety of the method and of meanings that are intentionally disguised. Each bit of information, says G. Norwood, "they quicken one another with newly discovered kinship of significance";[78] little by little the mind is playing with allusions and delicate understatements, in which the Greek taste for riddles is apparent.[79]

Theater can hardly allow itself this level of obscurity. It must, by contrast, guide the interest of the spectator along a single path. Yet it advances similarly, to the extent that it knowingly lays out episodes and themes in such a way as to allow a spectator, facing the characters alone, to draw from the whole a master principle, one that those same characters can embrace. Aeschylus provides numerous examples of this, the most famous, and the simplest, being that of *Agamemnon*. There we see not only that the ideas and feelings expressed by the characters are those that the situation and the unfolding drama demand, but also that, taking on a double meaning, they reveal, little by little, Agamemnon's guilt and make his death seem almost necessary.

Even without the night watchman's monologue, which suggests some threat, the play evokes a series of crimes from the beginning.

The first crime, and the most serious, marked the beginning of the expedition, and that is recalled right away in the first words of the chorus: for Helen, "for a woman who belonged to more than one man" (62), Agamemnon unleashed a brutal war. Even more he has sacrificed Iphigenia for this war; and the first chorus is dedicated to that event. It is recalled twice, separated by a prayer. First comes the memory of the primal presaging, and the prophecy that, in advance, condemns Agamemnon if he should sacrifice his daughter: "For there remains a treacherous warden

---

77. Croiset 1886, 343.

78. Norwood 1945, 99.

79. For example, in *Pythian* 4 Pindar uses a fable to support the request of the banished Damophilus: he celebrates the beauty of a large oak, damaged and trimmed. The oak represents Damophilus; a careful reader will know that; but he must be careful, and the fable begins with a warning: "Now, show the insightfulness of an Oedipus . . .".

of the house, terrifying, ready to rise again, the Anger that never forgets and will seek to avenge a child" (154–55).[80] The account of the sacrifice then appears to confirm, in some way, that curse: "And when he put on the yoke of necessity, breathing a changing wind of his mind, impious, impure, unholy, . . . He dared to be the sacrificer of his child, to aid the war to return a woman, and to ransom his ships" (218–27).

The second crime takes place at the very moment of the victory: it is the excessive sacking of Troy. Clytemnestra imagines it all, and her hypocritical hopes allow the danger to come through: "Let their pity simply revere the national gods of the defeated city and their holy temples, and they will not need to fear defeat after victory. . . . Let not their wrongful passion assail our warriors; let them not be moved to impious pillages . . . that they may yet return safely to their own homes" (338–44). After such warning as this, the words of the chorus celebrating the just punishment of Paris's crime seem to the spectator to apply just as well to Agamemnon, who was no less guilty. This entire series of laments clearly applies to his crime, ending the evocation, and to the warriors who fell "for a woman who was nothing to them." The chorus fears the glory of the conquerors; it knows the risk: "Whoever has shed rivers of blood holds the attention of the gods" (461–62) and "May I not be a sacker of cities" (μήτ' εἴην πτολιπόρθης, 472). After that, the spectator is duly warned. It is at this point that the herald arrives, and everything he says in honor of Agamemnon confirms the dual sins of impiety and pride, since Agamemnon had "destroyed the altars and the temples of the gods" (527) and was "of all the living, the most worthy of a cult" (531–32). From that moment, everything becomes a condemnation of Agamemnon: the speeches of the herald, evoking suffering and grief, the condemnations of the chorus toward Helen and of those "golden palaces where a bloody hand rules" (775–76); finally, even the chorus's expressions of respect, saluting the sovereign with the title to which he opened himself, that of destroyer of cities (πτολίπορθε, 783). Even the silence becomes accusatory, for the presence of Cassandra at the king's side serves as a concrete reminder of his wrongful triumph.[81]

---

80. The preceding lines (150–51) even allude specifically to "a monstrous sacrifice, which will give birth to discord in the heart of the family and will respect no spouse."

81. These prophecies will have further impact on the bloodiness of the tragedy, joining the distant past to the coming denouement.

It is still more fitting that his pride is affirmed in a third and final crime, one that symbolizes the others, when he agrees, upon entering his home, to walk on royal purple. The meaning of this act is made clear in the hesitancy he himself expresses beforehand. His final words, when he says: "I will enter my palace walking on the purple" (997), mark his acceptance of a fate that was preordained three times. Clytemnestra's vow clearly informs the spectator of the imminent outcome: "Zeus, Zeus, through whom all is done, grant my wishes and think well of the work I am bound to do" (973–74).

There is nothing obscure in all of this, far from it. But nothing is ever said directly, either. Aeschylus does not try Agamemnon: he does not let Clytemnestra expose her motives, nor does he judge them. But, by selecting, by setting up verbal connections, contrasts, pauses, repetitions, he sets up this trial before the spectator in a way no less subtle and no less thorough than Thucydides does that of Athens.

Moreover, so simple are the lines of such a construction that they still demand of the spectator, if he wishes to appreciate the full reach and impact of the drama, an attentive intelligence, capable of making connections, of grasping the allusions and of measuring the contrasts. And it helps to specify that in tragedy the choruses, whose link to the action is generally presented in an allusive form, may on occasion demand considerable effort on the part of the spectator. *Antigone* provides a famous example. There are few plays actually in which the connection between the choruses and the action is easier to see, because they celebrate first the victory, then, following the condemnation of Antigone, the disaster; after the scene of Haemon, love; after Antigone's farewell, the memory of the cruel fates experienced by women related to the gods. Yet there is one that is awkward. After the scene in which we learn that Creon's order has been violated, the chorus sings about human progress but shows that this makes no sense if it is not joined with respect for the laws of the state and with the law of justice ordained by the gods. Does this chorus condemn Antigone or Creon? It is debatable.[82] The truth seems to be that the chorus itself is mistaken in its application of the principle: not knowing who was responsible for the burial, it thinks of speaking about him; but its words, which do not seem to apply to Antigone, designate the king, who "thought only of his State,

---

82. Ehrenberg 1954, 61–66.

but in fact betrayed his country."[83] The chorus never suspects that its words must ultimately have a double meaning; they become clear only for the most attentive spectator, who is left to discover, by looking at the scenes together, a deep meaning, but one misunderstood at the time.[84]

What is, therefore, the trait shared by lyric and tragedy is found to a no less remarkable degree in philosophy and particularly the kind practiced by Plato. This helps explain both details of composition that may be surprising and even the relationship between thought and dialogue.

In terms of the composition, it is easy to see that it implies a subtle organization, one that contains pauses, contrasts, suggested connections. *Phaedrus* provides a good example. And first, looking at it from the outside, what should one think, in a philosophical dialogue, of an episode like the myth of cicadas? Obviously its initial function is as a parenthesis and interlude, separating the second speech of Socrates from the debate on rhetoric. But at the same time it merges two themes, one inviting the soul to turn away from physical pleasures to seek the divine, the other specifying that the sovereign Muse, whose interpreters are the cicadas, is that of the epic and of eloquence: thus it calls, in an allusive way, for public speaking to be taken up again in a new spirit.[85] This preparatory and allusive benefit reappears in the two passages that open and close the dialogue, the "mythology" and the "invention of writing": the same respect for the divine, the same internal effort toward truth, are united there. The digressions of the *Phaedrus*, like those of the other dialogues,[86] thus furnish a transposition of the idea, one that can then be grasped at the deepest level.

The different parts of the dialogue are organized no differently. That dialogue begins with a discussion of love and ends with a debate about

---

83. Mazon, note on *Antigone* in Dain and Mazon 1950, 20.

84. Ehrenberg 1954, 65: "Although we can perhaps understand this song as the expression of a weak and frightened chorus of ordinary old men, it gains its full significance only when we realize that the poet, by way of his famous 'irony,' made the chorus say things of a far wider and deeper meaning." This will compare with what is said of the *Heracleidae* in Zuntz 1955, 43 and 48.

85. One might be even more specific; see Robin 1933, xxxvi: "The subordination of Urania, muse of things from the sky, in relation to Calliope suggests the idea that the dual function of the latter stems in effect from some common principle, which can only be philosophy. There would thus be, at least in connection with public speaking, a sort of presaging of the existence of a philosophical rhetoric and of its necessary relationship to the study of heaven and of all nature."

86. Festugière (1936, 410ff.) shows a comparable connection between the "episode" of the *Theaetetus* and the demonstration: the latter completes it, since "two forms of life are in opposition at the same time that these two concepts about knowing diverge."

rhetoric: isn't love as an example chosen more or less gratuitously?[87] A closer understanding shows that love is presented, in the course of a series of self-correcting speeches, as a true initiation: it awakens a recollection of extrasensory realities and a desire entirely focused on the divine. Love is a psychagogic guide and proceeds according to the same movement as that of the dialectic;[88] hence the latter appears as the result. Not only is the close tie between the two subjects of the dialogue explained in this way, but also the order in which they appear.[89] The logical sequence between them, the guiding principle, becomes clear for readers from this intelligent juxtaposition. In other words, there is in the dialogue a deep organic unity, conforming exactly to the wishes Plato justly expressed there;[90] this unity is accessible only to a penetrating mind, one that is capable of going beyond the text to follow the path independently.

That would clearly seem to be the principle of the Platonic dialogue. Where does the reversal of positions in *Protagoras* end, where do the aporetic dialogues in general end, if not at a conclusion situated beyond, not expressed, and one that readers alone can and must discover? Such is the principle that A. Koyré (1945, 25) has sharply brought to light in his little book: "It is a mistake for modern readers to forget that they are readers of the dialogue and not interlocutors of Socrates. For if Socrates often makes fun of his interlocutors, Plato never mocks his readers." Koyré shows this by bringing out the meaning that appears in the *Meno*, *Protagoras*, and *Theaetetus*, without its being expressed; and he explains the reason for this process; it is that true knowledge cannot be imposed on the soul from the outside; "it is in and by itself that the soul attains it, discovers, and invents it." So it is not surprising that Platonic dialogue should be considered as a system of allusions to a concept somewhere beyond. For it is not just the conclusions as a whole but also the development of the ideas that are usually

---

87. The ancients argued equally about the true subject of the *Gorgias* or *Republic*.

88. The union of the two themes is marked at the end of Socrates' speech (*Phaedrus* 257b): ἁπλῶς πρὸς Ἔρωτα μετὰ φιλοσόφων λόγων τὸν βίον ποιῆται, "simply live his life with philosophical discussion according to Eros." On the related roles of love and dialectic, see 249b, compared with 265d.

89. On the composition of the *Phaedrus* as a whole I recommend the excellent article by Bourguet (1919).

90. *Phaedrus* 264c: "Every speech should be structured like an animate being: it should have its own body; it should not be without head or feet but should have a middle as well as two ends and should be composed in a manner that is internally consistent and coherent overall."

revealed in direct speech, as Schaerer (1938, 272) has shown. He finds the explanation for this in Plato's own concept of philosophy. Plato says in *Letter* 7 that this was something that could not be expressed; moreover, it could not be made accessible to the masses; it could be addressed only to an "elite, for whom just a few indicators would suffice to reveal the truth" (341e). In Plato, provisional truths bring out apparent contradictions, repetitions, detours. One must explore every mode of knowing before arriving at knowledge (344c): "That is why every serious man will be careful about treating serious questions in writing." And Plato's work includes not just formal exposition but also a game of allusions and suggestions.

It would not be possible here to look in detail at these procedures and difficulties; suffice it to say that we find the same subtle composition replacing direct discourse, and the same appeal to the minds of readers or spectators who must discover for themselves the deeper meanings, whether we are referring to an aristocratic poet like Pindar, a dramatist writing for the masses, or a philosopher possessing a penetrating mathematical mind obsessed with clarity. We can apply to all of them what Schaerer (77) says of Plato: "He leaves much more for readers to infer than do modern authors."

Examples and arguments could be multiplied. For the issue that concerns us here, I wish only to add that this trait does not distinguish, as one might imagine, a certain number of authors of exceptional difficulty and exceptional subtlety. The simplest of Greek authors and the least subtle is no doubt Isocrates: no one says at greater length, more fully or more clearly, what he has to say. And yet, one has only to read a work like the *Panathenaicus* to discover a surprising complexity. Even there the composition of a speech in its proper sense is far from simple; and there would be a great deal to say about the way the different themes on the glory of Athens are arranged, and the different responses to the objections tending to praise Sparta. When it is added that this discourse does not fill the whole work and is further extended by a double argument with a youth, we get the idea that this entire composition is serving more purposes than simply the demands of clarity. Most curious of all is the hypothesis that comes quickly to the mind of that youth when he hears the speech. He thinks that Isocrates, desiring to praise Athens cleverly but bothered by seeming to contradict himself, thought he could seem to blame Sparta, all the while praising the latter without anyone suspecting it; that because he sought "discourse with a double meaning, that could apply equally to praise as to blame, and would be open to argument" (*Panathenaicus* 240). According to this young man, his objective would have been "to compose a speech of a particular type, a speech that inattentive readers would find simple and easily understood, but that, in the opinion of thoughtful and deep readers, would be difficult to grasp, within reach of only a few people."[91] By explaining its intent, one would rob the speech of the glory that makes it worth all the pain and effort expended on its behalf. Also, this speech would have been addressed to "the wisest of all Greeks, to the true men of letters, those who were worthy of the name." Was Isocrates capable of proceeding with this subtlety? By leaving the young man with no response, he shows at least that he relied, on that occasion, on the discernment of his readers; and the very hypothesis that he imagines is characteristic of a certain mental attitude toward a literary work.

That attitude is confirmed by everything that we know about the Greek way of reading Homer. In such an atmosphere, he was clothed in multiple meanings. Xenophon's *Symposium* reveals that a cultivated young man was learning from Stesimbrotus and from Anaximander the ὑπόνοιαι, in other words the hidden meanings. And Plato seems to have considered it natural for one to see some episodes of Homeric poems as allegorical.[92] In his view, poets expressed themselves in allegories, if not in riddles.[93] This is not surprising for a people whose gods enjoy demanding some finesse from their interpreters. What Heraclitus said of the Delphic oracle applies to all the texts that we have examined: "It neither expresses nor hides; it furnishes a sign" (frag. 93: οὔτε λέγει οὔτε κρύπτει, ἀλλὰ σημαίνει).[94]

Obviously, it is far from the rigorous clarity found in Thucydides to these esoteric games. On the whole, the examples that we have just compared differ greatly in both intention and result. For Pindar, poetic freedom is allied with a desire, no doubt deliberate, for difficulty. In tragedy, there is almost nothing that is not the result of the material conditions of

---

91. *Panathenaicus* 246. See in particular: τοῖς δ' ἀκριβῶς διεξιοῦσιν αὐτὸν καὶ πειρωμένοις κατιδεῖν ὃ τοὺς ἄλλους λέληθεν, χαλεπὸν φανούμενον καὶ δυσκαταμάθητον.

92. *Republic* 378d: οὔτ' ἐν ὑπονοίαις πεποιημένας οὔτε ἄνευ ὑπονοιῶν, "neither those composed in hidden meanings nor those without them."

93. *Republic* 332b: Ἠινίξατο ἄρα . . . ὁ Σιμωνίδης ποιητικῶς, "Simonides then was telling a poetic riddle."

94. There are probably religious reasons behind this attitude too, but those were of no concern to Thucydides.

the work and the constraint on the author to speak only through his characters as intermediaries. In Platonic dialogue, the characteristics themselves of the thought account for the gap between the ideas expressed and the conclusions implied. But in every case alike these different conditions come down to a complex and subtle art, and a demanding reliance on discerning readers. We have no choice but to conclude that this discernment existed, that it was natural to reckon with it and refrain from saying everything on the assumption that it was accustomed to comprehending even what authors had not said.

Thucydides is for his part a difficult author; his style is sufficient proof that he did not mind putting readers to the test at times. But this difficulty is only in the expression; the clarity with which he organizes the historical material and the reliance itself on reasoning that characterizes its elaboration show that, when it comes to history, it is clarity that is the quality toward which he most naturally strives. And the type of evidence that his account includes surely attests that he achieved it.

Yet this clarity and reasoning are themselves able to take advantage of the resources that the widespread demand for discerning readers made available: this is actually what allows him to retain the most objective tone through his account, while letting the meaning emerge beyond the narrative, just as it does, from the works listed above, beyond their outward contents. He encloses it within by the same methods and lets it be read by the same minds. But in the process he never strays from that ideal of clarity, quite the opposite. In essence, on behalf of the historian's scrupulousness he voluntarily places himself in a condition analogous to that of Aeschylus: he abstains from any personal commentary; he lets the facts speak. And, in compensation for that restraint, the confidence of his writing enables him to achieve the superimposition of one level of clarity over another one, and the addition to the unfolding narrative, without its being obscured thereby, of a comprehensive interpretation: by examining the one, we discover the other; and the discovery is all the better the more attention we pay.

Against the backdrop of the Athenian practice of allusion and implication, what is it in Thucydides to which the facts, in their objectivity, allude, and what is it that they imply? The solution to their riddle, clearly visible to those who know how to read, is historical meaning.

2

Battle Accounts

Analysis and Narration

It is natural that the same patterns of selection and interpretation should recur in the particular narrative category consisting of battle accounts. They always appear there in a special light, since within this narrowly defined context they can operate with a unique rigor. Moreover, they are all the easier to perceive because they remain distinct compared to the genre's development and its very different origins. For this reason it may be helpful first to retrace that development, before determining by comparison the originality of Thucydides and his characteristic methodology.

Before Thucydides (Homer, Herodotus, Tragedy)

Greek literature begins for us with the story of a war, and the *Iliad* is primarily about a succession of battles.

There is, however, one stipulation to be made: the *Iliad*, a work about war, does not, strictly speaking, contain any battle accounts. It takes a very close reading of the poem to recognize the four days of fighting it relates. During those four days, the development of the situation is, generally, difficult to retrace and presents the commentator with certain very subtle problems.[1] It could hardly have been otherwise, since there seems to be no organizing principle. When Hector is on the left, he is ignorant of what happens on the right (11.498), and when he is in the middle, of what is happening on the left (13.675): even speaking of "center" or "left" seems an unusual effort to organize the battle as a whole.[2] As for advice from the generals, it is reduced to a minimum. Apart from an order given by Diomedes urging all Argives "to rally here" (5.823) it amounts to two orders of Polydamas, pointing out the obstacle presented by the trench (12.61) and the opportunity to await Achilles in the city (18.254). The latter order is in any case misunderstood by Hector.

So, if there was any rudimentary military technique in the Homeric period, the poet does not seem to have been concerned with depicting it.

For Homer, the entire battle was never more than a canvas. At the beginning of an account, the evocation of confusion serves primarily as introduction.[3] It is always very brief; it describes the noise, the deaths, the dust. Sometimes it injects a metaphorical quality to great effect, comparing the confusion to some natural phenomenon in which great forces are unleashed: in book 4 (452ff.) it is the clash of torrents, in book 11 (150ff.) a fire that devours the forest, or, in book 17 (735ff.), one that ravages the city; it is again, in book 15 (379ff.), the raging sea, or, in book 16 (765ff.), the collision of two winds.

The remainder of the story is made up of a series of single fights, presented in a series. The series tends to begin with πρῶτος δέ.[4] There is no

---

1. The battle for the ships unfolds exactly like a battle on an open field. Here we find the Trojans on the ships (15.389); twenty lines further, they are no longer there; they are back on them in 15.653. The trench destroyed in 15.355 is back in 16.369; this trench stops the army, but it does not stop Hector, who is in a chariot. Even if these difficulties relate to the conditions in which the *Iliad* was composed, it may be noted that the "arrangers" have little interest in strategy.

2. Similarly unusual is that the author of book 13 is familiar with the use of a sling and knows how little confidence one should have in archers "who don't know how to hold the front line and who must be massed in the rear" (13.713); note also his description of the phalanx (13.125–35), which also occurs in book 16 (211). For details, see Mazon 1948, 192.

3. At times it also serves as a conclusion, and, after individual exploits, abruptly expands the field of view. But in both cases its role as a canvas is the same.

4. This appears four times in book 16 alone.

systematic linkage that governs the order of these encounters, except that usually a given series is devoted to the glory of a particular hero. Yet each encounter is treated by itself. If there is in Homer an art of tactics, a battle technique, it may be found in the single combats, for Homer always says what type of weapon is used, what body part is struck, what kind of death results, and he never fails to highlight those unusual wounds that produce spectacular and unexpected effects.[5] In these descriptions, therefore, the interest is not only ethical, but also technical. In both cases, however, all the attention is focused on the worth of the individual.

Still, we should add a reservation, for these glorious exploits, ἀριστεῖαι, that Homeric battles are, are distorted in our eyes by one remarkable circumstance: the one who puts courage or fear into the heart of the fighter, the one who directs the lance or diverts it, is very often a god. Everything is miraculous and thus full of surprises,[6] and when we think we are heading for one particular result, we discover that this "would certainly have happened, if at that moment, a god" had not intervened.

This feature, moreover, contributes to the pathos, by helping us judge the weakness of mere mortals who are so often tricked. The "charming head" of Hector, rolling in the dust, and the "poor idiot" Patroclus, who runs to meet his death, draw our pity to the individuals; but the very atmosphere of the battle, charged with marvels, assumes a quality no less moving. It conveys the sense of man overcome by superior forces. As F. Robert (1950, 23 and 25) writes, "In a real battle, one would look in vain for a different explanation"; it is a combat "where one advances and retreats without understanding how or why."

Thus the epic battle, in all respects, is notably *not* intelligible.

To find some order in battle, we must look mostly to new genres, which are, moreover, roughly contemporary with each other: history, with Herodotus, and tragedy. But both start from Homer.

Herodotus knows tactics and strategy. With him we are in the modern world of cities and democracy, in which armies serve as a tool of strategic

---

5. Thus, book 16, lines 347, 405, 481, not to speak of the blow that knocks Cebriones' two eyes to the ground (741).

6. Nothing remains for the victim except to repeat that it was extraordinary: see 15.286; 20.344; 21.54: ὦ πόποι, ἦ μέγα θαῦμα τόδ' ὀφθαλμοῖσιν ὁρῶμαι ("Astonishing! Truly I behold with my eyes a great marvel").

intelligence. And he is interested in the knowledge the Greeks have acquired in matters of war.[7] He quite readily insists on the superiority that this knowledge gives them in contrast with the barbarians; the latter have numbers on their side, but the Greeks have skill; they know how to fight σὺν κόσμῳ ("with order") and κατὰ τάξιν ("according to arrangement"), while the barbarians do nothing συν νόῳ ("with intelligence").[8] Furthermore, being few in number, the Greeks are able to attack the troops of the King, who are dumbfounded by what to them looks like folly.[9] Moreover, they know to choose fields that make numbers ineffective for lack of space. The notion of lack of space (στενοχωρία) is prominently displayed at Thermopylae and Artemision;[10] and both times the result emerges clearly: the barbarians, "fighting in a narrow space, were unable to benefit from their numerical superiority" (7.211); and Xerxes' fleet "was itself encumbered by its own size and the great number of ships, such that they were impeding and bumping into each other" (8.16). It is the same at Salamis, where this time the idea is brought up in the preceding deliberation by Themistocles (8.60). Finally, it is the same at Plataea, where the generals sought to position themselves so that they would not be vulnerable to the cavalry, and where Amompharetus is shown to be quite absurd in refusing to make the slightest movement with the others, because he fears that fleeing in the sight of strangers would "dishonor Sparta."

Furthermore, scholars have been able to show that by and large Herodotus's battle accounts form fairly intelligible wholes.

But why go to such trouble to show that? And why, in stating this result, are there so many reservations? Both are explained by what is, in spite of everything, the very summary nature of the explanations furnished by

---

7. For the use of this knowledge on land, note the maneuver described for Marathon (6.111) and the movement carried out by the Lacedaemonians at Thermopylae (7.211). At sea, we see at Lade the Phocaean Dionysius attempt to teach maneuvers to the Ionians (6.12); he is not successful: the Ionians, who hate these exercises, fall ill! But the Athenians are not like them, and the account of the naval battles suggests an actual experience (see at Artemision the formation with sterns in the center, 8.11).

8. Herodotus 8.86; see the same terms used at Plataea, 9.59.

9. See the comparison of the words ὀλίγοι and μανίη in 6.112 (Marathon) and 8.10 (Artemision).

10. In the first case, the concept of στενόν is repeated four times in one chapter, 7.176; and the outcome, anticipated in 7.177 (οὔτε πλήθεϊ ἕξουσι χρᾶσθαι οἱ βάρβαροι), is precisely realized in 7.211 (οὐκ ἔχοντες πλήθεϊ χρήσασθαι).

Herodotus.[11] And this summary nature can in turn be explained by the fact that these tactical maneuvers, the guiding principle of which Herodotus understands, and which he even manages to expose right at the beginning of the account either indirectly or in a speech, are, however, not for him the real substance of the narrative. His model remains the epic. And this is seen not only in tone or style,[12] but in the structure itself of the account, which always yields to anecdote and to the celebration of exalted, isolated deeds.

After a fleeting word about military events (which has replaced the Homeric evocation of confusion) there follows always a burst of anecdotes to the glory of the most courageous, catalogs of exploits (ἀριστεῖαι), some more developed than others but always included. At Thermopylae, this is a list of the illustrious dead (7.224), followed by a kind of awarding of prizes: "The overall conduct of the Lacedaemonians and the Thespians was such, and they say that one man surpassed all others in bravery, the Spartiate Dieneces, who . . ." (7.226); "After him, the prize for bravery went to . . ." (7.227); "among the Thespians, the most distinguished . . ." (ibid.); "Of two of the three hundred, Eurytus and Aristodamus, they say the following . . ." (7.229). This is by far the longest part of the account. And we would find the equivalent at Artemision, Salamis, Plataea, Mycale; at Artemision, we even recognize the Homeric πρῶτος δέ. When by chance Herodotus ignores these κλέα ἀνδρῶν, he apologizes, as in the case of Lade (6.14).

If we add to these commemorations the anecdotes that precede or follow the narrative proper (for example, the four anecdotes about the spoils from Plataea), the miracles framing or accompanying the battles (for example at Marathon, where the account opens with the story of Hippias's

---

11. The number of books and articles on this subject is too great for me to try to summarize here; I will simply mention Ph.-E. Legrand's (1932) verdict passed on the battle of Salamis (book 8, *Notice* p. 30): "The account of the battle itself is little more than one of isolated and independent episodes the majority of which take place at the moment when the barbarians are already defeated and fleeing."

12. We see the similarity between a provocation like that of Mardonius (9.48), who dreams of a single combat, and mockeries like those of Polycritus toward Themistocles (8.92), for which Herodotus recalls the ἐπεκερτόμησε ("he taunted him") that Homer applied to the mockeries of Patroclus toward Cebriones (*Iliad* 16.744). The role of individual honor is the same, right up to the formula that Herodotus recalls at Plataea: οὔτε τις αὐτῶν ἀλκῆς ἐμέμνητο, "nor did any of them think of resistance" (9.70).

dream and ends with a reference to the miraculous blinding of Epizelus after he saw a kind of ghost in the battle), we will realize that the account, for Herodotus, was not primarily about tactics.

More seriously, sometimes these brave deeds are not presented separately at the conclusion of the account, or at either end: at Salamis and at Plataea, among others, Herodotus wishes to order them chronologically, within the actual narrative. At Salamis, the story of the attack is first interrupted by meditations on human worth; he then comes to the successful outcome of the attack, only to move right away to an isolated action of Artemisia; and lastly, when the barbarians try to take Phaleron, Herodotus mentions the heroic deeds of the Aeginetans and connects them with Polycritus's mocking Themistocles in the middle of the battle.[13] Such a procedure undoubtedly adds variety and liveliness to the narrative, but it has the effect of overwhelming our picture of the whole. One senses that the story hesitates between two points of view, trying unobtrusively to bring some order to contents in which the individual remains the primary center of interest.

Yet when we consider Herodotus's narratives within the history of the genre, and if we compare them with those of epic from which they derive, it is not the unfinished character of the transformation one will recall, but the transformation itself. For though he employs (from an intellectual, moral, literary, point of view) an epic structure, Herodotus actually modifies it quite profoundly. He introduces the idea of mass combat, very specific remarks about strategy, a way to set forth the plans of the leaders, and, lastly, the idea of an intelligence directing events, intelligence that triumphs over numbers and that sometimes, he imagines, can be worth more than courage itself.

Moreover, his effort in this direction is not an isolated one. And I should add that we recognize in his work other models besides the epic, since the story of Salamis in particular had been brilliantly told by Aeschylus.[14]

Yet before considering that unique story, it may be the time to consider later and less important tragic tales: these allow us to isolate better what is specific to tragedy in general and what is specific to Aeschylus.

---

13. Here too moreover we find, as Legrand (1932, 31) correctly observes, a ghost in chapter 84 and a mysterious craft that appears to have been "sent by the gods" in chapter 94.

14. Obviously here we are only glimpsing, in a rapid review, the principal literary works that have been preserved: Herodotus had at his disposal many other epics, historical and tragic or even lyric narratives that I do not mention for the sake of simplicity.

These are the narratives of *The Heracleidae, The Suppliant Women*, and *The Phoenician Women*. Setting aside other influences,[15] it is easy to recognize in these narratives of mythic battles a reminiscence of Homer, but a modified one, and modified in a different way than in Herodotus.

In Euripides' three versions, we find, as in Herodotus, a general description ending with individual exploits.[16] In both parts the imitation of Homer is perceptible.

It is extremely clear in the case of individual exploits, whether that of Iolaus, who benefits from a true miracle with a cloud surrounding his chariot and a rejuvenation of the hero, or that of Theseus, with his truncheon "knocking off necks and heads, with his cudgel reaping a harvest of helmets,"[17] or especially those of Eteocles and Polynices, who fought hand to hand in the best Homeric tradition. After offering prayers reminiscent of the *Iliad*,[18] they receive the honor of the metaphor of the boar, just like Idomeneus in book 13 (471), and then they fight, first with spears, each wounding the other, and then with a rock, a μάρμαρον πέτρον, just like Patroclus in book 16 (734), and finally with the sword. The blows are described in detail worthy of Homer, down to the "Thessalian feint," and to the double blows that hit the navel of one and the liver of the other.[19] Then, in the Homeric expression, they "bite the dust."[20]

In the confusion of battle, reminiscences of Homer occur equally. Although the battle scene in *The Heracleidae* is described somewhat summarily, in *The Suppliant Women* it evokes the "great cloud of dust that mounted to the sky," "the bodies dragged up and down by the leather reins, the blood flowing in streams," and even returns to the same sarcastic comparison that Homer put in the mouth of Patroclus, comparing his victim

---

15. It is possible that the narrative of *The Persians* in particular influenced the other tragic narratives.

16. The move from one to the other occurs in *Heracleidae* 844; *Suppliant Women* 707; in *The Phoenician Women* the story is divided into three parts: the battle in general (1090–1200), the single combat (1217–63), and lastly the battle between the two brothers (1356–1480).

17. *Suppliant Women* 717; the helmets are the Homeric κυνέαι.

18. *Phoenician Women* 1374; see *Iliad* 3.351.

19. It is amusing to note that in his eagerness to imitate Homer Euripides loses the correct tone and falls into implausibility: Eteocles, seeing the bare *shoulder* of Polynices, strikes him in the *chest*, whereas Polynices is not impeded from fighting by being struck in the leg.

20. *Phoenician Women* 1423; see *Iliad* 22.17.

to a "diver."[21] As for the battle chaos in *The Phoenician Women*, it joins, in a sort of last straw, the "divers," the movement from one hero to the next, the prodigy meant for Capaneus, the reference to "the altered earth was soaked with bloody streams," and even a mixture of minute detail and tenderness recalling the wounded, which seems so characteristic of Homer.[22]

Yet even in these three accounts, so closely faithful to the Homeric tradition, novelties emerge. By definition, tragic narrative unleashes anxious anticipation and addresses people who are moved; the story is told by someone who shares their emotion and feels it all the more keenly for having just been involved in the action or at least having watched it. The focus is thus necessarily much more centered on, much more oriented toward, the final outcome. And the new element of pathos, thus introduced, becomes at the same time a new element of order.

First the narrative is introduced either by a chorus or in a lyric dialogue. The messenger is expected: he must first answer some questions.[23] Thus it is in an atmosphere of profound participation that he launches his narrative.

Moreover, he has himself become involved in the emotions of the combatants and does not fail to demonstrate it. The exhortations of the generals contribute to this impression (*Heracleidae* 838; *Suppliant Women* 701, 711); they are completed by the reactions of one group or another, whether in the "lamentations mingled with groans" of the combatants in *Heracleidae* 833 or in the outbursts of the messenger himself: "I screamed, I danced, I rejoiced and clapped my hands" (*Suppliant Women* 719); when the battle is not general, it is rather its onlookers, who, "more even than the combatants, felt their sweat flow, so fearful were they for their friends" (*Phoenician Women* 1388–89).

How are we to imagine that such tension, such emotion, could wander off in scattered remarks? Precisely because everyone is interested in the outcome of the fight, it organizes itself, and the narrative comes together.

---

21. *Suppliant Women* 692; see *Iliad* 16.745; see also *Phoenician Women* 1149.

22. In particular, lines 1159–63. Homeric echoes are numerous in the detailed description: 1105 (see *Iliad* 13.339); 1168; 1234 (νίσσεσθε); 1246 (ἔσταν; and also χρῶμα οὐκ ἠλλαξάτην; see 13.279).

23. In *The Phoenician Women* this dialogue is restarted three times (1075–90, 1208–17, 1335–56), which makes perceptible the dramatic progress of the narrative: the two brothers live; they are going to fight; they are dead.

The phases of the battle are clearly distinguished;[24] the placement of the troops is explained. Thus the narrative of *The Suppliant Women* distinguishes three different armies and two wings, tells of the successive engagements between chariots and cavalry, and finally shows the two right wings winning on each side but the leader never fails to move to the point where his troops are weakening.[25] In *The Phoenician Women*, that is the very reason for changing leaders: Eteocles, like Theseus, goes from gate to gate, to every point where his army is in danger.[26] Consequently, a kind of unity of action, demanded by the situation in which the narrative occurs, almost perfectly sees to its arrangement.

Returning now to the unique example provided by Aeschylus, we will see that this same character is what gives the narrative of *The Persians* its exceptional force. There, the main point of the narrative and the central idea of the tragedy are joined; no one has ever taken further the art of sustaining emotion and keeping the narrative moving by distinguishing its successive phases, which are revealed one after another.

The play opens with the queen and the chorus anxiously awaiting news. Soon the messenger arrives with the announcement of the catastrophe: στρατὸς γὰρ πᾶς ὄλωλε βαρβάρων ("The entire army of the barbarians has perished!"). Forty lines further comes the surprise: Xerxes lives! But as a counterstroke comes the naming of those who died.

In the narrative itself, the speaker has joined large, well-constructed blocks: the battle, the episode of Psyttaleia, and the retreat. And each time, there is a shock as the latest disaster is learned. As for the troops remaining in Greece, they are reserved for a final episode, postponed until much later: the prophecy of Darius (798ff.) will thus bring the crowning blow of the disaster.

These three blocks represent three moments, each with its own emotional impact. Of the two battle episodes, the first ends with "groaning mixed with tears that rules alone over the wide sea, up to the hour when the dark face of the night comes and puts an end to everything" (426), and the second

---

24. See *Heracleidae* 834–36: τὰ πρῶτα μέν . . . εἶτα . . . τὸ δεύτερον δέ ("first . . . then . . . second").

25. *Suppliant Women* 709: ἐς τὸ κάμνον οἰκείου στρατοῦ ("to whatever part of his own army was tiring").

26. *Phoenician Women* 1163–64, 1170–71. See also the *teichoscopia* at the beginning of the play, which has a pathetic aspect but also serves to indicate the location of the troops.

with the "long groaning" of Xerxes before the abyss of grief, when he "tears his clothes and gives a harsh cry" (465–68). We finish in the presence of the combatants what we have lived through with them, knowing every stage of their fear, when they hear, then see the Greek army (391), their feeling that "there is no more time for delay" (407), finally their panic.[27]

And this panic itself is explained for us: neither Aeschylus nor his messenger is unaware of the role of Themistocles' ruse, nor of the rashness of Xerxes in posting his troops at Psyttaleia, and they are careful to say so: Xerxes "does not suspect a Greek's trick or the jealousy of the gods" (361–62), "he did not know the future that the gods were preparing" (373), "he was bad at knowing the future" (454). Even more, they experienced the battle and could grasp the principle that determined the result; the Persians suffered from being a great multitude in a small space: "When their multitudes massed together in a narrow space where they were not able to help each other and crashed their bronze prows against one another, and saw all their oars broken, then the Greek triremes skillfully surrounded and attacked them; the hulls capsized" (413–19). The relief in the description that follows, with its asyndeton and its metaphor ("as if they were tuna, like boned fish"), gives all the greater emphasis to a principle that Herodotus too understood and had brought out in Themistocles' speech before the battle.

Finally, it should also be said that this unity, this progression, this principle emerge all the more strongly in that, throughout this long narrative, there is no exploit by a single individual. Whatever Artemisia or the Aeginetans did is of no concern in the great drama that is playing out between the ambition of Xerxes and the will of the gods—a drama that is enacted by the messenger, the queen, and the chorus. Moreover, Themistocles himself is not named: the emotional and moral unity that is established sweeps away everything else.

Writing about the same battle, Herodotus and Aeschylus offered accounts that are very different in structure. In terms of strategy, they are

---

27. All of this is suggested in a way that is so immediate and so real that one is thrown into some confusion owing to the fact that the story is told by a Persian based on the memories of a Greek: the barbarian forgets that he is a barbarian, when, in the face of the Greek call "Go sons of Hellas, free the fatherland . . . ," he evokes the "clamor in the Persian language" responding from the other side (406).

comparable: neither of the two is wrong, neither of the two is complete. Yet the processes are reversed. In Herodotus, we see an attempt to offer a historical account, with speeches, explanations, exploits; but his curiosity about details feels haphazard. In Aeschylus's work, the anxiety of the combatants introduces unity mixed with pathos. Herodotus, concerned with memorable qualities, sees his characters from the outside; Aeschylus involves the audience in their feelings. And even though in the two works the same king, Xerxes, reacts with equal vividness, his action is in Herodotus the occasion of a picturesque remark made after the fact ("They say that during the attacks, the King, who was watching the battle, jumped up three times from his throne, seized with fear for his army"), but in Aeschylus it marks a single occasion, at a moment of decision, an irrevocable time in the unfolding of the situation. Herodotus universalized and explained battle; the tragedians unified and internalized it.

Thucydides' narrative is located at the intersection of these two methods: by pushing to its limit the development begun by Herodotus, Thucydides actually recaptures those qualities that characterize a tragic style.

Simple Forms: Patrai and Comparable Accounts

In Thucydides a battle narrative has an inevitable unity, just as do all his other narratives, and for the same reason: because Thucydides brings out, as elsewhere, the intention, the γνώμη, that governs the action.

Only here this intention is of an extremely precise and deterministic type: it becomes the plan of a general who finds himself grappling with a given problem, limited in space and time; and it gives rise not to the intentions of a group, but to a precise rationale about the means to be employed.

Furthermore, this intention must be set forth; it alone can account from the start for the arrangement of the troops. To be comprehensible, it must also receive a more or less detailed justification. As a result, in contrast to what was seen in chapter 1, the plan is no longer simply contained in a series of actions that reveal its existence: it is stated at the outset, in the form of a project that the facts will or will not be responsible for carrying out, and with the help of a rationale that the facts will or will not come to confirm. Just as the battle is the archetype of an action in which two adversaries confront each other with contrary plans, one may even say that, between two objectives and two processes of reasoning, the facts come to vindicate one set over another.

On this basis the battle narrative is distinct from narrative in general. It provides the same unity, certainly, the same absence of everything that is anecdotal, idiosyncratic, or accessory. But its structure is even more tightly developed, and the contrast between the two intentions in it is even more apparent, for the narrative is composed of two stages: preparation and proof, calculation and verification, between which Thucydides does not fail to weave those verbal webs that give even greater rigor to the confrontation.

The first stage can only have a scope that varies case by case. And this explains why the narrative may take on different forms, with greater or lesser complexity, each of which should be considered in turn.

For this purpose, the two successive battles of Patrai and Naupactus, in book 2, may be taken as examples, the one a simple account, the other more developed. These are in fact the first naval battles of the war. They pit experienced Athenian forces against the inexperienced but far more numerous Peloponnesian forces. One engagement follows the other almost immediately. The narrative devoted to them covers chapters 83–92 in this book.

The **battle of Patrai** is narrated in the first two chapters and is easily analyzed.

First of all, it contains a preliminary phase (2.83.1–4), in which Thucydides describes how the battle will unfold: the Peloponnesians were, he tells us, constrained (2.83.1: ἠναγκάσθησαν) from engaging. The Athenian general Phormio intended for the battle to be fought on the open sea (2.83.2: ὁ γὰρ Φορμίων . . . βουλόμενος ἐν τῇ εὐρυχωρίᾳ ἐπιθέσθαι, "Phormio . . . wishing to attack in a wide area"); the Peloponnesians had not anticipated (2.83.3: οὐκ . . . οἰόμενοι) this; but when they set out to cross the strait, they found themselves confronting the Athenians and compelled to fight in the middle of the straits: 2.83.3: κατὰ μέσον τὸν πορθμόν ("in the middle of the crossing") confirms 2.83.2: ἐν τῇ εὐρυχωρίᾳ ("in a wide area"); and 2.83.3: ἀναγκάζονται ("they are forced") takes up the preceding 2.83.1: ἠναγκάσθησαν ("they were forced").

Not all battles have this initial phase, since not all generals have Phormio's skill at fighting in the very place that suits him best. But after this initial phase—so characteristic of the pattern we will find—we return to the normal framework of a battle account.

The analysis of γνώμη ("intention") is linked to the description of tactical formations.

On the Peloponnesian side, after giving the names of the leaders, Thucydides defines this tactical formation (2.83.5: ἐτάξαντο, "they arranged"): it consists of forming a circle, with lighter craft in the center. This serves a dual purpose: it prevents the Athenians from penetrating and makes it possible for assistance to be brought to the point of attack (this dual purpose is expressed by a participle, then by a clause with ὅπως).

Seeing the Lacedaemonian formation, the Athenians maneuver. The formation itself is indicated in just a few words (2.84.1: κατὰ μίαν ναῦν τεταγμένοι, "arranged in a line of one ship each"), and the description of the movement begins (once again making it clear that the initiative was Phormio's); but that movement is immediately interrupted by an explanation, indicating Phormio's plan and the reasons behind it (2.84.1: προείρητο δ' αὐτοῖς ὑπὸ Φορμίωνος . . . ἤλπιζε γὰρ, "They had been given advance instructions by Phormio . . . because he hoped . . .").

Whereas the intention (γνώμη) of the Peloponnesians is expressed in two words and related only to the tactical situation, Phormio's is presented in the form of a process of reasoning, and its contents govern all the action that ensues. He is counting on the fact that the standard Peloponnesian tactical formation will be ruined by disorder. Two forces will cause that. The first depends on himself: he will force them to get too close to each other; the Peloponnesians had, in fact, made as wide a circle as possible, and by circling around them, the Athenians, as Thucydides said from the beginning, squeezed them. The other factor was circumstantial, but it was familiar to this highly experienced general, who did not fail to exploit it: it was the wind that typically picked up around dawn, whipping up the gulf. Overall then, Phormio drew on two probabilities; hence the words ἤλπιζε . . . ἀναμένων . . . ἐνόμιζεν, "he hoped . . . waiting . . . he thought . . ." (2.84.2).

These probabilities will be rigorously verified in the account, and the words used in the narrative are identical to those in the speech. The wind rises, as predicted (2.84.2: εἴ τ' ἐκπνεύσειεν ἐκ τοῦ κόλπου τὸ πνεῦμα . . . 2.84.3: ὡς δὲ τό . . . πνεῦμα κατήει, "if the wind should blow from the gulf . . . when the wind came down"); the lack of space becomes a factor (2.84.1: ξυνῆγον ἐς ὀλίγον . . . 2.84.3: ἐν ὀλίγῳ ἤδη οὖσαι, "they came together into a small space . . . now being in a small space"); as foreseen, the Peloponnesians are thus exposed both to the wind and to the collision of boats in the center (2.84.2: τὰ πλοῖα ταραχὴν παρέξειν, εἴ τ' ἐκπνεύσειεν . . . 2.84.3: ὑπ' ἀμφοτέρων, τοῦ τε ἀνέμου τῶν τε πλοίων, "the ships would cause confusion if it should blow . . . by both the wind and the ships"); chaos follows (2.84.2: ταραχὴν παρέξειν . . . 2.84.3: ἐταράσσοντο, "would cause confusion . . . they were confused"); the ships are thrown against each other (2.84.2: ξυμπεσεῖσθαι πρὸς ἀλλήλας τὰς ναῦς . . . 2.84.3: ναῦς τε νηὶ προσέπιπτε, "the ships would strike against each other . . . ship stuck against ship"); their inexperience leaves the Peloponnesians prey to worry and confusion; and then the expected signal could finally be given (2.84.1: πρὶν ἂν αὐτὸς σημήνῃ . . . 2.84.3: σημαίνει, "until he gives the signal . . . he gives the signal"); and this perfect correspondence between expectation and confirmation is underlined here by the use of an emphatic expression: 2.84.3: τότε δὴ κατὰ τὸν καιρὸν τοῦτον [σημαίνει], "Then at this crucial moment [he gives the signal]."

In a few words, Thucydides can thus hasten the Athenian victory; in fact, there is no resistance, owing to the chaos created (2.84.3: ὑπὸ τῆς ταραχῆς), and the account is quickly concluded when the trophy is erected (2.84.4).

Thus we see that the narrative of this engagement is constructed with perfect rigor and that not a word, not a phrase, appears to be used by chance:[28] what is properly called its narration is shown to be the plan laid out at the outset, and those few lines devoted to the confusion are the only descriptive element that is added to that blueprint.[29]

It would be easy to discover the same procedure in quite a number of accounts that Thucydides devotes to battles on both land and sea.

The **battle of Olpae,** in book 3, provides a very simple example. Thucydides provides the facts at the beginning: first the establishment of the two camps (3.107.1: στρατόπεδον ἐποιήσαντο; 3.107.3: ἐστρατοπεδεύσατο); then, the day of battle, the formation of the troops (3.107.3: ἐτάσσοντο), yet Thucydides does not stress this point, for it is specifically the study of the

---

28. A translation that could make this rigor perceptible would be desirable. Unfortunately, the effects of this are lost entirely in a modern translation, where we find (Voilquin 1948, 1:154 on Thucydides 2.154) "rétrécissait . . . sans cesse . . . causerait de l'embarrass . . . se trouvèrent gênés . . . se gêneraient . . . se bousculaient." Similarly, the translation "il attendait cette éventualité en continuant à tourner" transforms something reasonably precise (ὅπερ ἀναμένων παρέπλει, "expecting which he circled around and around") into a limp narrative.

29. See below, p. 93.

two armies before him that inspires in Demosthenes, on the spot, the plan he will follow.[30] This is explained by a participle and a preposition with ὅπως (3.107.3). Demosthenes has actually foreseen the danger that threatens him, that of being surrounded; and, in order to counter that possibility, he places four hundred men in an ambush ready to attack from the rear. Next Thucydides sets out the distribution of forces and moves on to the narrative: this fulfills exactly Demosthenes' expectations, of both the risk and the remedy. The risk was περίεσχε ("outflanked") and δείσας μὴ κυκλωθῇ ("fearing being surrounded") (3.107.3); and so we have περιέσχον ("outflanked") and ἐκυκλοῦντο ("were surrounding") (3.108.1). The remedy was κατὰ νώτου γίγνωνται ("get behind them") (3.107.3); and we have κατὰ νώτου προσπίπτουσι ("attack from behind") (3.108.1). The plan is executed precisely, and it proves sufficient: despite the victory by one wing of the enemy, which found itself isolated, the effect of the Athenian success on morale determined the outcome of the battle. A lull, and the Athenian trophy concludes the episode the next day (3.109.1–2). To this strict outline, Thucydides once again adds only a few words in passing bearing on the results obtained by the various contingents.

The **Athenian landing at Sphacteria**, in book 4 (31–38), presents analogous characteristics. This time it is the Peloponnesians who are unprepared for battle, and Demosthenes alone has a plan. That plan, first indicated by a clause with ὅπως, rests on real reasoning, and Thucydides explains it early and directly in about a dozen lines.[31] Here, as in the preceding examples, reasoning is shown in a form and in terms that will furnish the framework for the narrative proper. Demosthenes' idea consists of occupying the heights so that the enemy is always caught between two hostile forces, and occupying them with light-armed troops who can use all sorts of projectiles but will themselves be impossible to reach. The Lacedaemonians are indeed caught, as he planned, under attack from hostile elements positioned on

---

30. This plan is given here with the tactical disposition itself, and in a sentence structure that shows clearly, chronologically, the formation of the plan: 3.107.3: καὶ (μεῖζον γὰρ . . .) ὁ Δημοσθένης δείσας . . . λογίζει . . . , "and (because the Peloponnesian army was larger) Demosthenes, fearing he would be surrounded, sets hoplites in ambush."

31. As at Patrai (p. 73 above), Demosthenes' plan is set out in the form of an explanation once the action is under way, for, as at Patrai, the Athenian general has the initiative. Here too he takes them by surprise, and that is why the Peloponnesians have no plan in response: their troop formation is mentioned only to explain what the Athenians found confronting them.

both sides (4.32.13: ἀμφίβολοι... ὑπὸ τῶν ἑκατέρωθεν παρατεταγμένων, "hit from all around . . . by those stationed on both sides"; 4.33.2: οἱ γὰρ ψιλοὶ ἑκατέρωθεν βάλλοντες, "the light-armed troops hitting from both sides"). Those light troops actually do constitute a formidable opponent, as he wished: impossible to pursue, they became emboldened, employing every kind of projectile (4.32.4: τοξεύμασι καὶ ἀκοντίοις καὶ λίθοις καὶ σφενδόναις, "with arrows and spears and sling-stones"; 4.34.1: ἔβαλλον λίθοις τε καὶ τοξεύμασι καὶ ἀκοντίοις, ὡς ἕκαστός τι πρόχειρον εἶχεν, "They were hitting them with stones and arrows and spears as each had anything available"). Next (34.2–3) comes a concrete and thoroughly de-scriptive representation of the disorder, noise, and darkness: it corresponds to what was, in the battle at Patrai, the description of the confusion at sea; and the passage concludes the first part of the battle. Yet the episode, though decided, is not over: an important group of Peloponnesians takes refuge in the fort, where they cannot be surrounded. Thus there must be an adjustment in the Athenian plan. A Messenian commander arrives to show a way to take them from the back (4.36.1: περιιέναι κατὰ νώτου αὐτοῖς); he succeeds (4.36.2: περιελθὼν ἔλαθε, καὶ ἐπὶ τοῦ μετεώρου ἐξαπίνης ἀναφανεὶς κατὰ νώτου, "He went around them without their knowledge and, appearing suddenly above behind them"). After that, the Lacedaemonians are, once again, exposed to a double attack—that is, βαλλόμενοι... ἀμφοτέρωθεν and ἀμφίβολοι, "hit on both sides" (4.36.3). Soon all the Athenian leaders have to do is stop the massacre.

Of course the narrative is less schematic, less simple, than in the preced-ing examples: in the first place, confusion plays an integral role in the plan and must be described very concretely;[32] in addition, the battle happens to include a second phase, undertaken as an improvisation and depending on concrete means that need some justification[33]—the precautions taken by the Messenian commander, the reasons why the path was not guarded,[34]

---

32. See below, p. 100.

33. See below, p. 98.

34. In respect to this, we can turn to the account given by General Marbot (1988, vol. 2, chap-ter xii, p. 112) of the attack at Busaco. Many circumstances are the same: a frontal attack, bru-tal and deadly; the announcement that there was a path; the secret departure of a contingent; the enemy army turned back; the path unguarded because no one thought that it was usable. Thus the schema so clearly presented by Thucydides is repeated here exactly, amid all the concrete details, circumstances, and the regrets with which Marbot has enriched it.

the impact of surprise on morale. But if the narrative seems more detailed as a result,[35] it is obvious that the structure of the narrative is, especially in the first part, identical to the one that precedes it.

At the **battle of Potidaea** (1.62–63), the connection between plan and action is marked just as plainly, particularly as here it has a somewhat negative role. Thucydides, after having indicated the names of the Peloponnesian leaders, presents, along with the tactical layout, their plan (1.62.3: ἦν δὲ ἡ γνώμη τοῦ Ἀριστέως, "It was the plan of Aristeus"). This plan involves a division of their own forces in order to take the Athenians from the rear. But the Athenian general dashes this hope (1.62.4: Καλλίας δ᾽ αὖ..., "Callias on the other hand ...") because he too divided his forces in order to (ὅπως) pin down his adversary. These two plans fill ten lines. There follows one of the simplest battles, in the course of which the Peloponnesians, victorious on one wing, lose their advantage by letting themselves become carried away in too long a pursuit. But Thucydides moves on quickly;[36] what really interests him is that, during this time, the cavalry troops massed at Olynthus do not take the Athenians from the rear, as they are supposed to do. They do attempt, as planned, to go to help (1.62.3: βοηθοῦντας; 1.63.2: ὡς βοηθήσοντες), but, as the other side had planned, the enemy cavalry blocks their way (1.62.4: ὅπως εἴργωσι; 1.63.2: ὡς κωλύσοντες): Athenian foresight foiled the Peloponnesian plans. Although the two γνῶμαι were, in a way, paralyzed, here again it was the interrelation of the plan and the action that, for Thucydides, gave structure to the account.

It may happen, moreover, that this interrelation brings out a contrast: the confrontation between plan and action brings into sharp focus the theme of defeat. This is what happens with the account of the **battle of Mantinea** (5.71–73). Agis's plan, to prevent his left from being surrounded,

---

35. Apart from the details just mentioned, it is important to note the comparison with Thermopylae, which is the only element being added, unexpectedly, to the traditional schema. Thucydides seems to have been struck by the existence of some characteristically disastrous situations: a comparison of the same genre recalls specifically in 7.71.3, the situation of the Lacedaemonians being cut off at Sphacteria.

36. He mainly gives the results and isn't interested in details other than Aristeus's predicament (ἠπόρησε μὲν, "he was confused"; ἔδοξε δ᾽ οὖν, "he thought"). This confusion is between the two directions, Olynthus and Potidaea, and thus is directly related to the failure of the maneuver that was planned from Olynthus.

involves moving certain contingents, and filling the empty space they left with others. But in fact the two cohorts that are supposed to fill the gap (5.71.3: διάκενον) do not carry out the orders they received; the result is that the enemies penetrate κατὰ τὸ διάκενον (5.72.3), and the encircle- ment on the left that he wanted to avoid (5.71.3: κυκλωθῇ) happens in this area (5.72.3: κυκλωσάμενοι). Here it is a defeat that emphasizes the rigor of the story; and we see at the same time the reason for this failure: the plan was not carried out for lack of sufficient experience. Thus Agis's calculation is definitively proved correct and verified: only it is his fears that are confirmed, and not his hopes or wishes. The principle, however, remains the same.

Of course, it would be an exaggeration to claim that this principle ap- plies all the time without any exception. There are battles where there is no plan.[37] There are also cases in which a general's actions are marked es- sentially by a series of improvisations.[38] Lastly, there are cases in which his actions are too varied and specific to be described clearly in advance. Even in those cases, however, one can say that Thucydides arranges to bring out a common idea and a determining feature governing all the particulars; we can judge this for ourselves from an extreme case and an engagement that, while strictly speaking not even a battle, seems to lend itself about as badly as possible to the analysis that we have just offered: this is the case of the **escape from Plataea**, in 3.20–24.

This event corresponds to a detailed plan that is supposed to include all sorts of concrete circumstances occurring in succession. Thucydides gives all the details as the narrative progresses in order to explain the success or the difficulty of each step in the action. But, primarily, he isolates what he considers the most important factor, specifically the bad weather (rain and wind), along with the lack of moonlight (3.22.1: τηρήσαντες νύκτα χειμέριον ὕδατι καὶ ἀνέμῳ καὶ ἅμ' ἀσέληνον, "waiting for a stormy night with rain and wind and also no moon"). It is the double explanation that marks out the main stages in the Plataean success. First of all, their at- tempt goes unnoticed; the enemy does not see them because of the darkness,

---

37. For example, among the naval battles, that of Corcyra (1.49) and, among land battles, that of Corinth (4.43–44). In many cases the plan reverts to the simplest of tactical formations, and the fight is reduced to a clash between two lines.

38. As was the case at Delium (4.96), or in Brasidas's retreat (4.127–128.1).

does not hear them because of the wind (3.22.1: ἀνὰ τὸ σκοτεινὸν…ψόφῳ δὲ … ἀντιπαταγοῦντος τοῦ ἀνέμου, "in the dark … because of the noise … with the wind rattling"); and then, when the sentinels grasp the situation, confusion erupts. Why, if not because of the darkness and the storm (3.22.5: σκοτεινῆς νυκτὸς καὶ χειμῶνος ὄντος)? This insistence[39] is all the more remarkable in that the Plataeans do not rely on this circumstance alone: to be specific, they take care to observe a certain distance between themselves; they take care also to launch an attack from the other side in order to fool the enemy. Thucydides mentions it, but in his eyes it is incidental; he introduces these remarks with a ἅμα δὲ καὶ…ὅπως… ("at the same time, in order that …") (3.22.2), and a καὶ ἅμα… ὅπως… ("at the same time … in order that …") (3.22.5), just as he introduced other details with a simple ὅπως or ἕνεκα ("for the sake of"), or with a participle.[40] So each show of ingenuity emerges (intention and action) to meet each obstacle; but, prefacing it all, Thucydides has brought out what seems to him to be most general and closest to an overall plan.

Nevertheless, it is obvious that such an account constitutes, compared to Thucydides' customary method, a limit and an exception. At no other point is the preliminary analysis so brief nor are the successive narrative details so varied. On the contrary, the normal tendency in the account is rather to make the objective, the general's plan, encompass in advance as much of the action as possible, and as a result be related as fully as possible. To the simple "in order that…" Thucydides prefers a more reasoned analysis; and most of the examples we have examined (and there could be a great many more of them[41]) contain, in recounting the plan, what is actually indirect discourse.

This is why it will not be surprising to see this recounting, in some cases, take the form of direct speech.

Thucydides found a model for this in Herodotus, and the nature of his accounts ensured that he would be turning to it. And he does so whenever

---

39. Again, see, in what follows, the other advantages of darkness and the storm: ἐκ τοῦ σκότους (3.23.4: "because of the darkness"); ἀνέμῳ, ὕδωρ (3.23.5: "wind, rain"); μετὰ λαμπάδων (3.24.1: "with torches").

40. Hence, in the first stage (the surprise approach), they are wearing shoes only on the left foot, as a security measure on account of the mud (3.22.2), and others carried their shields in order to (ὅπως, 3.22.3) facilitate their progress; during the second period (the confusion), they have their torches all ready, in order to (ὅπως, 3.22.8) confuse their signals.

41. See, for example, Brasidas's battles: 4.73, 4.126.

the plan, or the personality of the general, calls for it. To do otherwise would have been surprising, and the whole series of simple accounts culminates logically with the introduction of a speech; the transition from the first type of account to the new one occurs without any alteration of the general principle.

One example will suffice to prove the point; for this we can take the **battle of Amphipolis** in book 5 (6–11), and we may treat it just as we did the earlier ones.

The initiative in the battle belongs to Brasidas, just as it did to the Athenians at Patrai. He actually anticipates (5.6.3: προσεδέχετο, "he was awaiting") the movement of Cleon, who in fact finds himself forced to carry it out (5.7.1: ἠναγκάσθη ποιῆσαι ὅπερ ὁ Βρασίδας προσεδέχετο, "He was forced to do what Brasidas was waiting for"). Next, Brasidas develops a battle plan relying on a stratagem (5.8.2: τέχνη). This plan, being subtle, is first justified to readers in an indirect speech; then, since there is a risk it might shatter the courage of the soldiers who are not aware of it, it is set forth in a direct speech to the troops (5.9.1–10). This presents a process of reasoning based on probabilities ("I believe it likely . . . it seems to me . . . it can be presumed . . ."). The plan itself consists of creating a double surprise, by attacking at an unexpected moment and in two stages. For that, Brasidas looks for an opportune moment (5.10.5: καιρόν) and then unleashes two successive attacks. The first frightens the enemy, which is, as expected, in disorder (5.9.3: ἀτάκτως, "out of order"; 5.9.7: φοβοῦντα, "afraid"; 5.10.6: πεφοβημένοις, "frightened"; ἐκπεπληγμένοις, "stunned"; ἀταξία, "disorder") The second came, as planned, by complete surprise (5.9.7: αἰφνιδίως, "suddenly"; 5.10.7: ἀδοκήτῳ καὶ ἐξαπίνης, "unexpecting and suddenly"). The result was the hoped-for victory: the left wing was routed, then the right wing, and finally Cleon's hoplites.

This example confirms what is found in other accounts, and Louis Bodin, in his fine article "Thucydide et la campagne de Brasidas en Thrace,"[42] did not overlook this characteristic: "De nouveau aussi, mais de façon plus appuyée encore, le récit corrobore le harangue; d'avance, il a

---

42. Bodin 1935; the quote is taken from p. 49; the earlier example to which it refers is the battle described in 4.125–28, of which he wrote: "Qu'on lise là-dessus le récit, qui suit, de la bataille: il vérifie trait pour trait, on dirait volontiers mot pour mot, la thèse de la harangue." (One should read for this the subsequent account of the battle: it confirms feature for feature, one could readily say word for word, the argument of the speech.)

légitimé toutes les considerations ... sur lesquelles s'appuie le plan de Brasidas; le combat engage, il en confirme toutes les prévisions. ... Tout est ainsi mis en oeuvre pour faire sortir la leçon, et, comme la première fois, celle-ci vise le lecteur au moins autant que les soldats." (Once again, but in a still more forceful way, the account corroborates the speech: first, it gave legitimacy to all the considerations ... on which Brasidas's plan rested; once the battle was under way, it confirmed all expectations. ... Everything that is put in the work is there to teach a lesson, and like the first time, the lesson is aimed at readers at least as much as at the soldiers.) Thus the principle is the same, the rigor is the same.[43] Only the form given to the preliminary analysis distinguishes this example from the others, because a direct speech has replaced an indirect account. But that is nothing but an enhancement: in all the preceding examples, the most characteristic element is actually the very importance that Thucydides accords to this preliminary analysis; that importance only increases with the introduction of a speech.

In any case, although in general this trait constitutes a simple expansion of the process used elsewhere, it is impossible not to recognize that it carries with it a great many increased possibilities: the use of a speech is what allows for the transition from what we have called simple forms to more complex ones, from the account of Patrai to that of Naupactus.

An Account with a Debate: Naupactus

A speech differs from indirect discourse in that it is supposed to be convincing, and can be used for this purpose. The statement of the intention gives way to justifications. And, in order for intention to appear feasible, it must rest on a calculation of probability. Moreover, in order to meet its objective, the speech must give courage and dispel fear; in other words it is supposed to—and may—no longer furnish merely the outline of a plan but the complete analysis of a situation.

---

43. The verbal repetitions may be slightly less striking here: everything happens as if the presence of more detailed explanations, taking more fully into account the precision of the expectations, removed the need for more external linkages.

Perhaps there are also more concrete details in the narrative that are not related to the theoretical frame; it is certainly of interest to note that all relate to Brasidas personally, or to his death and that of Cleon.

Moreover, it usually happens that two plans oppose each other;[44] in that case, two different analyses of the same situation are found side by side: they lead to opposing conclusions, since, from the same conditions, each adversary must draw reasons to believe in the victory of his men. From that point on the readers will have before them not one, but two analyses, which will be mutually complementary in showing the precise chances of each side. This double analysis will be all the more instructive, as the positions will be argued more tightly, and their structure will make it easier to determine the superiority of one over the other.

Thus we reach a rather remarkable result: whereas, in the preceding examples, Thucydides showed in the events the more or less successful execution of a plan laid out at the outset, we will now discover that in the case of narrative with speech, the plan is replaced by a kind of dual dialectic, in which the battle is fought in advance intellectually. It is a battle of argument, in which the principal element is prediction; whoever presents a more complete system of arguments is seen to be the victor. But this victory is further confirmed by the victory of fact; events tally the points in favor of one side or the other; and the real battle takes into account the strength of the arguments; it confirms step by step what was foreseen by one or the other, and, ultimately, by one of the two. Hence the battle itself becomes more fully intelligible, since readers are thus able, by systematic comparison, to attribute to each moment of the action its precise cause, in accordance with the event's falling into one of the two systems proposed, or the other, or neither. The explanation of facts becomes clearer, just as it becomes more complete; and the element prior to the action is linked more tightly to the narrative and at the same time becomes fuller.

The two speeches at Naupactus should provide an example. Louis Bodin studied them in a talk given in 1914 to the Association des Études Grecques.[45] The example they provide is actually a particularly instructive one, as becomes readily apparent from a single reading.

Obviously, these two speeches are constructed antithetically, and their arguments correspond closely.[46] The order that each adopts varies from

---

44. If only one leader speaks, it is because he alone has the initiative and manages the operations: cf., on the silence of Cleon at Amphipolis, Bodin 1935, 50.

45. A summary, unfortunately a brief one, can be found in Bodin 1914. It indicates the different role played by moral and tactical considerations.

46. See Luschnat 1942, 26–32.

speech to speech, but they represent both sides, Phormio's skill consisting in answering precisely the arguments of the Peloponnesian leaders.

Their troops, recently defeated at Patrai and aware of the experience of the Athenian fleet, have to be afraid: the Peloponnesian leaders therefore have to try above all to dispel those fears (2.87.1: φοβεῖται, "fear"; τὸ ἐκφοβῆσαι, "frightfulness"); to do that, they remind the troops of their own bravery, and of the numerical superiority on their side. These two elements, inversely, are frightening to the Athenians; and, in a move similar to that of the other speech, Phormio also tries to allay the fears of his own men (2.89.1: πεφοβημένους, "frightened"; ἐν ὀρρωδίᾳ ἔχειν, "consider terrifying"); to do so, he shows that numbers, on the Peloponnesian side, are a mere proof of self-doubt, and they do not have a monopoly on courage. Thus the Athenians have nothing to fear (2.89.5: μή . . . δείσητε, "Do not fear"): it is the Peloponnesians who are afraid (φόβον παρέχετε, "You give them fear"; πεφόβηνται, "They are frightened"), and their fear grows when they see the Athenians attacking despite their number.[47]

So Phormio has ruined the whole Peloponnesian argument: in terms of the two successive factors supporting the argument—one of numbers and the other of courage—his reasoning is more subtle.

Concerning numbers, he overturns their argument in two stages. The Peloponnesians had said: Don't be afraid, because there are more of you. To this he replied: They are afraid; their number proves it. And he added: They are even more afraid, since, if we attack with a numerical disadvantage, it is because we are counting on something else (in other words, they are more afraid precisely because there are more of them)![48]

As for courage, the case is the same. The problem that presents itself to the two adversaries is to deal with different advantages, with one side known for its courage, the other for its skill. As early as book 1, when the Corinthians face this problem when they want to show that Athens will be defeated, the substance of what they say is this: we Peloponnesians have an innate superiority that they can never acquire, namely courage;

---

47. Thus although Phormio has already dismissed the Peloponnesian argument, at the very end of his speech he can return to their original idea, to destroy or counterbalance it: the Peloponnesian troops cannot help but be frightened by their recent defeat (2.89.11). See below, p. 117.

48. For more on the "inversion" (using someone's own argument against him) effected here, see the next chapter, p. 125.

they, the Athenians, have an acquired superiority that we can obtain, naval skill; by equalizing our chances where we can, we thus obtain the advantage.[49] The reasoning of the Peloponnesian leaders at Naupactus treated the same issue, applied to the immediate action, and provided a more subtle response, since it said basically this: Athens has skill, we have courage; now a psychological analysis shows that skill is useless without courage. But Phormio's response weaves between these same ideas[50] a relationship more subtle still, one that rests on a more nuanced psychological analysis: courage, he says, is really just the confidence gained from experience;[51] the Peloponnesians might benefit from it on land, but not at sea; there is no such thing as innate courage.

This is not the place for a detailed study of the rules of this type of dialectic, nor of its principles. But we can see from our first look that two systems are opposed to each other with unusual rigor.

Each is dominated by a different analysis of morale; in the first, emotional power dominates; in the second, intelligence; and the question is to decide which of these two qualities should in practice guarantee victory. While it might seem difficult to settle the question in debate, it happens that the narrative furnishes an answer. The end of the battle proves Phormio right; and what determines the victory is that in the initial surprise, the Peloponnesians are frightened (2.91.4: φόβος, "fear"); they became confused and made mistakes (2.91.4: ἀτάκτως, "without order"; ἀξύμφορον, "counterproductive"). The Athenians, by contrast, were encouraged (2.92.1: θάρσος, "boldness"): they followed orders closely (2.92.1: ἀπὸ ἑνὸς κελεύσματος, "from a single command"). After this, the Peloponnesians are beaten. Thucydides, in describing their defeat, takes pains to repeat the reasoning, and so one hears again the mention of their "mistakes" and "disorder" (2.92.1: ἁμαρτήματα . . . ἀταξίαν).

Of course the narrative does not enable us to evaluate in depth the two preceding analyses; it simply confirms one of the two conclusions and

---

49. On the arithmetical aspect, see p. 135.

50. Numerous verbal connections naturally underline the close thematic relationship: Louis Bodin remarks that the Peloponnesians call Athenian knowledge "what you most fear" (2.87.4: ἣν μάλιστα φοβεῖσθε), and Phormio calls Peloponnesian courage "what they most rely on" (2.89.2: ᾧ μάλιστα πιστεύοντες).

51. In this inversion, as in the one about numbers, Phormio establishes a causal relationship between two notions that the Peloponnesians set in balance: see below, p.125.

possibly reproduces certain terms that the preceding arguments were able to show as linked together. It can do no more; it is not reasoned out; it can prove nothing. But, precisely because it is separate and placed on a different level, the enrichment is done in reverse, so that the narrative is the beneficiary. The isolated terms it offers add to the known linkages. At every moment in the action, readers, armed in advance with two complementary arguments, are in a position to add to what they read, to understand which factors might arise to prevent or provoke such an outcome, to pick out an easily understandable relationship by which these factors ought to be more decisive than those. A whole reasoned system surrounds each statement of fact, and gives it a new dimension. The action, in the smallest details, takes on a wider importance; the Athenian victory at Naupactus itself becomes, in the eyes of the readers, the triumph of experience over innate courage; it illustrates the consequences for morale that accompany technical progress. And this is a kind of explanation that cannot be achieved through indirect discourse nor so neatly defined in a single speech.

Can we say, however, that the Athenian success was inevitable, obvious? Far from it, since this success almost does not happen. Here too Thucydides has to offer an explanation.

One can say, actually, that Phormio's speech included a whole supplementary element that does not relate to anything in the speech of the Peloponnesians: that is the purely tactical part, concerning the battle plan. It is found in 2.89.8, and it is rather remarkable that this analysis should have fallen to Phormio, since it was not he, here, who had initiated the operation, and he knows it: his talk indicates only why it is unfavorable to the Athenians to fight in a tight space; he lets himself say only that he would not do so willingly.

But this is exactly what Peloponnesians are able to make him do against his will; and here the narrative repeats the terms of the analysis, but to confirm Phormio's fears: he had said that he would not willingly (ἑκών) fight in the gulf (ἐν κόλπῳ); then the narrative shows that the Peloponnesians, wishing to force Phormio's men to enter there[52] against their will

---

52. The word ἔσω ("inward") at 2.90.1 recalls the words at 2.91.1, ἐς τὸν κόλπον καὶ τὰ στενά ("into the gulf and the narrows"), that preceded it; these recall both the actual conditions and the analysis of the speech of Phormio, who says at 2.89.8 first ἐν τῷ κόλπῳ, "in the gulf," and then ἡ στενοχωρία, "a narrow space."

(ἄκοντας), actually bring it about that he acts against his will and soon finds himself in the gulf.

Moreover, the account underlines rigorously this Peloponnesian success through phrases like ὅπερ ἐκεῖνοι προσεδέχοντο, "which they were expecting" (2.90.3), and ὅπερ ἐβούλοντο μάλιστα, "which they had especially aimed at" (2.90.4).[53] And one might note that this first part of the battle seems to lead to a decisive conclusion, with many killed or taken prisoner: actually only a small unit escaped the massacre.[54]

The tactical section in Phormio's speech is explained in relation to this early phase: it makes clear why skill is not instantly triumphant. Skill would have required fixed conditions, and the combination is not always to be found. The two adversaries know that; also fear in one is confused with hope in the others; each has to recognize that Athens' naval superiority emerges when the fleet has a clear field. The tactical part of Phormio's speech, by evoking these conditions, explains the beginning of the battle.

The question that remains then is which of the two qualities will prevail—in other words, how the action will move from one phase to the next. Since the Peloponnesians have the ability to constrain Phormio to enter the gulf, and since, once there, Athenian superiority will be lost, how does it happen that the Athenians win? It is here in the narrative that a concrete circumstance arises that no one could have predicted: the presence of a small boat lying at anchor. Thucydides presents clearly and openly this element that has defied prediction with the verb ἔτυχε. But not everything about the incident is random: the Athenian ships take advantage of the opportunity and are saved mostly by the speed with which they move (2.91.1: φθάνουσιν, "They outrun them"; 2.91.3: φθάσασα καὶ περιπλεύσασα, "outrunning them and sailing around it"); for the Peloponnesians, on the other hand, the initial surprise immediately turns to fear; suddenly the danger in their disarray is apparent, and their inexperience prevents them from putting up any useful resistance. So owing to chance, the normal order is reestablished, according to the terms of the debate; and the superiority or inferiority

---

53. We have seen the predominantly intellectual value of these expressions that describe the correctness of their predictions. It is a complete break with Thucydides' thinking to translate them simply on an emotional level (for example, "which they had so much wished for").

54. See 2.91.2: ὡς νενικηκότες, "as if victorious."

of the two adversaries, which until then has been masked by the exceptional circumstances, is quickly apparent once they must adapt to a change in circumstances.

This is doubtless why the tactical considerations are attributed to Phormio and treated separately. If it were otherwise, if the Peloponnesians claimed to be counting on the lack of space to paralyze Athenian experience, and if chance then intervened to ruin their plan, then the Athenian victory would be viewed as a surprise, pure and simple. But that is not the way Thucydides sees it. What is normal, in his view, is that the Peloponnesians make mistakes and become discouraged; the slightest stroke of fortune should ruin their plan; and the lack of space represents extraordinary and risky conditions of battle. Thus, in focusing the debate on what is deep and lasting, on the normal conditions of battle, conditions that will soon be reestablished, Thucydides brings out the deep cause and presents the final outcome as more necessary than it is fortuitous. This analysis not only sheds light on those elements that are causal in the battle and the reasons for its outcome; it even establishes an order of precedence among the diverse explanations, distinguishes the essential from the incidental, orders, selects, comments. The battle account becomes a theory.

This feature also offers an explanation for some contents that are rather surprising, namely those of the speeches (both military and political); for they must give an account of events, but at the level chosen by Thucydides. There are, in fact, different ways of accounting for them:

1. Explaining specific maneuvers of the fleet, its battle order, circumstantial motives determining one movement or another, constitutes the first level: Thucydides, to the extent that he feels obliged to refer to these, does so in the narrative itself.
2. Showing that the Athenian victory resulted from knowing how to exploit the carelessness of the Peloponnesians, who, in success, succumb to chaos, is the simple kind of strategic explanation that Thucydides furnishes in the accounts without speeches.
3. But showing the opposing qualities of each side, deciding in what measure the outcome of the battle might be explained by general causes, those that would have the same effects in other cases, and seeking to know the ways in which the psychological reactions of the two adversaries were typical, or necessary, that is what only the speeches can do.

This is the source of their abstract quality. But this is also what explains the exemplary value they give an account. Linked to ideas—courage and experience, number and confidence, prediction and chance—the account may now clarify numerous general traits: τῶν μελλόντων ποτὲ αὖθις κατὰ τὸ ἀνθρώπινον τοιούτων καὶ παραπλησίων ἔσεσθαι, "what, given humanity, is going to happen once again in an approximately similar way" (1.22.4). As Louis Bodin wrote, "In the enormous imbalance of forces in conflict, in the huge readjustment that, in the midst of the action, shifted the victory from one camp to the other, the battle engaged the contemporary imagination intensely. Such failure, followed by such success, held a lesson. . . . Now, an historical fact, taken in its raw state, is a dead letter. It cannot be an object of thought and become exemplary unless it has first been submitted to analysis; only analysis can reveal whether it contains any eternal truth."

This role is particularly remarkable in the case of the military speeches. These in fact manage to reconcile two apparently very different requirements. To the extent that, unlike other speeches, military speeches are related to simple narration that serves as an immediate control on them, they should reconstruct an explanation that corresponds perfectly to the facts and is adapted in each case to the circumstances. But at the same time, like other speeches, they function to clarify a situation in depth, completing a general analysis of the forces facing each other.[55] They depart from the immediate to rise intellectually to the level of the great political speeches. And because of them the battle account, resting on a certain number of broad themes more or less known in advance, ultimately emerges with the clarity of a proof.

A Highly Complex Account: Syracuse

Yet it may happen that speeches, beyond these general references, relate to still other elements.

---

55. This is what is shown by Luschnat (1942, esp. 113–14). He considers particularly the passages of exhortation, those that insist on the importance of the battle and on what is at stake. These are the passages that are least directly related to the narrative, and that consequently are of least concern to us here (see the difference that he himself notes on p. 72 between his view and that of Bodin 1935).

Let us consider a case in which the form of the battle account becomes even more complex and is no longer limited to two speeches before the narrative.

Such a case occurs when a series of battles arises from similar conditions and includes actions both sequential and recurring. Such is the case of the battles joined in the harbor region of Syracuse, in book 7, particularly the final three battles (7.36–41, 51–54, 59–71), following the Athenian loss at Plemmyrium (7.24.3): all three are conditioned by the fact that, from this point on, Athens no longer has a large enough space at its disposal to exercise its maritime skill.

Thus the problem is the same one encountered in the battle at Naupactus, but here the situation is even more serious. At stake is a battle to the death between the two cities: Athens has met its match, for Gylippus is a brilliant commander, and the Syracusans are experienced on the sea; lastly, locked in a prolonged, face-to-face deadlock, the adversaries have time to pursue options and improve their military methods.

So Thucydides does something unusual: in 7.36, the indirect statement ascribed to the Syracusans, he portrays the general conditions of the conflict preceding the first of these three battles. The frame is simple: one plan, one narrative. The plan is simple as well, consisting essentially of one innovation in weaponry: in order to optimize the battle conditions, the Syracusans shorten and strengthen their prows. But the analysis does not stop there: for this innovation is linked to the tactics, which are themselves linked to the lack of space; and so, the reasoning concludes with the realization that the lack of space can be an advantage.

The passage is difficult in both structure and content[56] owing precisely to Thucydides' desire to emphasize quite systematically the coherent nature of the Syracusan campaign: everything is linked, everything intersects; the text shows how weapons, tactics, and topographical conditions affect each other; and it also shows how, in each of these areas, and owing to their interconnectedness, the Syracusans prevail over the Athenians. Thus he mentions first the weaponry (7.36.3, beginning) and then the differences in tactics ("because [the Athenians] did not employ prow-to-prow

---

56. Louis Bodin was very thorough in his analysis of 7.36; I made a great effort to summarize his conclusions in a corresponding note in my edition (Romilly et al. 1953–72, 7:168–69), and use them here.

[διὰ τὸ μὴ ἀντιπρῴροις] ramming rather than side-to-side"). The Syracusans think that the Athenians are not equipped to resist their new tactic. He then turns to the topographical factors, also linking them to tactics: "[The narrow area] would be in their favor, because charging prow to prow (ἀντιπρῴροις) . . .". The Syracusans reason that the Athenians will not have room to respond to these new tactics with new ones of their own. Finally come the tactics themselves ("colliding prow to prow," τῷ ἀντιπρῳρον ξυγκροῦσαι . . .), now linked to the topographical factors in general on land as well as on sea. Syracuse thinks that, given the uneven coastline, Athens will not have room to avoid battle by retreating. The outcome will be thus assured, since the Athenian defense itself will risk further disorder and defeat by creating even less room in which to maneuver. And so every point of view is considered, all Athenian options are removed. And against them Syracuse mounts a systematic opposition.[57] In fact, one could say that here we have not the usual indirect statement, but one similar to the outcome in a dialectical struggle, in which one side prevails over the other in every respect. In this respect, the indirect statement found in 7.36 is without equal in the entire work: it is presented in purely dialectical form.

The reason for this is clear. If the battle of Naupactus, where Athenian experience triumphed, has been the subject of the kind of deep analysis that we have observed, it is easy to see that the three battles of Syracuse constitute a response to Naupactus: in the account in book 2 we witness the triumph of Athenian experience, as long as they maintain εὐρυχωρία ("large space"); the accounts of book 7 show the possible defensive tactic, provided one is in στενοχωρία ("narrow space").

From this fact we can draw an additional conclusion: this exceptional indirect style is significant only if it represents explanatory γνώμη ("intention"), not only in the battle that immediately follows, but in the sequence of battles leading to the Athenian disaster.

This sequence alone, moreover, leads to the final confirmation.

---

57. As always, the structural junctions are reinforced by verbal repetition, as Louis Bodin has remarked. Thus we find, at different stages, the infinitives at 7.36.3 οὐκ ἔλασσον σχήσειν ("not fare worse") . . . πρὸς ἑαυτῶν ἔσεσθαι ("be in their favor") and at 7.36.5 πλεῖστον . . . ἐν αὐτῷ σχήσειν ("fare best in this") with the corollaries τοῖς Ἀθηναίοις οὐκ ἔσεσθαι at 7.36.4 and οὐκ ἔσεσθαι τοῖς Ἀθηναίοις at 7.36.5 ("not exist for the Athenians"). These facts are mentioned, as are others, in my edition.

The first battle (7.37–41) is well commanded, according to the analysis; but a counterplan intervenes. After an initial, inconclusive engagement, Nicias actually has time to respond in one respect to the Syracusan strategy. In order to draw Athens into disorder and defeat, Syracuse is counting on difficulties encountered in attempting to backwater (7.36.5–6: τὴν γὰρ ἀνάκρουσιν . . . καί . . . ἤν πη βιάζωνται . . . ταράξεσθαι, "backing up . . . and . . . if somehow pressed . . . would be in confusion"). Nicias minimizes these by anchoring his supply ships "in order that if any ship was pressed it would have a secure place to flee and a place from which to sail out again without being attacked" (7.38.3: ὅπως, εἴ τις βιάζοιτο ναῦς, εἴη κατάφευξις ἀσφαλὴς καὶ πάλιν καθ' ἡσυχίαν ἔκπλους). The measure is not without effect. In fact, after a period of chaos, owing to a Syracusan ruse (a different level of detail), the battle gets under way; it happens in two stages. The first fully justifies the Syracusans' indirect statement; in effect, the benefit of the Syracusans' weapons is quickly shown; the power of prow against prow is successful (7.40.5), as are all the tactics used,[58] in paralyzing the great Athenian fleet. Syracuse is victorious. But the next battle justifies Athens' counterplan; this time Syracuse is unable to exploit fully its victory; Nicias's supply ships halt the pursuit.[59]

Demosthenes' arrival changes none of these facts; on the contrary, his failure at Epipolae manages to discourage the Athenians, and that is their state of mind when the next battle begins. Furthermore, Demosthenes recognizes the problem and wants to leave Syracuse to fight in open water (7.49.2: "not in the narrow space, which is more to the advantage of the enemy," οὐκ ἐν στενοχωρίᾳ, ἣ πρὸς τῶν πολεμίων μᾶλλόν ἐστι), but no one listens. Since the conditions are the same, Thucydides furnishes no new explanation of naval tactics before the battle; he simply relates, in an indirect-statement analysis (7.50.3–51.2), the shift that has occurred in morale and the desire the Syracusans now have to prevent the Athenians from getting away. In terms of the way the events occur, the analysis of chapter 36, without corresponding perfectly to the facts, is again proven

---

58. Here two kinds of fighting are involved that are not described in the indirect statement: the attacks by the soldiers on the bridge and by the light boats. As always, Thucydides prioritizes, and his analysis involves only the principle.

59. Note here repetition of the word κατάφευξις ("place to flee") in 7.38.3 and 7.41.1, as well as the proper nouns designating the merchant ships and the anchorage.

correct; and the account shows simultaneously the validity of Syracusan predictions, and the thinking that prevented their ultimate victory. First, a tactical error by Eurymedon puts him in the position—the words themselves underline it—that is essentially the one predicted by the Syracusan analysis:[60] his units are pushed too close to the shore and sink. Yet the Athenians once again are saved from total disaster, this time because their allies guaranteed success on land, permitting the sailors to disembark outside the normally protected area without too many losses.[61]

After this new Syracusan victory, troop morale changes dramatically once again (7.55–56), and consequently Syracuse closes the great port. All signs indicate that this time the battle will be decisive, which is why Thucydides puts the catalog of allies first. The fullness of the account itself is exceptional.

It includes the following elements: Athenian positions (7.60); Nicias's speech (7.61–64); Syracuse's position (7.65); speeches of the Syracusan leaders and of Gylippus (7.66–68); the final appeal by Nicias (7.69); the battle (7.70–72). Only for this battle is the structure even more comprehensive than for Naupactus.

Without going into the details of the contrast between the two speeches, there are three principal points to be made.

The first deals with the reasons for confidence. Like the Peloponnesians at Naupactus, the Athenians have just been defeated here. At Naupactus, the Peloponnesians had to overcome the memory of their defeat by justifying the reasons for it, and by reassuring themselves with thoughts of their valor and their numbers. At Syracuse, apart from their number, the Athenians have to rely on luck. The Syracusans, on the other hand, know that the experience of their earlier defeats has to discourage the Athenians (7.66.3), and that their own number will be an encumbrance (7.67.3), and

---

60. 7.36.5: ἐξωθουμένοις . . . ἐς τὴν γῆν, "pushed onto the land"; see 7.52.2: πρὸς τὴν γῆν μᾶλλον, "more toward the land," then ἐξεώθουν ἐς τὴν γῆν, "They pushed him to the land." Yet the case is not exactly identical, because the accident does not result from prow hitting prow, nor from a defensive withdrawal. That is doubtless why Thucydides is so terse in his explanation of this battle.

61. The Syracusans had thought that the Athenians could not withdraw except κατ' αὐτὸ τὸ στρατόπεδον τὸ ἑαυτῶν ("through their own camp," 7.36.5); they manage to escape by disembarking ἔξω τῶν σταυρωμάτων καὶ τοῦ ἑαυτῶν στρατοπέδου ("outside of their own stockades and camp," 7.53.1).

that their fear is in fact despair, since they can rely only on luck. All the wise reasoning of the past now works for the Syracusan side, and the very nature of Athenian hopes gives comfort to the enemy, so irrational do they now appear.[62] The weakness of the Athenian position becomes apparent from the speech, from the contrast between the two speeches, and even from the contrast between the two debates.

The second remark bears on the question of what is at stake. Although the two antithetical speeches are roughly parallel, this issue comes first for Nicias, and last for the Syracusans; the situation of the two adversaries is, in terms of risk, very different. Only the urgency of their risk can motivate the Athenians, while the Syracusans are inspired by the exceptionally positive consequences of total victory. Here again, the arguments are made with rigor, but only to render more apparent the weakness of the Athenian position.[63]

That leaves, finally, the role of the tactics themselves. Here Nicias provides something new, for he too wishes to adapt to the battle conditions analyzed in 7.36; he changes the usual position: since the battle will have naval maneuvers, he takes on board many men who will fight on deck and, as the enemy's reinforced prow-extensions will provide protection against the shock of prow against prow, Nicias will use iron grapplers to immobilize the Syracusans' ships after these assaults (7.62).[64] As he says himself, he rejects traditional naval tactics for the Athenians, since

---

62. Similarly, the speech in 7.77 is entirely based on hope (which, as we know, arises only when the situation has grown hopeless) and on εὐτυχία, "good luck," i.e., a τύχη, "luck," that Nicias attributes to the gods. The narrative is, in fact, a contradiction of his speech rather than a confirmation of it (for example, concerning the forced marches or the fidelity of the Sicels): his argumentation foreshadows the result.

63. Here again we find many verbal echoes. We could even say that, despite an appearance of parallelism between the beginnings of the two speeches, Nicias's first lines and the final lines of the Syracusans are presented as stark opposites. Nicias begins (7.61.1–2) with a remark on the stakes, the words ὁ μὲν ἀγών, "the contest," being followed by information of a twofold objective (τε . . . καί); then comes the hypothesis of success (ἢν γὰρ κρατήσωμεν, "for if we prevail"), and finally information about the proper attitude (οὐ χρή . . . οὐδέ, "we must not . . . nor . . ."). The Syracusans conclude (7.61.3) with information about the proper attitude (μή . . . πρέπει . . . μηδέ . . . , "it is not suitable . . . nor . . ."); then comes the hypothesis of Athenian success (καὶ ἐὰν κρατήσωσιν, "and if they prevail"), and finally the indication of the double objective (τε . . . καί), concluding with the stakes (καλὸς ὁ ἀγών, "The contest is noble").

64. The introduction of this refinement has a place within a rigorous logical progression. Diodorus (13.16), on the other hand, writing after Thucydides, reveals the iron hooks by accident, in an aside, in the account of the fourth battle.

the conditions preclude their use; in their place, he adopts the principle of "ground fighting on the deck."[65] But, as with all the other elaborations, this project finds a response[66] in the Syracusan speech (7.67.2 end). They observe that the Athenians, by changing their ways, will adopt methods that were well known and normal for their adversaries (ξυνήθη, "customary"; οὐκ ἀνάρμοστοι, "not unsuited"), but unusual for themselves (παρὰ τὸ καθεστηκός, "contrary to custom"; χερσαῖοι . . . ἐπὶ ναῦς, "land-based . . . on ships"); this, combined with the number of ships, will immobilize them. So, whereas in other areas the contrast between arguments revealed the Athenians' inferiority, it could be said that here we have come full circle: in order to adjust, the Athenians are compelled to change; and it is this very change that will lead to their defeat.[67]

The battle of Syracuse thus becomes a kind of ratification of the battle of Naupactus. After great trial and error, the Syracusans have succeeded in doing what the Peloponnesians tried in vain to do at Naupactus: they denied Athens the εὐρυχωρία ("wide space"), by limiting its space both on land and on sea; they forced the Athenians gradually to modify their armaments, their battle formation and even basic tactical principles. In the naval battle that ensued, Athens no longer enjoyed the benefit of its long experience.

After this, the battle unfolds in precisely the ways foreseen by the Syracusans in their analysis of chapter 36, and very soon repeated in the chapter on tactics in their last speech: the battle is fought between many ships in a tight space;[68] maneuvers such as pulling back (withdrawing) and breaking

---

65. For anyone pondering retreat, Nicias has but one exhortation; he reminds them in that case of how little land the Athenians occupy (7.62.4 and 7.36.5; see the repetition in 7.63.1).

66. The answer to the iron grappling hooks will be leather coverings, introduced in the narrative with a purpose clause (ὅπως, 7.65.2).

67. Syracuse, on the other hand, can effectively employ a procedure previously condemned (7.36.5), because it was its own; Athens, in the last battle, has to relinquish at once its habitual ways and advantages.

68. 7.70.4: ἐν ὀλίγῳπολλῶν, "many in a little space," reinforced by πλεῖσται . . . ἐν ἐλαχίστῳ, "most . . . in the least space"; see 7.36.3: οὐκ ἐν πολλῷ πολλαῖς ναυσίν, "many ships in a little space"; 7.62.1: τὸν μέλλοντα ὄχλον τῶν νεῶν, "the coming mass of ships"; and 7.67.3: ἐν ὀλίγῳ γὰρ πολλαί, "many in a little space." The term στενοχωρία, "narrow space," is used again further on (7.70.6); see 7.36.4 (twice).

through become impossible and are replaced by simple assault;[69] soldiers on deck assume great importance.[70] Everything transpires amid ferocity and chaos, and after relentless fighting we witness the turning point (7.71.5: πρίν γε δή, "until at last"): the Athenians turn and flee to the shore; the disaster is total.

Here, then, the narration of the battle is introduced, not simply by indirect speech, or by a direct speech, or by contrasting direct speeches, but by an entire complex,[71] including an initial analysis, that ushers in a series of accounts and stretches over two-thirds of the book.

One might, moreover, take this conclusion even further, for what is true from the point of view of tactics is also true with regard to the analysis of morale or even face-to-face formations of forces. In these two areas, as in that previously considered, the texts reinforce each other, and all the clues that precede the final battle are themselves the product of comprehensive preparation still earlier.

What must be remembered is that in this vast composite, Thucydides is not content to relate, as would many good historians, every new phase and the importance of every factor; he weighs, compares, explains, everything in advance. When his account grows richer, it is always the same part that expands: the part that precedes the action. Facts are not more detailed; they are more analyzed, more explained; an increasingly elaborate dialectical system traces a kind of outline that soon comes to include everything. From that point on, no aspect of events can any longer be mentioned in the narration without revealing immediately to the readers its meaning and its causes, its truth or necessity, its gravity. Nothing happens that is not either a confirmation or a refutation of the calculations worked out by reason; nothing appears that is not an adaptation, that is not a concept, nothing that has not been given its shape and foundation by the mind.

---

69. 7.70.4; see 7.36.4 and 5.

70. 7.70.5; see 7.40.5 and n. 4 above.

71. The second appeal of Nicias, in the last battle, cannot be taken into consideration; it is not helpful to an understanding of the narrative and appears there to make the extreme gravity of the situation felt. We might compare it to the second appeal of Brasidas in 5.10.5.

Pathos and Detail

This suggests that the battle loses any anecdotal quality,[72] but it does not mean that it lacks either pathos or concrete realism. The account of the battle of Syracuse itself, often cited as an example, should suffice to prove it. But here the pathos and realism take on a special quality.

In Thucydides, as in tragedy, pathos is tied to structure; and it is manifested in the battle accounts as well as elsewhere. Yet whereas in tragedy it is the narrator's emotion that, quite naturally, gives the narrative its form, in Thucydides it is the narrative form that excites the emotions. The readers, already initiated into the plans of the two adversaries, and informed of the significance of every event even before it occurs, are led, by prior knowledge, to invest the text with sympathy, hope, and fear. They are thus in the position of participants.

Even more, in the exceptional example just examined, we observe that Thucydides is not content simply to create pathos by the rigor of intellectual preparation. To make it felt, he uses the very technique used in tragedy to describe the way participants feel themselves affected by events.[73]

First, their suffering corresponds to the suffering in tragedy expressed by people who are outside the battle but who will be affected by the outcome, of which they are as yet ignorant. Thus, for readers, Nicias's final warnings function here in a way similar to the tears of Jocasta or Atossa, or to the anxious anticipation of the chorus before the narrative.

But above all we see how the account itself is interrupted by the evocation of the emotional reactions of those who were involved in the fighting or were witnesses to it. In tragedy, in one place there are "lamentations mixed with wailing,"[74] and in another, "witnesses, more than actors feeling

---

72. This is easily shown for book 7 when we compare the accounts of Thucydides with those of Plutarch (p. 24 above). When Thucydides offers an anecdote in a battle narrative, we can be sure that it concerns an individual of particular importance (such as the fall of Brasidas, wounded, in 4.12.1) or a particularly catastrophic event (such as Timocrates' suicide in 2.92.3).

73. Finley (1942, 321–22) shows with great precision that Thucydides' narrative of the battle of Syracuse is more evocative of Aeschylus or Euripides than of Herodotus. Numerous excellent comparisons are found in his book. Here I am concerned only with their meaning as related to the problem of technique I am considering.

74. Euripides, *Heracleidae* 833; see p. 67 above.

their sweat run, so afraid were they for their friends";[75] above all, in *The Persians* it is the cries and appeals resounding in the two camps, mixed with sobbing, echoing the two stages of the fighting.[76] These devices, so natural to tragedy, are precisely the ones employed by Thucydides.

In the account of the battle of Syracuse, in addition to a division of the battle into two phases (inconclusive fighting, followed by the Athenian retreat to the shore), we actually see another division: for each of these two phases is considered in turn, first directly and then indirectly, through the reactions of witnesses (7.71.1: ὅ τε ἐκ τῆς γῆς πεζός, "the infantry on land"; 7.71.6: ὁ δὲ πεζός, "the infantry"); each time, the feelings of these witnesses are analyzed (7.71.1–2: the anxiety, the tension, the mood, the fear for the future; 7.71.6: ἔκπληξις, "panic"); they are perceived through gestures (7.71.3: "The very movement of their bodies, in this extreme suffering, follows the fluctuations of their mood"), and in particular they express themselves through their cries: first, wailing mixed with cries as they observe the spectacle of defeat (7.71.3: ὀλοφυρμῷ τε ἅμα μετὰ βοῆς, "lamentation simultaneously with shouting"), then, an entire concert of exclamations, for which Thucydides has found stylistic effects and asyndetons that are worthy of Aeschylus (7.71.4):

πάντα ὁμοῦ ἀκοῦσαι, ὀλοφυρμὸς βοή, νικῶντες κρατούμενοι, ἄλλα ὅσα ἐν μεγάλῳ κινδύνῳ μέγα στρατόπεδον πολυειδῆ ἀναγκάζοιτο φθέγγεσθαι.

It was possible for all things to be heard together, lamentation, shouting, conquerors, defeated, every other sound of many kinds that a great camp in great danger could be forced to make.

And finally the great moans of defeat, recalling the long wail of Xerxes in *The Persians* and his piercing sob (7.71.6: οἰμωγῇ τε καὶ στόνῳ, "lament and grief").

As in tragedy, moreover, this evocation specifically helps to emphasize the duration of the battle and contrasts two parts of unequal importance:

---

75. See p. 67 above.
76. See p. 68 above.

the long sustained effort on both sides, then the sudden panic. This sort of descriptive pathos can only make the personal suffering more moving as a result of the intellectual preparation.

In fact, even when dealing with a battle less noteworthy for its significance or for the care Thucydides devotes to it, it does appear that the account is presented in such a manner as to direct the sympathy of the readers, leaving them to interpret, in a literary way, the emotional value of different stages of the action. Whereas there is nothing, in the account of the battle of Naupactus, to correspond to the sights and sounds evoked in book 7, there can be no doubt that the logical commentaries in 2.90.3 (ὅπερ ἐκεῖνοι προσεδέχοντο, "as they expected") and in 2.90.4 (ὅπερ ἐβούλοντο μάλιστα, "as they especially had wanted") help, as much as any cry of joy, to make one feel the Peloponnesian success at Naupactus; or that the contrast between the battle cry announcing this almost final success, and the ἔτυχε δέ (2.91.3: "And it happened that there was . . .") that erupts at the beginning of the sentence, draws attention to this development or surprise; or that words like φόβος (2.91.4: "fear") and θάρσος (2.92.1: "daring"), coming into the narrative at that point, translate the intelligible cause of the final result, and at the same time the psychological value of the catastrophe. These sentiments are not, as they are at Syracuse, those of powerless witnesses; they form part of the action, where their causes and their consequences are read; as such, they are part of a rational system, but that does not make their emotional value any less immediately accessible.[77]

The preliminary analyses give the narrative its intellectual transparency; it is that very transparency, when projected in time in the narrative, that assumes a lifelike rhythm and is converted to pathos.

Similarly, it is its intellectual character that defines when and how concrete reality takes its place there.

---

77. The emotions of the combatants are evoked in a rather detailed way at the battle of Pylos, as are their cries (4.34.1: τοῦ θαρσεῖν, "boldness"; καταφρονήσαντες καὶ ἐμβοήσαντες, "feeling contempt and shouting"; 4.34.2: τῆς βοῆς, "shouting"; ἔκπληξις, "confusion"; 4.34.3: τῆς μείζονος βοῆς, "louder shouting"; οὐκ ἔχοντες ἐλπίδα, "without hope"; 4.35.2: ἔτι πλέονι βοῇ τεθαρσηκότες, "emboldened with still louder shouting"). Here, though, a new way of fighting is the issue: the confidence assumed by the light troops allows them to scatter and horrify the Peloponnesians by their loud and tumultuous attacks.

It may, certainly, occur in an initial case, as an integral part of the intention (γνώμη)—in other words, when the latter is used either to improve the material at hand or as a supplement for what is missing.

The first of these two cases is what is often found in the sieges; sieges allow for more leisure than the actual battles and give rise to similar inventiveness. The siege of Plataea (2.75–76) is characteristic of this. There we find, clearly argued and analyzed, the dialogue between the two intentions (γνῶμαι) of the two adversaries; however, this dialogue makes sense here only in precise, concrete detail. Thucydides begins by describing at some length the construction of the earthworks put up by the Peloponnesians in front of the city wall (2.75.2: "Tree trunks, cut on Mount Cithaeron, ran the length and width of the two sides of this construction, to prevent a collapse [ὅπως μή]. . . . The hole was filled with wood, stones, earth"); the details are explained by the fact that the battle is one of practical initiatives. In order to defend themselves against the earthworks, the Plataeans begin by raising their fortification by means of a wooden wall whose construction is described for us with the same precision (2.75.4–6: "They fortify it with bricks, taken from neighboring houses; the pieces of wood served as support and prevented [τοῦ μή]. . . . They hang skins and hides on the outside of the scaffold so as to provide the workers protection from the burning arrows [ὥστε] . . ."). But at the same time the Plataeans begin to remove the embankment that supported the earthworks. What will the Peloponnesians do? They invent (2.76.1) a new system involving reed baskets filled with clay to prevent the removal of the earth (ὅπως μή . . .). How will this obstacle be met? The Plataeans begin to remove it from below: they invent (2.76.2) a new method that involves digging a tunnel from the city. At the same time, they begin a new construction. What can be done against these efforts? The Peloponnesians resort (2.76.4) to machines. How can the damage of the machines be stopped? The Plataeans have the idea of using slipknots, or heaving heavy posts to break the head of the battering ram (2.76.4: "They hung the two ends of giant posts from iron chains, which slipped on two leaning masts that jutted out from the wall"). Every invention is answered with a new effort, and practical results abound; this is about practicality informed by intelligence to meet certain practical goals, calling on very practical skills.

When, instead of improving skills, intelligence had to compensate for the lack of alternatives, relying on one's wits plays the same role with less ingenuity and more brute force; an example is the action of the soldiers at Pylos, who made up for the absence of tools in choosing their stones, and for the absence of troughs by carrying the mortar on their backs: "bending in order to hold it, and crossing their hands behind their backs to keep it from slipping off" (4.4.2). This vivid picture is shown with the same ὡς and ὅπως as every other γνώμη. Moreover, its presence is even more justified in the passage, since Thucydides insists, for the entire episode, on the fact that Demosthenes' plan could not be carried out except thanks to a felicitous coincidence of luck and the soldiers' spontaneous goodwill.[78]

Occasionally, this type of information is found in the battles themselves, but rarely, as the situations hardly lend themselves to these kinds of initiatives. Yet we notice, in the case of a series of battles, such as those of Syracuse, the role that modification of material plays.

On the other hand, battle contains one element that eludes rational interpretation, for by its very nature it is irrational; this is where Homer opens, with a scene of chaotic confusion.

For Homer this marks the beginning, out of which a whole series of individual exploits arise. For Thucydides, it marks the end, the result of a whole system of well-reasoned calculations on the part of the generals; it is the conclusion.

The naval battle of Leukimme (1.47–54) alone begins right off with the chaos of rioting, accompanied by θόρυβος, "tumult" (1.49.4: πανταχῇ μὲν οὖν πολὺς θόρυβος καὶ ταραχώδης ἦν ἡ ναυμαχία, "Everywhere there was much tumult, and the sea battle was in a state of confusion"); but this is precisely because this involves a battle of the old-fashioned kind, in which everyone fights "with more heart and vigor than skill" (1.49.3: θυμῷ καὶ ῥώμῃ τὸ πλέον ... ἢ ἐπιστήμῃ). Otherwise, to attack this way is barbaric (4.127.1: πολλῇ βοῇ καὶ θορύβῳ προσέκειντο, "They attacked with great shouting and tumult"): Brasidas devotes one whole speech (4.126) to showing the contrast between this behavior and that of the always disciplined and orderly Greeks. For an intelligent Greek, θόρυβος ("tumult") is, in fact, accidental. But they all attempt to produce it in the enemy. As Thucydides says of the naval battle at Corcyra (3.78.1), ἐπειρῶντο θορυβεῖν, "They tried to create tumult."

---

78. On the element of luck, see Romilly 1963, 174.

Accordingly, disorder, which can only be described in its concrete reality and its very incoherence, arises from within a rational system; it is foreseen by one of the adversaries; it marks the success of one line of reasoning or a failure of the other.

It may stem from a style of fighting with which one of the combatants is unfamiliar, in particular, the use of light-armed troops. That is the case at the end of the Aetolian campaign, in 3.98. Demosthenes should not have exposed himself to such risk;[79] and the result is not long coming: the Athenians "were exhausted and very burdened with their repetitive task, while the Aetolians kept up the pressure and threw spears. At last they turned and fled, and falling into gorges with no way out and unfamiliar places, they were killed; for their guide to the roads, the Messenian Chromon, had by chance been killed. Many of them, as they turned and fled, the spear-throwing Aetolians, who were swift and lightly armed, chased and caught them right there, but the majority, wandering the roads . . ." (3.98.1–2). It was the same at Pylos: "They didn't know which way to look, incapable of seeing anything in front of them or hearing the orders of their commanders, drowned out by the cries of the enemy. Besieged on every side, they had no hope of withdrawing. A great many were already wounded" (4.34.3).

Elsewhere, a similar effect is obtained by surprise:[80] the Plataeans' attack (3.22.5–6, with, in particular, ἐθορυβοῦντο μὲν οὖν, "They were in a tumult"), the return to Megara at night (4.67–68), and especially the battle of Amphipolis, when the element of surprise that was so important to Brasidas[81] causes exactly the result anticipated in the narrative (5.10.8: ξυνέβη τε . . . θορυβηθῆναι, "And it happened that . . . they were placed in tumult").

Again elsewhere, it may be overconfidence that leads to panic.[82] In any case, of all the examples, the most remarkable is the one that adds to this

---

79. In fact he made two serious mistakes that the report exposes fully: 3.95.1 (Μεσσηνίων χάριτι πεισθείς, "swayed by partiality for the Messenians") and 3.97.2 (ὁ δὲ τούτοις τε πεισθεὶς καὶ τῇ τύχῃ ἐλπίσας, "swayed by them and hopeful because of his luck").

80. Sometimes a surprise attack leads to early chaos that is immediately remedied; see 7.3.1: ἐθορυβήθησαν μὲν τὸ πρῶτον, παρετάξαντο δέ, "At first they were in tumult, but put themselves in order"; also 7.37.3 and 7.40.3.

81. See above, p. 79.

82. At Potidaea, for example (1.62 end to 1.63; see p. 76 above), and, on the sea, at Naupactus (2.91–92; see p. 83 above).

two important circumstances: the fact that the battle takes place in unknown territory and that it is fought at night. Undoubtedly, Thucydides emphasizes this exceptional and illustrative battle all the more because it is the one that, by causing the Athenians to lose any chance of taking Epipolai and thus benefiting from the arrival of Demosthenes, would prove to have the direst consequences (7.43–44). From the ἀταξία, "lack of order," of the victors (7.43.7) to the ταραχή, "confusion" (7.44.1),[83] then to θόρυβος, "tumult" (7.44.4); and no part of the description of the chaos is as concrete, nor as complete: the quality of the light, the tumult of the voices, the movement in all directions, are evoked in a chapter that fills no fewer than forty-six lines in the Oxford edition; even the troubled spirits are made perceptible in the narrative,[84] up to the moment when total chaos reigns at last, when "the ranks have broken down, and fall on each other, friend against friend, citizens against citizens" (7.44.7), when even those who escaped became lost and perished.

Disorganization at sea may arise for the same reasons: ships are surprised before even getting out to sea; that was the case at the first battle of Pylos, where we saw the Lacedaemonians "rush into the sea in their heavy armor, grab their ships, and try to drag them back, each man thinking that all would be lost without his own effort. The tumult (θόρυβος) was great." But what really impedes the ships' ability to maneuver is the lack of space, with the result that each is in the other's way; we saw this happen to the Peloponnesians at Patrai (thanks to an Athenian maneuver),[85] and to the Athenians at Syracuse (owing to a whole series of Syracusan operations). In this last battle, we see the confusion of battle brilliantly drawn, the noise so great that the pleas of fellow soldiers could not be heard (7.70.6). The passion of each man, the feelings and behavior of combatants and spectators alike, combine in this description of θόρυβος ("tumult") and give

---

83. The idea of ταραχή is repeated: 7.44.1 (ἐν πολλῇ ταραχῇ); 7.44.3 (ἐτετάρακτο); 7.44.7 (ἐταράχθησαν).

84. Πῶς ἄν τις σαφῶς τι ᾔδει, "how anyone could know anything clearly"; ἀπιστεῖσθαι, "disbelieve"; χαλεπὰ ἦν ... διαγνῶναι, "it was difficult to recognize"; ἐζήτουν τε σφᾶς αὐτούς, "They looked for each other"; μὴ εἶναι ἄλλῳ τῳ γνωρίσαι, "There wasn't any other way to know."

85. 2.84.3; see above, p. 72; the confusion (ταραχή) was predicted by Phormion's indirect speech (2.84.2: ταραχὴν παρέξειν, "will produce confusion"; see 2.84.3: ἐταράσσοντο, "They were confused"; and ὑπὸ τῆς ταραχῆς, "because of their confusion").

it meaning.[86] The concrete description of the battle, with its visual and auditory elements suggesting psychological realism, adds to its emotional power. The θόρυβος, in which individual suffering overtakes discipline, marks the point at which Thucydides is unable to confine his narrative to pure strategy or thought.

But this θόρυβος, which cannot be described intellectually, is meaningful only in the context of rational analysis, of which it is the culmination. A reflection of individual suffering, it is the sign most feared and most hoped for by the strategist and is joined with his γνώμη.

Chance and Intelligence

As narrated by Thucydides, the battle, though neither dry nor disembodied, may be offered chiefly as a lesson.

It is first of all a lesson to the strategists: the causes of θόρυβος are shown clearly so that they may learn how to protect their own armies from it, and how to instill it in their enemies. That is, no doubt, a rather broad lesson. Xenophon and Caesar, military experts more than dialecticians, would offer more instructive details in this regard. But what Thucydides loses in technical precision, he gains in forcefulness. Unlike Caesar, he does not provide information on the number of divisions, on the topography, or on the particularities of complex movements;[87] he simplifies in order to highlight only the general principle and to show it with perfect clarity. Moreover, he reveals this general principle first, and in such a way that the whole exposition comes to refute or confirm its value. This is what other

---

86. See above, pp. 96–97. Here again the ταραχή, "confusion," was predicted in the analysis given in 7.36.6 (ταράξεσθαι, "will be confused"), and, more aptly, in Gylippus's speech (7.67.2: ταράξονται, "They will be confused").

87. The battle of Mantinea (5.66–75) is the one where Thucydides comes closest to this type of narrative. There we find much information about the methods of the Lacedaemonian army in general (5.66.3–4, 5.73.4), the numbers and organization of the troops (5.68.3), and finally the role of each corps in the battle—all unusual for Thucydides. Of course there he is concerned with a battle on land, which is exceptionally important: Thucydides was able to take the opportunity to study the organization of the Lacedaemonians in a battle on land as elsewhere he studies the organization of the Athenians for a battle at sea; it is a fact that some details prefigure Xenophon.

historians almost never do.[88] It is precisely this aspect that gives Thucydides' lessons their rational and privileged quality: owing to the combination of reason versus reason and reason versus action, the readers perceive at every instant not only the how of every measure taken, but also the why of every success.

The lessons that emerge have significance beyond the level of strategy. More than the triumph of this or that tactic, what Thucydides shows us is in fact, in any battle, the triumph of reason. Precisely because any military victory corroborates reason, it is obvious that reason can and must be the agent of victory. The art of foresight, always essential for Thucydides, thus finds its most striking justification.

There is no question that moral qualities are necessary; but in Thucydides we find them subordinate to intellectual ones. The question that Herodotus raises à propos of Amompharetus[89] is thus settled; and Thucydides insists, in Brasidas's speech, on the merits of a strategy based on observation and trickery. Even the courage of the troops, always indispensable of course, rests ultimately to some extent on reason. The speeches, by their very inclusion in the narrative, imply that the soldier will be more or less valiant as he understands the advantages of his situation;[90] besides, we have seen that Phormio neatly disposes of the concept of innate courage, preferring a notion of confidence based on experience. This same distinction appears again, as Louis Bodin (1914) has shown, in Plato (*Protagoras* 351a); but in particular it corresponds to the concept frequently defended by Pericles.[91] Whereas for Homer, the gods could alter a man's courage, in Thucydides courage is tied to experience, to superior skill and to reason.

---

88. Cf. in Caesar the very clear narrative of Sabinus's victory that lacks any advance preparation (*Gallic Wars* 3.17–19). When the plan is given in advance (the battle of the river Sambre, 2.16ff.), the subsequent narrative wanders off into thousands of details.

89. See above, p. 63.

90. The Lacedaemonian Brasidas apologizes twice for addressing his troops with this διδαχή, "didacticism" (4.126.1 and 5.9.2): these habits of thought, this principle of clear courage, appear no doubt less natural for a Peloponnesian than for an Athenian.

91. 2.40.3, 2.62.4–5 (in the first case, the notion is more modest; we know in fact, despite Louis Bodin, that knowledge of what is formidable and welcome does not *stop* the Athenians from facing danger—nor does it *enable* them to do so). Compare these intellectual ideas of courage with the definition given by Nicias in the *Laches* (196d). Thucydides, however, knows how to recognize the importance of bravery at the time (in 5.72.2 it compensates for the lack of experience, but Thucydides adds no analytical commentary).

Thus, in the end, every human means is subordinate to intelligence. A single aspect remains outside, and that is τύχη, "chance." Thucydides recognizes it and emphasizes its role. In fact, that is the word he uses for everything that cannot be foreseen by even the most astute analysis. Yet it is precisely for that quality that it has a place among the leaders' calculations. Their job is to minimize its role; and to do that, they must first imagine as many circumstances as possible, but then allow it as small a role as possible; leaders and soldiers must be, like the Athenians at Naupactus, sufficiently disciplined to avoid becoming disheartened, sufficiently informed to improvise on the spot a new solution. τύχη is therefore what distinguishes reality from reasoning, and to which the best reasoning must be able to adapt.

And so we progress imperceptibly from modest lessons to generals to a lesson of infinitely greater import. The true battle is one of intelligence, which is always looking to triumph over reality—the power of the mind, which can never be absolute but which strives constantly, more and more forcefully, to become so. We might say that Thucydides' battle narratives strive for an ideal point, always beyond reach, at which we could view two speeches fighting each other, while the narrative offers, in comparison to them, the least possible new information.

Clearly this attempt to encompass reality and to meet it with the highest level of intelligence possible establishes Thucydides' overwhelming originality. We saw, in the first part of this chapter, that the structure he adopted for the battle narratives could be considered as the culmination of an evolution beginning with Homer and tending, more and more, to rationalize combat. But here it has reached the limit; it can go no further. After Thucydides, nothing is the same.

The facts may be partly responsible for this. As battles themselves, from Homer to Thucydides, became more thoughtful and systematic, more subordinate to intelligence and strategy, so perhaps did the art of war, continuing to develop, become inseparable from more detailed and less simplistic analysis: one may analyze, at the beginning of an account, general principles of strategy but not the reasons behind complex movements, involving on all sides particular knowledge of multiple technologies.[92] Moreover,

---

92. The way that Xenophon explains the movements of Spartan armies in *The Constitution of the Lacedaemonians* chapter 11 shows quite well that one can be concerned with military actions from a less general point of view than Thucydides'.

the very scale of subsequent battles makes it more difficult to fit them into a Thucydidean schema.[93]

Yet even more than the facts themselves, history has changed.

The problem history faces is actually seen most clearly in the case of the concrete and complex action involved in a battle. Everyone who has ever tried to write about battle has experienced the difficulty of introducing order into something that seems so lacking in it; one has only to read Marbot's confession on this point: "Most military authors are apt to confuse the readers' mind by overcrowding their story with details. So much is this the case that, in the greater part of the works published on the wars of the Empire, I have been utterly unable to understand the history of many battles at which I was present, and of which all the phases were well known to me. I believe that in order to preserve the clarity of the narrative of action in war, one must limit oneself to an indication of the positions of the respective armies before the battle, and to relate only the principal and decisive facts of the battle."[94] But how is one to choose? Is it possible to go as far as the asceticism practiced by Thucydides? Is it possible to be satisfied with the sacrifice of so many details, particularities, specifics? And why? In the name of what duty?

In fact, no historian has ever gone as far as Thucydides in this direction, or required so much intelligibility: after Thucydides, the two concepts, intelligibility and foresight, separated; narrative superseded description. Thucydides' attempt, perhaps an unreasonable one, to reduce everything to reason, has remained exceptional.

To demand a rational accounting of battle may be something that few would attempt, and perhaps only a mind stimulated by the very novelty of the scientific method and dialectical rigor. The first methodical and rational historian was also, very clearly, the one whose method and reason went furthest. So the pressure to intellectualize that, after Homer, had been growing stronger might finally account for this extreme character, which leads Thucydides to reject compromises that history, after him, could no longer avoid.

---

93. If it is true that, after Homer, battle becomes more organized and more democratic and more easily studied, the opposite also happens: the great Roman or Napoleonic battles, and even modern ones, are fought on such a scale that in most cases the process would be incoherent. The battle of Waterloo in Stendhal is a well-known illustration.

94. Marbot 1988, vol. 1, chapter xviii, p. 196.

3

THE ANTITHETICAL SPEECHES

Although the battle accounts written by Thucydides tend to stress analysis to the greatest possible extent, as we have seen, nowhere is such analysis richer or more complete than when it is expressed in debate, in the confrontation between different reasonings. Isolated speeches introduce ideas; antithetical speeches, by putting those ideas in opposition, sharpen them. These debates allow Thucydides to exhaust every aspect of a situation. Thucydides' marked preference for analysis in general leads him to multiply these debates and to use them to address decisions of every kind. In fact, without counting the great debate in 1.66–87 (in which there are four opposing speeches), we find in the entire work a series of these "antilogies," or paired speeches. In book 1, we find the debate between the Corcyraeans and the Corinthians (1.32–43) and then one between the Corinthians and Pericles (whose opposing speeches are not adjacent: 1.120–24, 1.140–44); book 2 includes the two speeches at Naupactus (2.86.6–89); in book 3 there is the debate between Cleon and Diodotus (3.37–48), followed by that between the Plataeans and the Thebans (3.53–67); in book 6 there is first the debate between Nicias and Alcibiades (6.9–19), then the one between Hermocrates and Athenagoras (6.33–41), and then that between Hermocrates and Euphemus (6.76–87); lastly, in book 7, there are the two speeches before the last battle (7.61–68). Such a list suggests a systematic use of and strong preference for this formula.

Protagoras and the Origins of the Method

Thucydides was adopting a widespread tendency of his time, one that was almost a fad: this is the ἀγὼν λόγων, "contest of words," or oratorical debate, found almost everywhere; the legal argument provides the simplest example of it, but all literary genres used it, from Herodotus's *History* to tragedy, and including comedy, where in some ways it constitutes the very core.[1]

Nevertheless, these debates could not have contributed to the analytical process in Thucydides' work as much as they do—as the example of Naupactus shows—had they not been deployed in his own particularly rigorous format, and had a specific intellectual process not shaped the composition. Thucydides' method, which marks its most extreme and original development, thus merits further examination.

To start with, it would be good to know something of the origins of this method; since it existed independently of Thucydides' writing and preceded him, it had undoubtedly been a topic of instruction. It is not improbable that it was Protagoras who founded and expanded it. At the very least, from what we know of his work we can discern the principle behind such a method.

Protagoras's teaching was characterized by two ideas passed down by tradition.[2] The first of these is the best understood and the clearest. It states that for every question there are two opposing sides or arguments. The witnesses to this are explicit: "First, he has said that there are two opposing sides to everything (λόγους ... ἀντικειμένους)," wrote Diogenes Laertius

---

1. There is a good summary of these points in Duchemin 1968, 1–37.

2. Readers are referred to both the edition of fragments by Diels and Kranz (1951) and the summary of Navarre (1900, 48ff.); the latter does not, however, detail the entire dialectical aspect. See also Dupréel 1948, 38–45.

(9.51 = Diels and Kranz 1951, A 1, p. 253); "Greeks claim, following Protagoras, that, for every speech there is one that opposes it (λόγον … ἀντικεῖσθαι)," wrote Clement of Alexandria (*Stromateis* 6.65 = Diels and Kranz 1951, A 20, p. 260). So it is not surprising that Protagoras was proclaimed the initiator of ἀγῶνες λόγων, "contests of speeches" (Diogenes Laertius), or that he would have written a τέχνη ἐριστικῶν ("art of disputes") and two books ἀντιλογιῶν ("of antilogies");[3] or lastly that he would have taught his disciples the art of practicing, on the same subject, to praise as well as to blame.[4] The expression "paired speeches" (δισσοὶ λόγοι) clearly illustrates the principle behind such a method. Used in a fragment of the *Antiope*,[5] the expression is sometimes used as a title for these anonymous διαλέξεις ("disputes") that have come down to us through the works of Sextus Empiricus and subsequently developed as thesis and antithesis (good and evil, beauty and shame, etc.).[6]

This "invention" by Protagoras is first understood in a broad sense: in this case it means that on all questions one can hold opposing theses. But precisely because it is an invention, derived from philosophy and ending as a τέχνη, an art, it should also have a more specialized meaning. In that case, it means that for any given argument it is possible to argue its opposite. Not only do the two speeches tend toward opposing conclusions, but each particular point contains its opposite; they are systematically parallel inverse constructions.

The art of argument next consists in finding the opposing elements and making them more convincing. This introduces the second element of Protagoras's teaching. Aristotle refers to it in the *Rhetoric* (2.24.1402a = Diels and Kranz 1951, A 21, p. 260): "Making the weaker of two arguments the stronger consists precisely in this; so one is rightly indignant about

---

3. One could also cite the καταβάλλοντες, or *Destructive Speeches*, if the meaning of that title were more certain.

4. Stephanus of Byzantium, s.v. Ἄβδηρα.

5. Frag. 189 Kannicht: ἐκ παντὸς ἄν τις πράγματος δισσῶν λόγων/ἀγῶνα θεῖτ᾽ ἄν, εἰ λέγειν εἴη σοφός, "On any subject he could make a competition of two speeches, should he be wise in speaking."

6. It serves as an introduction to each antithetical series: Δισσοὶ λόγοι λέγονται ἐν τᾷ Ἑλλάδι ὑπὸ τῶν φιλοσοφούντων περὶ τῶ ἀγαθῶ καὶ τῶ κακῶ … λέγονται δὲ καὶ περὶ τῶ καλῶ καὶ αἰσχρῶ δισσοὶ λόγοι, "Two speeches are spoken in Greece by philosophers about good and evil … there are spoken also two speeches about beauty and ugliness."

Protagoras's teaching; for it is a deception, a false appearance of similarity that is found in no art except rhetoric and disputation."

Here too we can take the words in the broadest sense, to mean simply making the less worthy case prevail. This is the aspect most readily encountered, and the one that most quickly elicits criticism. This is what Aristophanes addresses in the *Clouds* (112ff.): "Among them there are, I am told, two arguments, the stronger, whatever that may be, and the weaker. They say the weaker of these two, in cases of injustice, wins."[7]

But once again we might equally imagine a more specific meaning. If we give to *logos* the same value it had above, in the expression λόγον λόγῳ ἀντικεῖσθαι, "speech is pitted against speech," and if we consider the logical implication of this effort, we get a better idea of Protagoras's teaching, from the technical aspect that he must have presented.

Basically this involves weakening an argument by means of another one which directly refutes or offsets it. This implies art, the art not only of making one's arguments strong, but also of effecting a certain movement of thought, allowing for the replacement of one idea by an idea that makes the opposite case. This is, if you will, a dialectic.[8]

Of course there is no theoretical text that allows us to be more specific, or to imagine this artistic process. But we can fairly easily classify *a priori* the best means to reach such an end.

The simplest, logically, is refutation proper: when the occasion offers itself, the argument of the adversary is shown to rest either on false data or on faulty reasoning. This example, quite common in practice,[9] would naturally be infrequent in collections composed systematically for that purpose by authors like Thucydides and Antiphon. There are other means. Among them, most natural is one consisting of finding an offsetting argument, one that annuls the argument of an adversary (my adversary is right about this, but I am right about that). This cannot, however, constitute a really decisive argument. The most decisive methods are those that consist

---

7. Compare this criticism with Plato, *Republic* 539b.

8. There is always a certain fluidity in the use of these words. Here I call logic the science of reasoning, in its pure and disinterested form; dialectic a method of argumentation applied, in this case, to argument; and rhetoric the art of persuading, particularly by means of expression itself. But there is continuous shading from one to the other as the concern for truth or for creating an illusion increases. See below, p. 130.

9. Consequently, Aristotle devotes considerable attention to this.

in turning the adversary's very own argument against him: in that case one shows that what he thought favorable to him was actually not favorable, or is rather favorable to oneself. In one case, there is a reversal; in the other, a true inversion: this completely disarms the opponent.[10]

There is no way we can know for certain whether or not Protagoras used these methods. All one can say is that they follow naturally from principles he established. Undoubtedly he used some of them; and in any case there clearly are some that, to varying degrees, both Thucydides and Antiphon seem to have practiced.

In fact, when we examine the argumentation in Thucydides' antilogies and then compare them to Antiphon's *Tetralogies* we cannot help feeling that a precise and subtle method—even more precise and more subtle in the work of Thucydides—governs their composition.

To prove this point it seems best to start with a very concrete example and analyze it first as a whole. Only then can we proceed to organize the results and discover the general characteristics of the method followed by Thucydides, and then, in light of certain commentaries from his time, try to understand both its principle and its value.

The Antilogy of Camarina (6.75–88)

If we wish to study Thucydides' methodology, the two speeches given at Camarina by the Syracusan Hermocrates and the Athenian Euphemus provide an excellent example. They enjoy a privileged position for analysis because in them Thucydides feels considerable freedom in terms of history. The real debate is actually without consequence; it concerns whether Camarina would openly join the side of the Athenians or the Syracusans; the end of the debate leaves Camarina just as divided as it was previously. In addition, one of the two speakers, Euphemus, is an obscure person whose views and personal habits have no relevance. Thucydides, therefore, is neither bound by the action resulting from this or that argument nor constrained by individual personalities. At any rate, his decision initially cannot have been prompted by the desire to provide an account of

---

10. What is true for an argument is also true for any judgment: an advantage, a wrong, a responsibility can be turned around in the same way.

them; perhaps more than any other, this antilogy is justified because of the analysis it provides of an entire situation.

Thus the antilogy can be seen as particularly instructive in terms of methodology.

The two arguments contrast sharply. Hermocrates accuses Athens of wishing to attack the freedom of all Sicilians. Euphemus replies that Athens seeks only to ensure its own security and to defend Sicilians at large against Syracusan ambitions.

As one would expect, the first and most important part of Hermocrates' speech is devoted to making the case against Athens. First, he refers to the Athenians' actions in Greece itself: the pretexts they allege for intervening in Sicily are not, he says, consistent with that action (6.76.2: οὐ γὰρ δὴ εὔ-λογον, "not at all plausible"). On the contrary, it all becomes obvious when one observes that both here and there the method is the same (6.76.3: τῇ δὲ αὐτῇ ἰδέᾳ, "in the same way"). Yet in that case, the right approach is to unite against Athens; it is wrong to be indifferent to the fate of Syracuse (6.78.1: καὶ εἴ τῳ ἄρα παρέστηκε, "if it has occurred to anyone") or selfishly to wish it ill (6.78.2: εἴ τέ τις φθονεῖ ἢ καὶ φοβεῖται, "if anyone envies or fears"): Camarina should help Syracuse. The last part of the speech addresses the possible objections. Hermocrates mentions two of them and deals in turn with questions of law and security (6.79.1: δειλίᾳ δὲ ἴσως τὸ δίκαιον, "perhaps out of cowardice, when it comes to justice"; 6.79.3: καὶ μὴ φοβεῖσθαι, "and do not be afraid"). Finally, he has only to conclude by showing the people of Camarina the consequences of their choice, which will mean victory for one side or the other and prove their choice right or wrong.

One can already see that in the very structure of the speech the art of argument plays a role: combined with argumentation is the refutation of possible objections. Right after he has accused Athens, Hermocrates begins to reject all the bad solutions to which one might turn (from indifference toward Syracuse to wishing some harm to befall it). And once these ideas are rejected, he begins to counter the arguments that one might use against him (arguments of justice, of security). These latter two refutations are particularly characteristic. The first consists in denying the adversary his argument, annulling it (6.79.1): "But such an alliance is not contracted against your friends, but against any of your enemies, who should march against you; and to help the Athenians if they should suffer wrong from another and not, as is the case, if they should do wrong against others."

The double contrast of the positive with the negative makes the annulment of the argument real (οὐκ . . . δέ, "not . . . but"; καὶ μὴ . . . ὥσπερ νῦν, "and not . . . as currently"). It returns in the second refutation, and this time it leads to a true reversal (6.79.3): "Athenian preparation is not frightening if we are all united; but rather it *is* so if—as they wish to happen—we stand separately in hostility" (οὐ γὰρ ἦν . . . ἀλλ᾽ ἦν, ὅπερ οὗτοι σπεύδουσι, τἀναντία διαστῶμεν).

But of course it is especially in the relationship between this speech and that of Euphemus that the dialectic is present. How, in fact, will the latter respond to the accusations brought against Athens?

Hermocrates had begun by saying that Athenians were proceeding in the same way in both Greece itself and Sicily: no, responds Euphemus, what is similar in the two cases is their motivation (6.76.3: τῇ αὐτῇ ἰδέᾳ, "in the same way"; 6.83.4: διὰ τὸ αὐτό, "on account of the same thing"); here as there, he explains, Athens aims to assure its security, and this reasonable objective leads to different methods in different circumstances. Euphemus thus uses as justification the very actions with which he was reproached. He even takes care to say so (6.83.3): "We prove this from the same things which the Syracusans cast against us and which you somewhat too fearfully suspect." So it is concern for their empire that, according to him, explains the Athenian strategy in Sicily; but this concern requires them to come to defend the Sicilians, and not to subjugate them. With that he completely reverses the argument.

What is more, Euphemus exploits this reversal nearly phrase by phrase to show the emptiness of Hermocrates' claims. Hermocrates had begun with the idea that the Athenian strategy was not logical (6.76.2: οὐ γὰρ δὴ εὔλογον); and he had compared two aspects of this strategy, both there (in Athens) and here (6.76.2: τὰς μὲν ἐκεῖ. . . . τὰς δὲ ἐνθάδε), with respect to Leontini (6.76.2: καὶ Λεοντίνων μέν . . . Χαλκιδέας δέ) and the Chalcidians: it is Euphemus who concludes with the idea that the Athenian action was entirely logical (6.84.2: εὔλογον), precisely in that it was different in the two places and particularly with regard to the Chalcidians and Leontini (6.84.3: τὰ μὲν γὰρ ἐκεῖ . . . καὶ ὁ Χαλκιδεύς,[11] . . . τὰ δὲ ἐνθάδε

---

11. At this point there is actually a formal reference to the other speech (6.84.3: ὃν ἀλόγως ἡμᾶς φησὶ δουλωσαμένους τοὺς ἐνθάδε ἐλευθεροῦν, "whom he says it is illogical for us to have enslaved if we are freeing those here").

καὶ Λεοντῖνοι καὶ οἱ ἄλλοι φίλοι). The notion of self-interest, which linked the different aspects of Athenian policy, actually defined the logic (6.85.1: οὐδὲν ἄλογον ὅτι ξυμφέρον, "Nothing is illogical if it is in one's own interest").

Having reversed the argument, Euphemus finds himself on equal footing with Hermocrates, in having rejected the accusation. But now he becomes the accuser. In order to cement his interpretation further, he examines the situation in Sicily as the result of Syracusan ambition. Hermocrates had warned Camarina of Athenian imperialism and wanted to make the Camarinaeans suspicious: Euphemus seeks to allay those fears (6.85.2: ἀπιστεῖν δὲ οὐ χρή, "must not distrust"), but, in allaying them, he uses them to effect a true inversion. According to him, those very suspicions of the Athenians that Hermocrates planted are being used by Syracuse to prepare its own domination (6.85.3: καὶ βούλονται ἐπὶ τῷ ἡμετέρῳ ξυστήσαντες ὑμᾶς ὑπόπτῳ . . . , "by uniting you in suspicion of us they plan . . .).[12] Yet he must give proof: he does this by recalling a detail not yet mentioned, the appeal some Sicilians have made to Athens.[13] He can then conclude that they must not mistrust the Athenians' words: rather, their mistrust should be directed against Syracuse (6.86.2: πολὺ δὲ μᾶλλον τοῖσδε ἀπιστεῖν, "but much more to distrust them").[14] This time, the accusation itself is entirely reversed, and in the most brilliant way. Besides, Euphemus is able to respond to both the question of security (see 6.85.3: ἀρχῆς γὰρ ἐφίενται ὑμῶν, "They desire to rule over you") and that of justice (6.86.2: καὶ νῦν οὐ δίκαιον, "And in the current circumstances it is not just").

After that, all the roles are reversed. Hermocrates showed that by saving Syracuse the Sicilians would save themselves (6.78.3: λόγῳ μὲν γὰρ τὴν ἡμετέραν δύναμιν σῴζοι ἄν τις, ἔργῳ δὲ τὴν αὑτοῦ σωτηρίαν,

---

12. As later he recalls that these suspicions are the means by which Sicily would lose (6.86.5: ἢν εἰ τῷ ὑπόπτῳ ἢ . . . ἢ . . . ἔτι βουλήσεσθε καὶ πολλοστὸν μόριον αὐτῆς ἰδεῖν, ὅτε οὐδὲν ἔτι περανεῖ παραγενόμενον ὑμῖν, "which if with suspicion either . . . or . . . you will wish to see just a fraction of someday when, if it does arrive, it will be of no help").

13. Similarly, later in 6.87.2: οὐκ ἄκλητοι, παρακληθέντες δὲ, "not uninvited, but appealed to"; the latter detail responds at the same time to the passage in which, in a purely hypothetical fashion, Hermocrates envisioned an appeal from Camarina to Syracuse (6.78.4: δεόμενοι ἂν ἐπεκαλεῖσθε, "You would be begging and appealing to us") and calls on the Camarinaeans to model their current behavior on that hypothetical appeal.

14. Hermocrates had guessed correctly about this fear, but he devoted only a few words to it, for good reason.

"speciously one would save our power, but in fact [save] his own salvation"). Now it is Euphemus who becomes the real savior (6.86.5: πολὺ δὲ ἐπὶ ἀληθεστέραν γε σωτηρίαν ἡμεῖς ἀντιπαρακαλοῦμεν, "We rather call you to a more true salvation").[15]

Similarly, Hermocrates had reminded them of the regret that those who did not support Syracuse would feel later (6.78.3: τάχ' ἂν ἴσως καὶ τοῖς ἐμοῖς ἀγαθοῖς ποτὲ βουληθείη αὖθις φθονῆσαι, "Perhaps he might desire some day to envy my prosperity once again"), and Euphemus gladly returned to this theme (6.86.5: ἔτι βουλήσεσθε καὶ πολλοστὸν μόριον αὐτῆς ἰδεῖν, "You will yet wish to see even a fraction of it"). Moreover, the consequences of an Athenian failure, which he leaves to their imaginations, have already been fully described, just as Hermocrates had described a potential Syracusan defeat; the participles of 6.85.3 (ἀπράκτων ἡμῶν ἀπελθόντων, . . . ἡμῶν μὴ παρόντων, "if we return in failure, . . . if we are gone") responded to those of 6.77.2 and 6.78.1 (τοῦ ἄπωθεν ξυνοίκου προαπολλυμένου . . . οὐ προδιεφθαρμένου ἐμοῦ, "when a distant countryman has already been destroyed . . . if I have perished first").[16]

We will not try to determine just what rules govern this reversal, but at least two facts emerge clearly. The first is that Euphemus's speech adheres closely to that of Hermocrates and reverses not just the general positions in it, but also the details themselves. The second is that Euphemus wishes, through both the choice of words themselves and the phrasing, to make sure the connection between the two is obvious.

This observation can perhaps be taken further. When we consider the structure of each of the two speeches independently of each other, we see that a certain number of words, by themselves without any great significance, are used very systematically to draw attention to the phrases. These words often echo each other.

---

15. Here he mentions another speech; see above, p. 112 n. 11.

16. Similarly, note that Hermocrates had alluded to the various (6.76.3: ὡς ἑκάστοις, "as for each one") pretexts that Athens borrowed; Euphemus's defense ends by showing first that it is the treatment itself that varied (6.85.1: πρὸς ἕκαστα, "toward each one"; 6.85.2: ὡς ἕκαστοι, "as individually"), according to different aspects of usefulness: so he draws from this theme a reassuring element (reversal); then he chooses to mention the various (6.86.3: ὅταν καιρὸν λάβωσιν ἑκάστου, "when they seize on each opportunity") opportunities Syracuse itself had seized (a case of inversion).

Thus Hermocrates' attack, in the first part of his speech, was given impetus by two similar expressions (6.76.1: οὐ . . . ἀλλὰ μᾶλλον, "not . . . but rather . . . "; and 6.77.1: ἀλλ' οὐ γάρ . . . πολὺ δὲ μᾶλλον, "but not . . . much rather . . ."); these words, without really belonging to the thought expressed, marked stages of it. Hence one comes to see that this correction via comparison serves perfectly Euphemus's twofold restoration in 6.86.2 (πολὺ δὲ μᾶλλον, "much more") and 6.86.5 (πολὺ δὲ ἐπὶ ἀληθεστέραν, "much more true").

Inversely, the words used to introduce Hermocrates' most precise accusation (6.76.3: καὶ τὰ ἐνθάδε νῦν, "and things here, in the current situation") are exactly the ones that from beginning to end mark by their repetition Euphemus's junctions in his speech. Its clear structure makes this easy to confirm. In the first part (that of direct justification, 6.82–83.2) the demonstration is shown twice: (1) by justification of the empire in Greece (ending with an aphorism at 6.83.2: "One does not incur censure by seeking to guarantee one's security") and (2) by καὶ νῦν (6.83.2: "and in the current situation"), applying it to Sicilian politics (the whole argument ending with the aphorism at 6.85.1: "Whether a tyrant or an imperial city . . ."). The denunciation then follows. This also appears twice: first (6.85.3–86.2), the real people to mistrust are the Syracusans (an idea expressed in the καὶ νῦν, "and in the current situation,"[17] in 6.86.2 and ending with the reversal πολὺ δὲ μᾶλλον τοῖσδε ἀπιστεῖν, "much rather distrust them"), and second, the true saviors are the Athenians (an idea expressed by a καὶ νῦν, "and in the current situation," in 6.86.4 and ending with the reversal πολὺ δὲ ἐπὶ ἀληθεστέραν, "to a much truer . . .").

Such close links cannot occur by accident. Joined with others, they are the best measure of the subtlety of this dialectic and the extent of its capabilities. These are not limited to the argumentation itself but bear equally on the general approach, on the expressions used, and on the slightest details.

In each of these ways, Thucydides' method suggests a true art both well trained and precise.

---

17. The same καὶ νῦν appears in the summary that introduces the conclusion, in 6.87.2.

Characteristics of the Antilogies

The conclusions that emerge from studying the antilogy of Camarina can be extended to include other antilogies. This is confirmed by returning to the remarks that were made in the preceding chapter, regarding the antilogy of Naupactus, or of the indirect speech of 7.36 (constructed, we have said, as an antilogy).[18] We can also look again at the conclusions published in the remarkable study of Cleon and Diodotus by Bodin (1940). More generally, when considering any of the antilogies mentioned at the beginning of this chapter, we will find that to varying degrees they all clearly show in arrangement, expression, and manner of argumentation similarities with the Camarina antilogy,[19] and that these similarities themselves relate, often very directly, to the *Tetralogies* of Antiphon.

Arrangement

These traits can be equally well explained as resulting from a common tendency to pursue an adversary as much as possible on his own ground.

In terms first of arrangement, it generally results in an overall parallelism between the two speeches.

We have shown that Euphemus begins by refuting the attack with which Hermocrates began, and then in the second part addresses the issues of justice and security that formed the second part of Hermocrates' speech. So too Cleon and Diodotus both have a first part relating to the general principle of reopening discussions (3.37–38 and 3.42–43) and a second part relating to the specific case of Mytilene (3.39–40 and 3.44–47). And again, Alcibiades and Nicias both have a first part devoted to the examination of the situation in Sicily and in Greece (6.10–11 and 6.17–18.4), then a second part devoted to personal attacks (6.12–13 and 6.18.4 to end).

---

18. See above, p. 88.

19. Perhaps the only one we should exclude is the Hermocrates-Athenagoras antilogy in 6.33–41. This proposes two plans of action based on different hypotheses: Hermocrates pronounces the Athenian expedition to be imminent, and Athenagoras refuses to believe it; so they do not have the same bases of discussion. This exceptional situation, while portraying the divisions within the city, highlights the unreasonable nature of the Athenian strategy; but it denies the two men the usual dialectical methods.

Yet this is not at all a rigid parallelism; the demands of the dialectic may themselves introduce certain irregularities.

First, it might happen that the second speech, having to deal with refutation more than the first one does, consequently finds itself in charge of a task, as it were, doubled, the refutation coming first and then complemented by the inversion. That is, on the whole, quite normal. There is evidence of this even in the *Tetralogies* of Antiphon, as rigorous as they are in the way they respond to one theme after another, from one speech to another.[20]

The author is himself aware of this when he has the accuser in the second *Tetralogy* (3.3) say: "I did not imagine that he would make a defense (ἀντειπεῖν); otherwise I would not be restricted to a single argument in place of two, and deprived myself of half the accusation; and he would not have, thanks to his audacity, a twofold superiority, since he has been able in his defense speech not only to respond to an attack but at the same time to launch additional unanswered charges."[21] Assuredly, the text allows us to see that a prudent dialectician would not let himself be taken by surprise in this way: he would refute in advance the arguments that one could use against him. And that is what Thucydides does almost every time. We have seen, in the speeches at Camarina, the first one takes on the quality of a refutation, by attacking possible objections or positions. Similarly, the Corcyraeans, for example, examine in sequence all the possible criticism first of their position, then of their statements (1.34.1: ἢν δὲ λέγωσιν ὡς οὐ δίκαιον, "if they say that it is not just"; 1.36.1: καὶ ὅτῳ τάδε ξυμφέροντα μὲν δοκεῖ λέγεσθαι, φοβεῖται δέ, "and if someone thinks this proposal is beneficial, but is afraid"). So too the Lacedaemonian generals examine whatever might frighten the army (2.87), and so on.

Still, it is not unusual for an argument that is "unleashed" in the discussion, or even an entirely new one, to bring to a close the second speech. The first is the case found in the antilogy of Naupactus, in which, at the end of the discussion, an idea returns that the Peloponnesians' speech had

---

20. We can show this by comparing, for example, the second, third, and fourth speeches of the third *Tetralogy*; the same ideas are gradually repeated: the dead man had been the aggressor (β1 = γ2 = δ2); he died several days later, which suggests that the doctor was responsible (β4 = γ5 = δ8); on the other hand, what counts is intent (β5 = γ4 = δ4).

21. The interpretation of the beginning is conjectural, but the ending is certain and quite clear.

claimed to eliminate—that is, the idea of the psychological influence that the memory of the preceding battle might exercise (2.89.11).[22]

The other case is more common. This is the one found, for example, in the antilogy of Corcyra: the Corinthians, after having answered the charges and the justifications of the Corcyraeans, are able to invoke an argument of their own and call for the repayment of a favor (1.41).[23] And again, the Thebans, after defending themselves for their "Medism" (submission to the invading Persians in 480) and after overturning all the Plataeans' self-defense relative to their conduct during the recent events, introduce, in the form of proof, a new accusation, founded on a new fact: Plataea, in the course of those events, has violated its agreements (3.66).

Lastly, it may also happen that this double approach (refutation and attack), without involving any material addition, undergoes a kind of dialectical shift: in this case the initial arguments—whether they consist of one or more parts—are negative and support the refutation: only the final one is positive and may thus serve as its counterpart in the whole.[24]

Yet such shifts have little effect on the parallelism of the whole and actually only complete it. It is rather the movements of arguments within each part that are notable.

Within detailed reasoning, ideas can actually occur in a new relationship: most often because their order has to be changed. In their respective opening sections, Nicias begins with Greece itself, and Alcibiades with Sicily—in other words, each opens with the area he considers strongest and most favorable to his own argument. Similarly, while the Corinthians, in thinking about means of acquiring a fleet, quickly dispense with the financial question (1.121.5), Pericles stresses at length the financial difficulties that threaten the Peloponnesians (1.141.3–142.2), in order to dismiss as

---

22. The possibilities for action of the Athenian fleet are also "vented" at the end of the discussion, in Pericles' first speech.

23. This argument simply corresponds, however, to an equally independent argument in the other speech: the Corcyraeans call the Athenians' attention to the fleet that they have brought them; it is interesting to see that the two theses here rest on arguments of a different order. But, at the same time, the χάρις that the Corinthians call for is the inversion of the one that the Corcyraeans promised them.

24. Thus in 7.36.5 the final branch of the argumentation completes the inversion by showing that the Athenians' maneuvers must in the final analysis destroy them. The dialectical plan, in two parts, does not fit perfectly with the linear plan, in three parts. Louis Bodin found this particularity in Protagoras, in the pastiche made of him by Plato.

a result the hypothesis that they might have a fleet, a hypothesis he considers out of the question (1.142.5–9).

Moreover, these very obvious and natural displacements lead to a number of others. It should not be forgotten that the argument needs to revisit the opponent's facts, ideas, words, and distinctions as much as possible: so it inevitably happens that these were used, in the new system, in different places. This aspect of Thucydides' work may be what is most disorienting for modern readers: the matching formulations actually appear in passages on different topics. As a result all the order that seemed to govern the whole, when examined in detail, disappears into a snarl of complex relationships impossible to disentangle. Pericles' speech cited above confirms this. Pericles actually returns to several themes that appeared in the Corinthians' speech: the contrast between the Peloponnesians, who pay with their bodies, and the Athenians, who rely on money (1.121.3 = 1.141.5), and the contrast between a long war and a short war (1.121.4 = 1.141.6), among others. But each of these concepts appears in a different context with a new role, which subordinates them in a different way to the leading idea. In one case as in the other, a more dense dialectic is making its claims felt.

Expression

At the same time, however, the last example shows that expression also feels the effects of this dialectic: what it takes away outwardly from compositional norms is compensated for by these verbal connections, which are woven with subtlety from one speech into another.

These speeches are of different types. In the case of the speeches at Camarina we have seen first that there were pivotal words, corresponding in each speech to overall junctions; that on the other hand these words might be taken up again from one speech to another; and naturally the same is true for all the words, expressions, and distinctions that directly constitute the thought itself. We noted these with regard to Naupactus and also in 7.36,[25] and Louis Bodin emphasized these verbal correspondences in his article on the Cleon-Diodotus antilogy (1940, 36). The same might be said for all of the antilogies. We note, for example, two small oddities in the

---

25. See p. 83 n. 50, and p. 89 n. 57.

Corcyraean antilogy: in it we see that the key words are actually repeated; thus the Corcyraeans make a distinction between a maximum advantage and a minimal one, in their attitude and that of Athens: 1.32.1: ἀναδιδάξαι πρῶτον, μάλιστα μὲν ὡς . . . , εἰ δὲ μή, ὅτι γε . . . , "to show first especially that . . . but if not, that . . ."; 1.35.5: ἀλλὰ μάλιστα μέν . . . εἰ δὲ μή . . . , "but especially on the one hand, otherwise on the other hand . . ." (see 1.35.4: ἤ . . . ἤ . . . μάλιστα δέ . . . , "either . . . or . . . but especially . . ."). The Corinthians make the same distinction regarding the degree of justice (1.40.4): δίκαιοί γ' ἐστὲ μάλιστα μέν . . . εἰ δὲ μή . . . , "You are on the one hand especially just . . . but otherwise . . .". But we also find a repetition of words characteristic of the thinking: the Corcyraeans, at the beginning, made a virtue of their isolation (1.32.5): αὐτοὶ κατὰ μόνας ἀπεωσάμεθα Κορινθίους, "We alone, by ourselves, repulsed the Corinthians"; whereas the Corinthians repeat the same expression to depict the Corcyraeans' guilty selfishness (1.37.4): ὅπως κατὰ μόνας ἀδικῶσι, "in order to commit injustice by themselves."

From the simple conjunction with the idea already discussed, it would seem that all the elements of a speech must be repeated by the other, in such a way that these small transpositions of detail soon leave nothing standing of the original construction.

The task that Louis Bodin set himself was to commit to finding all of these and to explaining the mechanism governing them; it was perhaps an impossible task, in that some of these connections may have been fortuitous and others gratuitous, in other words, tacked on to suit the occasion. Yet by seeking this comprehensive explanation one may at least measure the subtlety of this dialectic, and the variety of its applications.

The problem that concerns us today is a different one, and a simpler one, since, while the applications are varied, the fundamental principle itself always seems to remain the same.

Argumentation

Moreover, all the verbal echoes, whatever their type or wherever they appear, arise, like the composition itself, from the same tendency, whether through annulment, reversal, or inversion, to adhere as closely as possible to the arguments of the opponent while drawing the opposite conclusion.

Hence this dialectical mechanism is clearly most interesting, and on it rests the originality of the method.

The methods that are used vary and are of varying subtlety; yet the principle they share is easily found: it consists above all in altering the point of view when considering the same events.

The simple form, *par excellence*, is the one Antiphon taught future advocates in his second *Tetralogy*. A single event—in this case the death of a young man, killed in the gymnasium by the blow of a javelin—is shown to have a number of different meanings, depending on whether it is seen in one light or another. The young man has died from the blow (α1); yes, but it was he who entered the javelin field (β4); yes, but he was obeying the coach, and it was not the time for the javelin throw (γ6). The orators in Thucydides proceed no differently.

Most often it is the moment under consideration that changes from speech to speech.

If a single project is involved, each side in turn takes up the cause and effect. Nicias, at the beginning of book 6, constructs his argument on an idea: if we fail, it would be disastrous (both here and there). Alcibiades responds that there is no reason for us to fail (either here or there). He is putting himself in a point of time anterior to the one Nicias imagines.

Similarly, regarding the revolts of allies Cleon is thinking about origins, Diodotus about later developments. An indulgent politician, says Cleon, encourages (3.39.7); but, replies Diodotus, if we admit that a rebellion is inevitable, a harsh politician may face a worse outcome (3.46.2), for people will no longer hope for pardon or for any distinction between the guilty and the innocent, and they will not be willing to surrender.[26] The conclusions vary according to which future time one is considering.

And when the past is involved, the same is true. It is normal to see Thucydides' orators—like Antiphon in the example cited above—go back in time, in order to discover different causes and contrary explanations.

---

26. Diodotus is using two considerations, expressed, as Louis Bodin has clearly shown (1940, 52), by two twinned σκέψασθε; the first is that the uprising at Mytilene failed; the second is that the people ultimately made an about-face. Cleon knew that but didn't stress it; each retained the part of the facts that was favorable to his side.

So the Corcyraeans, clearly guilty of rebellion against Corinth, their me-
tropolis, explain: but it was really they who (*in the first place*) wronged us,
because they mistreated us (1.34.1). To which the Corinthians answered:
no, because they were (*in the first place*) ungrateful colonists, who failed to
respect us (1.38).

In the same debate, the Corcyraeans offer as proof of their good faith
that they had requested arbitration. To which the Corinthians answered:
yes, but you had (*in the first place*) committed your wrongs, rendering that
offer meaningless (1.39.1).

The principle is the same in book 3, when the Thebans, accused of having attacked Plataea in peacetime, answer: but it was you, Plataea, who
called us (*in the first place*), and we just followed. With that, they remove
their responsibility (3.65.2: οἱ γὰρ ἄγοντες παρανομοῦσι μᾶλλον τῶν
ἑπομένων, "It is leaders who break the law more than followers")[27] and
contribute to the complete reversion through which Plataea becomes, in
this respect, the more guilty party.[28]

Contrariwise, in the same antilogy the Plataeans, accused of having concluded an alliance with Athens, respond: but it was you, Peloponnesians,
who (*in the first place*) had rejected us. Thus they absolved themselves of
responsibility (3.55.1: ὑμεῖς δ' αἴτιοι . . . , "But you are to blame . . .").

Moreover, we might note that in general in this same antilogy the Plataeans, when interrogated about their actions in the course of the war,
immediately revert to the Persian Wars, which offers a more favorable
territory; the Thebans, in turn, go back even further, to the foundation of
Plataea, in order to connect all the facts cited by the Plataeans to different causes. In this, the two sides recall Helen of Euripides' *Trojan Women*
(919–20), who turns the accusation brought against herself against Hecuba
and reproaches Hecuba for causing everything, for being the one who gave
birth to Paris.

Yet at the same time this little game of avoiding blame clearly shows
that by viewing a different moment in the action, the speakers wish to

---

27. With rare elegance they repeat this distinction from the speech of the Plataeans itself,
when the latter defend themselves for having followed Athens: see the citation in the passage
(3.55.4) below, p. 123.

28. This inversion draws the conduct of the Plataeans into the action. It follows another that,
in itself, relates to the grievance of "Medism"; see below, p. 123–24.

show the cause as different. They can also do this directly, and they do not fail to do so. In such a case, they go from saying: "Yes, but in the first place . . ." to "Yes, but that was because . . .".

There are some simple and easy examples of this. The neutrality of Corcyra is a fact. According to the Corcyraeans, they were trying to avoid "mixing in the perils of a foreign alliance based on the whim of another" (1.32.3–5). In the eyes of the Corinthians, it was "scarcely virtue, but the taste for evildoing that guided their politics" (1.37.2);[29] the geographical situation of the island provides further proof.[30]

It is also a fact that the Plataeans acted against Sparta. But according to them, that fact does not show hostility toward Sparta; rather it is the result of their fidelity to Athens. Thus they conclude that they are not responsible (3.55.4: οὐχ οἱ ἑπόμενοι αἴτιοι . . . ἀλλ' οἱ ἄγοντες ἐπὶ τὰ μὴ ὀρθῶς ἔχοντα, "It is not followers who are guilty, but those who lead them to what is improper").[31] This argument enables them to carry out a brilliant inversion, making the very thing for which they were reproached their greatest virtue (3.56.6: "Today we fear that we perish for conducting ourselves according to the same principles, that is by acting with Athens according to justice rather than with you for our profit").

This kind of reasoning, applied properly, allows easy inversions. We saw that above, in the antilogy of Camarina, when Hermocrates accused Athens of coming to Sicily to pursue imperialist ambitions there in the same way (6.76.3: τῇ δὲ αὐτῇ ἰδέᾳ) as it had in Greece, Euphemus answered, generally: "You mistake the motive; in both places Athens is acting, by different methods, to achieve the same benefit: ensure its security."

Now in book 3, in response to the Plataeans, the Thebans twice use a singularly similar argument in the section relating to "Medism."

The first time the argument addresses the Plataeans' famous pride in the fact that they had not collaborated. True, reply the Thebans, but why? Simply because in all circumstances they followed Athens (3.62.2: διότι οὐδ' Ἀθηναίους, "because the Athenians did not . . . either"). Their

---

29. On the verbal connection in this, see above, p. 120.

30. In the same antilogy, the possibility that neutral states would rally to one side or the other was allowed or rejected on the basis of motivation (see 1.40.2).

31. Compare the citation of 3.65.2, just above. The words ἄγοντες and ἑπόμενοι are taken in a slightly different way, but the argument is just the same.

behavior since then could excuse their present mistakes: on the contrary, it is this behavior that is now taking a regrettable direction. Proceeding toward the Plataeans as Hermocrates had toward the Athenians, the Thebans lay out the overall conduct of Plataea against a single, negative standard (3.62.2: τῇ μέντοι αὐτῇ ἰδέᾳ ὕστερον ἰόντων Ἀθηναίων ἐπὶ τοὺς Ἕλληνας μόνους αὖ Βοιωτῶν ἀττικίσαι, "In the same way when the Athenians attacked the Greeks, they alone of the Boeotians Atticized").[32]

The fact remains that it was Thebans who had "Medized." True, they reply, but in this case you must make a distinction: it was the oligarchy alone that was responsible for a policy to which the people never adhered; and the proof lies in the very conduct of the city when it was faced with defending the freedom of Greeks being threatened by Athens. Here we have an argument of justification comparable to the one Euphemus used against Hermocrates. Like Hermocrates, the Thebans lay out against Plataea a coherent series resting on a common motivation; and like Euphemus, in order to justify themselves, they lay out certain distinctions corresponding to different circumstances.

The result of this double transposition is to reverse the roles: Plataea no longer has anything to do with Greek liberty, of which Thebes becomes the true defender. And the formula of retorsion is as neat here as in Euphemus's speech, when, like him, the Thebans, in 3.63.1, move to the accusation,[33] "Rather it is you who are guilty toward Greece and who deserve the ultimate penalty."

These parallelisms between the two antilogies can likely be explained by the fact that both cases involve discussing an accusation and resolving a case. But above all they teach us about the method of inversion. In each case, the principle is the same (τῇ αὐτῇ ἰδέᾳ, "in the same way," as

---

32. In this they proceed in a way directly opposite to the Plataeans. In order to justify their conduct during the war, the Plataeans had recalled the Persian Wars (we followed Athens in this war, as we had done against the Persians): at present, in order to minimize their conduct during the Persian Wars, they recall their conduct during the war (they went with Athens against the Persians, just as this time they follow them against the Greeks).

33. We can add that, in developing the accusation that follows, we see the same type of refutation and inversion: it is not in order to guarantee their security that the Plataeans sided with Athens during the war, since the Lacedaemonian alliance would have sufficed to protect them (3.63.2); furthermore, while there was shame in betraying Athens, there was much more shame in betraying Greeks to help Athens (3.63.3).

Thucydides would say!); it is always a matter of starting from the fact used by an adversary and giving it a different meaning: from a positive, it becomes a negative, and in place of strengthening a thesis, it weakens it.

Yet the best means for reaching this result, and the most elegant, is still to establish between two given elements put forward by an adversary, a different, and, if possible, opposite connection. In that case, gliding to another point of view is almost imperceptible. One need not draw attention to a different moment or to a new cause: one retains only those terms from which one's adversary derived his strength, and discards the relation that he saw between them, thus inexorably destroying his argument. In place of "Yes, but . . ." this time the response is "On the contrary, since . . .".

The most characteristic form of this argument consists in showing, whenever an adversary has contrasted two ideas, that they are actually joined with a view to a single goal.

For example, one will say that good actions in the past, instead of redeeming you, only make you guiltier. The Thebans do not hesitate, toward the end of their speech, after so many well-schooled attacks, to let fly a new charge (3.67.2): "Past virtues . . . for those who act disgracefully ought to involve double punishments (διπλασίας ζημίας), since their crimes come after a different past." This was the very argument that Sthenelaidas had already used against the Athenians (1.86.1): "Yet, if they behaved well against the Persians in the past but are evil toward us now, they deserve double punishments (διπλασίας ζημίας) for having become bad after being good."[34]

This form, the simplest of all, contrasts with the most elaborate form, such as appears twice in the antilogy at Naupactus.

The Peloponnesians said: "They have more experience, but we have courage" (2.87.4: ὑμῶν δὲ οὐδ' ἡ ἀπειρία τοσοῦτον λείπεται ὅσον τόλμη προύχετε, "In your case, inexperience itself is not as great a disadvantage as your bravery is an advantage"). Phormio's analysis, set beside this, brilliantly shows that courage is actually a function of experience (2.89.3: ἐπεὶ εὐψυχίᾳ γε οὐδὲν προφέρουσι, τῷ δὲ ἑκάτεροί τι εἶναι ἐμπειρότεροι θρασύτεροί ἐσμεν, "since they are in no way superior in courage, but we

---

34. See later Demosthenes, *Against Timocrates* 127: οὐ τοσούτῳ μᾶλλον αὐτὸν ἔδει δεδέσθαι, εἰ χρηστοῦ πατρὸς ὢν τοιοῦτος ἦν; "Isn't it all the more necessary that he be arrested if, despite his good father, he behaves in this way?"

are bolder to the extent that each of us is more experienced in something"). And to this one might add that such an argument rests on a rigorous distinction between the meanings of words, perfectly in keeping with Prodicus's lesson. Antiphon follows that example when, in the third *Tetralogy* (γ4), he states: ἔστι δὲ ἡ μὲν ἀτυχία τοῦ πατάξαντος, ἡ δὲ συμφορὰ τοῦ παθόντος, "To the one who delivered the blow belongs misfortune, but to the one who received it belongs catastrophe."[35]

The Peloponnesians had said: you have been defeated, it is true, but our number gives us confidence (2.87.6: περιγίγνεται δὲ ὑῖν πλῆθός τε νεῶν, "We have a surplus number of ships"). Phormio's speech again makes a causal connection between these two opposing elements: the number of Peloponnesian ships can be explained only by their earlier defeat (2.89.2: οὗτοι γὰρ πρῶτον μὲν διὰ τὸ προνενικῆσθαι καὶ . . . τὸ πλῆθος . . . παρεσκευάσαντο, "First, they have acquired more ships because they were defeated before").

Has not Pericles, however, already done the same when, responding to the Corinthians' plans, he takes up again the terms of their analyses, in order to show a new and even inverse relationship? To the Corinthians, who had suggested that they could offset Athens' naval superiority by training,[36] he responds by saying that training itself would be denied them by that same naval superiority.[37] So once again two ideas, meant to balance each other, ultimately depend on each other. And the result is that, once again, what should have been the Peloponnesians' strength ultimately shows up their weakness.

---

35. ἀτυχία designates the case of someone not accomplishing what he intended; it is linked to ἁμαρτία; συμφορά on the other hand designates the case of the victim who suffers.

36. This very training was for the Corinthians the benefit resulting from a long war (1.121.4); according to Pericles (1.141.6), however, a long war would bring out the lack of unity on the Peloponnesian side. A long war goes from being something favorable to something unfavorable, by a change in the point of view.

37. 1.121.4: μελετήσομεν καὶ ἡμεῖς ἐν πλέονι χρόνῳ τὰ ναυτικά, "We will ourselves train at seafaring given a longer time"; and 1.142.6–9: οὐδὲ μελετῆσαι ἐασόμενοι διὰ τὸ ὑφ' ἡμῶν πολλαῖς ναυσὶν αἰεὶ ἐφορμεῖσθαι, "nor allowing them to train, because of their being blockaded by many of our ships." The Corinthians also affirm that the Peloponnesians' strength rests on their people, whereas Athens' strength is in its money: they see in that a weakness for Athens, since its sailors can be corrupted. Pericles again makes the same distinction; but he sees it as a sign of weakness for the Peloponnesians, for they will be bothered by a lack of financing; conversely, the risk for Athens is illusory: Athens' naval superiority itself will prevent the corruption of the sailors.

Here again is an example of a method matching perfectly the two anti-logies; and here again we can say that they belong to the same type, since in each case they involve a deliberative debate bearing on available forces.[38] This recurrence also allows us to grasp more readily the dialectical inver-sion in its most perfected form. It is also in this category that it would be best to classify its most characteristic argument of all—that which we might call "plausibility arrived at by reasoning." Given a connection be-tween two ideas that is initially plausible, one can invert this connection adequately simply by predicating a subject who has been informed of it.

Aristotle, in a passage already cited above (*Rhetoric* 2.1402a), provides a classic example of this, writing: "It is of applications of this topic that Corax's *Art of Rhetoric* is composed: if a man does not lend credence to the charge against him, if for example a weak man is accused of assault, his defense will be that it is not plausible that he is guilty; but if the accused *does* lend credence to the charge, if for example he is a strong man, then his defense will be that it is not plausible that he is guilty because it was plau-sible that he would be thought guilty. And it is the same in other cases; for either one lends credence to a charge or one does not; the two cases seem plausible; but one is truly so, the other is not absolutely so, but only in the way that we have described it."

That was no doubt a famous case. It is merely a refinement of Plato's simpler case given in *Phaedrus* 273b and attributed to Tisias: "If it hap-pens that a weak but brave man has harmed another who is strong but cowardly, the major argument he should use will be 'How could I, made as I am, have attacked him, made as he is?'" About this classic case, there henceforth exist two contradictory plausibilities.

A second form, one that is the subtlest and that Aristotle describes, is found in Antiphon and Thucydides.

For Antiphon the two examples most often cited are both borrowed from the second speech of the first *Tetralogy*. In both, the hatred of the ac-cused for the victim creates a plausibility, which, assuming the accused is well informed, is reversed: "Actually," says the accused, "if the violence of my hatred is in your eyes a sign of plausible guilt, it is actually even more

---

38. Actually, the issue in both cases was how to take on the Athenian naval strength, just as previously it was to judge Athens and those who had acted as it had.

plausible that before acting I would have anticipated the suspicion that would attach to me; if, in fact, I knew that someone else was premeditating murder, I would have had to stop him, far from committing murder myself and exposing myself to the suspicion that was obvious in advance" (3); and later: "Or else those who hated him no less than I—there are many who do—are they not even more likely than I to be his murderers? It was obvious for them that the suspicion would fall on me, while I knew very well that I would be incriminated in their place" (6).

The antilogy of Naupactus is no different when it too uses psychology in order to counter probability. As I have already shown, numbers meant nothing, owing to the fact that the Peloponnesians were aware that these numbers were an indication of their feeling of weakness.[39]

But what is more, the inferiority of Athenian numbers should itself frighten the Peloponnesians: they would say that Athens, in order to attack under such circumstances, must be motivated by great confidence (2.89.5–6): "Rather, it is you who give a fear that is greater and more justified, in accord with your prior defeat of them and because they think that you would not be opposing them unless you intended to achieve something to offset their great advantage;[40] for most of their enemies, as they do, go into a fight relying on strength rather than a state of mind; but those who do so with much fewer numbers, and are not forced into it, are emboldened by an unshakable resolve that is great. Since they have calculated this, they fear you more because of our inscrutability than because of our sensible preparation."

Hence, without changing the facts in any way, the basis for the entire explanation is inverted. We can see why the discovery of such possibilities had a striking effect on contemporaries and filled them with admiration and anxiety.

So we can clearly say that Antiphon and especially Thucydides employ a variety of forms of refutation, inversion, and retorsion, from the very simple to the most subtle, aiming to achieve, with virtually no alternation of the evidence, the greatest reversal of the conclusions drawn.[41]

---

39. 2.89.2, cited above, on p. 126.

40. Both text and meaning are in doubt.

41. One must add that in the absence of any particular argument, arguments can themselves recur; the very fact of the accusation betrays the ill will of the accuser: Thucydides 6.85.3 (see above) and Antiphon 3.β7 (also δ11).

Such a consistent approach, applied in such an elaborate way, thus constitutes a true art. This was no doubt an object of instruction at the time, since one finds many a trace and consequence of it throughout contemporary texts, but Thucydides appears to have pushed the method to the point of perfection, to its ἀκμή ("high point").

What accounts for this impulse, this urge in Thucydides? What is this somewhat suspect art doing in the work of a historian? Are we to believe that he was simply following, out of a desire for historical accuracy, the customs of the time? It seems hard to imagine that he should have applied these methods with such consistent success if he had not found in them some advantage for his work. What then was the advantage? First of all, it was to dazzle; and these sophistic games allowed him to dazzle, as did stylistic patterns, for example. But this is not the only explanation of either the sophistic games or the stylistics. If he went further than his contemporaries, it was because in both cases something in his own thinking pushed him to do so: he found this dialectical mode intellectually satisfying. To understand his reasoning, we need in a broad way to be able to grasp its meaning and its influence.

The Principle of the Antilogies

Above all, in order to judge the method fairly, we must not minimize the accumulated details on which it is built.

The Instrument

Obviously, such model arguments as we detect behind all these reversals hardly seem *a priori* to constitute a serious logical method. The methodology itself is worrisome. With it, we are closer to rhetoric than to logic.[42] In any case, the disadvantages in this kind of mixing are obvious.

---

42. Each time one must invent an argument or carry out a process of refutation there is an appeal to a method of reasoning. But here this method is again hindered by its utilitarian aims. Moreover, conforming to the double meaning of the Greek λόγος, it does not separate form and function, reflection and the art of persuasion. The τέχναι ("methodologies") of the sophists and Antiphon's *Tetralogies* belong to rhetoric.

First, the argument may also be a specious one. Rhetoric requires only that the argument be convincing. Moreover, whenever there is a technique, surprising, unexpected results will be sought; the desire to dazzle will take over; and thus the door will open to the parade of paradoxes and sophisms. The dialectic ends, following this path, with the eristic. From these lessons are born the λογίδια, "mini-arguments," which Isocrates scornfully said "would lead to a host of evils for anyone who remained faithful to them in practice" (*Against the Sophists* 20). Moreover, even if these λογίδια were less open to criticism, there is always the problem, from the intellectual aspect, that they are simply examples. A series of formulas, even legitimate ones, never constitutes a method of reasoning. Aristotle will observe, at the end of the *De sophisticis elenchis*, that before him the eristic teachers provided the kinds of instruction that was quick but not methodical (ταχεῖα μέν, ἄτεχνος δέ), since what they taught was not theory but applications, like someone who promised to teach the art of the cobbler and instead simply offered different kinds of shoes (34.7).

All these features are sufficient explanation for the hybrid nature of such teaching and the criticisms it provoked. Isocrates was the first to free rhetoric from it: he blamed the sophists, the "authors of treatises," the teachers of eristic; and for him dialectical research was reduced to the rank of propaedeutic exercises, not to be pursued too long (*Antidosis* 261–68). Yet the definitive classification would be done by Aristotle alone. It was in his work that everything would find its place: rhetoric was distinguished from dialectic; and from dialectic sophistic, with its impure intentions, was tossed aside. The art of reasoning could then be treated in a scientific manner: Aristotle identified the rules of the *Topics* and attached the *Topics* to an analysis of pure and rigorous reasoning, provided in the *Analytics*.

Nevertheless, although the progress thus achieved was enormously necessary, and although Aristotle's teaching was defined by its opposition to what had preceded it, it is nonetheless true that it was a continuation of it and owed its existence to what had gone before. The evolution leading to Aristotle's logic began with the dialecticians of the fifth century. From those predecessors to Aristotle there was a transformation, but also continuity.

The very idea of a commonplace, as it is seen to evolve from the antilogies of Protagoras to the treatises of Aristotle, is evidence of this dual relationship.

Even in antiquity the invention of these commonplaces was traced back to Protagoras. Cicero states this explicitly,[43] and the expression he uses designates without any doubt prefabricated arguments, applicable to multiple examples and demonstrating for their subject the case for as well as the case against. Overall, arguments of this type were taught by teachers of eristic. It is in opposition to the somewhat simplistic manner in which they did this that Isocrates objects in *Against the Sophists* (particularly 16ff.). It is he who uses the term ἰδέαι,[44] translated according to context as "procedures," "general themes," and "commonplaces." In any case it is clear that, in his mind, it always refers to types of argument to be applied according to circumstances. Yet the meaning tends to become more general; and, in certain examples, it clearly must include "genres of argument" such as eulogy, comparison, commemoration of the past, and so forth; such was the case, in particular, in *Philip* 143, and in the letter *To the Children of Jason* 8. Aristotle himself, indicating an even greater generality, uses the word τόπος, "place." For him, "place" means that to which the enthymeme pertains, and what provides it (*Rhetoric* 2.26.1402a: ἔστιν γὰρ στοιχεῖον καὶ τόπος εἰς ὃ πολλὰ ἐνθυμήματα ἐμπίπτει, "An element is also a commonplace to which many enthymemes are relevant"). Yet one must admit that in fact Aristotle does not use the word without a slight hesitation. Some of the "places" are still defined by content of a general sort; the place consists in "saying that . . ."; thus in *Topica* 3.2.3.117a, "The same things accompanied by pleasure are preferable to those same things without pleasure." Others are defined by their principle: the "place" consists in "to examine whether . . ." (ἐπιβλέπειν εἰ . . .); thus in *Topica* 2.2.1.109a, "One place is to examine whether someone has described as an accident something that happened in some other way." So this expression "commonplace," which is used so widely today to designate an argument of a banal and well-known character that is used in very different circumstances,[45] happens also to be

---

43. *Brutus* 12, 46 (Diels and Kranz 1951, B 6, p. 256): *scriptasque fuisse et paratas a Protagora rerum illustrium disputationes, quae nunc communes appellantur loci*, "that there were disputes on famous topics written and prepared by Protagoras, which are now called commonplaces." The passage was inspired by Aristotle, Τεχνῶν Συναγωγή frag. 137 Rose; see also Quintilian 3.1.10 and 12.

44. See *Against the Sophists* 16 and *Antidosis* 183.

45. This use is completely legitimate. One must only be careful not to confuse commonplace, in this sense, with a maxim or aphorism. Both had a role to play for ancient dialecticians, but very different ones. The aphorism, which Thucydides uses regularly, appeared in reference to

a technical term for a rule of logic defining the possible uses of the enthymeme, and belonging to a system that, if not one of pure reasoning, is at
least clearly and narrowly established.[46]

Clearly it is far from the *Analytics* to the *Topics,* and even farther from
the *Topics* to the Δισσοὶ λόγοι. Yet just as one could, regarding Aristotle
himself, somehow rehabilitate *Topics* (the study of "places") and see in it a
science in the modern sense of the word,[47] so one should be aware that this
science had its roots in fifth-century B.C.E. sophistic and dialectic practices.

The rigor and the subtlety that Thucydides deploys in the antilogies
clearly, then, are part of an effort that would conclude with the beginnings
of logic.

The Method

That does not necessarily mean that the instrument of logic invented in
this way had been used with much discernment. And it remains to be seen
to what extent a method that consists of always contrasting the pro and con
as a series of two speeches can be a good method intellectually.

Its disadvantages or dangers were evident at the outset, and contemporaries recognized them clearly. To the extent that the method conveys
the feeling that everything can be defended equally, it leads first to a sense
of paradox. This happens when Helen becomes the incarnation of inno-
cence and accuses Hecuba, when Pasiphae accuses Minos,[48] and so forth;
in this way all values are at risk of a change of meaning. We must consider
this technique, like Gorgias's rhetoric, as a risky tool in any case, one that
can be used for good or ill, according to the intentions of the one using it.
Rhetoric, like any weapon, should be used justly. But what is more, by its
very nature, a technique that consists in always discussing, refuting, invert-
ing argument, risks losing the very concept of truth. That is a danger to

---

the known—for example, to recall a theorem that had already been proven. Generally, it defined
this εὔδοξον ("accepted opinion"), to which one wished to assimilate some idea or another. It concluded an argument, for which the commonplace was its model.

46. See Weil 1951, 313 n. 1: "We are not speaking of logical rules in the strictest sense of the
work, in other words, of actual *loci communes.*"

47. This is what Weil (1951) undertook to do, even though Aristotle could not, as Weil recognizes, separate sophistic from dialectic completely.

48. See Duchemin 1968, 207 and n. 11.

which Plato was especially sensitive, and that he denounced on numerous occasions. In particular, in the *Phaedo* (90b-c) he decried the skepticism that arises among those accustomed to antilogies ("those who spend time on antilogy speeches," οἱ περὶ τοὺς ἀντιλογικοὺς λόγους διατρίψαντες); and, in the *Republic* (538e), he laments the influence of dialectic on young people, who want only to contradict (ἀεὶ εἰς ἀντιλογίαν χρώμενοι).

Yet we may also wonder if it is not precisely when it works, as Protagoras wanted, to defend two opposite theses, that it is really justified. For the point of an antilogy is that two theses are juxtaposed, that they are both presented, both defended, both heard. To support *or* overturn one of these leads only to the success of the one who manages it: to support *and then* overturn a thesis is the means, and the one that seems best, of showing the listener the truth. There can be two interlocutors, two theses, two speeches, four speeches, as there will be later in dialogue; but there are always two complementary sides. And what was oratorical or sophistic artifice, considered from the point of view of Hermocrates or Euphemus, becomes, considered at the level of Thucydides as author, a powerful method of analysis and discovery from the point of view of his readers.

The principle of the antilogy has always seemed to the Greeks the very essence of wisdom and understanding. Antilogy means deliberation. It means weighing the pro and con. And that, according to Herodotus, is by far the best method of discernment: "O King," says his Artabanus, "if conflicting views (γνωμέων ἀντιέων) are not expressed, it is not possible to choose the one that is best to adopt, but one is forced to limit oneself only to the one that was expressed; but if they are, then it is possible; it is the same for gold: one cannot recognize pure gold when looking at it alone; it is by rubbing it on the stone next to another one that one recognizes the real thing" (7.10).

From this comes their habit of always wanting to hear both sides, presented as forcefully as possible. It is what one does in court; it is what one does in the assembly. And from a juxtaposition of two opposite speeches the truth may come out. The procedure is so natural that it sometimes reappears in someone as averse to antilogies as Plato. His Glaucon is not content with the discussion between Socrates and Thrasymachus, so he is going to take up Thrasymachus's argument and support as forcefully as possible an argument that is not his own: "That is why I am going to make the greatest effort (κατατείνας) to praise the lot of an unjust man, after which I will show you how, in turn (αὖ), I would like to hear you denounce injustice and praise justice."[49] Those who criticize too quickly the eristic are forgetting that the purpose of antilogy is precisely the confrontation of two theses.

How is that confrontation possible? Once again, Plato may guide our understanding. Moreover, its principle is quite simply one of measurement, of addition and subtraction—in short, of arithmetic. This is what we see clearly when Plato analyzes and criticizes it in book 1 of the *Republic* (348a): after having heard Thrasymachus list the advantages of injustice, Socrates proposes, once again, to replace antilogy with dialogue, and then summarizes the principle of antilogy: "So I say if, gathering our forces and matching speech for speech, we enumerate all the advantages on the side of justice, and he replies and we respond, we would have to count the advantages and measure what we each said in our respective speeches, and we would need judges to decide the matter. If, on the other hand . . .".

Here we see the principle of the tetralogy: there was a speech, and there would be a response (αὖ), then again a speech on each side (καὶ αὖθις οὗ-τος καὶ ἄλλον ἡμεῖς, "then he . . . and we once more"). The answering speech would line up with the one to which it responded (λόγον παρὰ λόγον, "speech beside speech"); and each of the two would provide the very best arguments possible (ἀντικατατείναντες, "exerting themselves in opposition").[50] What would remain to be done in order to learn the truth is expressed in two characteristic words: count (ἀριθμεῖν) and measure (μετρεῖν).

Despite the implicit criticism in this passage, these two words illustrate the value of the method and show how it could become, more than simply a rhetorical game, a true intellectual tool. In fact, this counting and measuring may first be applied to simple units. In that case the antilogy puts forth two lists, enumerating, for example, the various advantages that one would have in acting in such or such a way: it suffices to say which list is the longest or offers the greatest advantages. This is the very natural form, without malice, that antilogy takes in tragedy, or in comedy or

---

49. *Republic* 358d; see 367b: "For myself, I don't want to conceal that it is in order to hear you support the opposite argument that I have supported my position with all the force I could (κατατείνας)."

50. Note the same word as in the citation given above on book 2 and in the summary of 367b. The use of αὖ ("once again") in the first two cases is equally natural.

even, to cite a famous example, in Heracles' fable of Vice against Virtue (Xenophon, *Memorabilia* 2.1.21). But the comparison will actually be all the more convincing when the parts being compared are most alike, so that the same units are found in each part: for that, the terms must be reduced in some way to a common denominator so that there are the closest links and clearest parallels between one list and another. Obviously, if the speakers themselves do the calculation, either by removing their adversary's arguments or by offsetting them, or by making them their own, they will make the outcome more obvious, the conclusion easier, victory more secure: the subtleties of dialectic are justified by their ties to the comparative and arithmetic nature of the method; these give it its real rigor. In fact it has been noted that these constitute precisely the original and distinctive feature of Thucydides' antilogies.

Arithmetical Reasoning

This rigor, which strives to transform all the elements of the argument into comparable data, suitable for addition and subtraction—in other words, interchangeable—is actually made to stand out in Thucydides' work by the detailed expression itself. In his antilogies a speech does not attempt to acquire precision by the use of any deductive method. Nor does it strive to make a direct effect by synthesizing a mass of relevant information. On the contrary, it tends to isolate each term; not without some stiffness, it tries to give every argument the almost schematic clarity that simple units would have, and then proceeds to treat these units as one would numbers: antilogy, in the effort to be rigorous, becomes an arithmetic of arguments.

The fact is quite clear in antilogies relating to the analysis of troops. Thus the Corinthians, in book 1, speak of equalizing skill in their jobs as sailors, and thus surpassing others in courage (1.121.4: ὅταν τὴν ἐπιστήμην ἐς τὸ ἴσον καταστήσωμεν, τῇ γε εὐψυχίᾳ δήπου περιεσόμεθα, "When we place our knowledge on an equal level, obviously we will be superior in courage"): this could be diagrammed in an arithmetical operation, consisting of eliminating the common elements from each side.[51] Moreover, this

---

51. This concept was a familiar one to the Greeks; see Demosthenes, *On the Crown* 231, which uses the word ἀντανελεῖν ("make a corresponding subtraction"). For more on the metaphor employed in this passage, see the note below.

idea of elimination is well shown by the commentary that follows: "For the advantage that we owe to nature they can acquire only by learning, but the superiority that they owe to knowledge, we can eliminate through training." "Eliminate" (καθαιρεῖν), "restore balance" (ἐς τὸ ἴσον), "gain superiority" (περιεσόμεθα), are all terms perhaps relating to combat; but they express, in the same way, a comparison between larger and smaller forces; they convey in an active and concrete way what the arithmetical operation conveys abstractly.[52] And they all can suit equally well the description of such an operation.[53]

The same element of comparison and calculation is found at Naupactus. This is the case where the Peloponnesian leaders, laying out one argument in opposition to another, think that the surplus is in their favor: "Compare, against their greater experience, your greater courage (πρὸς μὲν οὖν τὸ ἐμπειρότερον αὐτῶν τὸ τολμηρότερον ἀντιτάξασθε), and, with regard to your fears about our losses, the fact that we were unprepared then: and on your side there is still the superiority (περιγίγνεται δὲ ὑμῖν) of numbers of ships and the prospect of a naval battle close to the shores of your ally" (2.87.5). Here the words themselves describe the two parallel columns (ἀντιτάξασθε), giving a clear view of the arithmetical result (περιγίγνεται); and the neuter comparatives (ἐμπειρότερον . . . τολμηρότερον) correspond well to the advantages of one side or the other. In fact, a few lines above, we see the respective advantages compared directly: "In your case, inexperience itself is not as great a disadvantage as your bravery is an advantage" (2.87.4: ὑμῶν δὲ οὐδ' ἡ ἀπειρία τοσοῦτον λείπεται ὅσον τόλμῃ προύχετε).

---

52. The same is true for the examples cited further on, for ·ἀντιτάττειν ("compare") and even for ἀπώσασθαι ("subtract") (see below, p. 139), which itself has clearly military roots.

53. This is known for the last two and probable for the first: a word like ἀναιρεῖν clearly shows these two meanings, "destroy/subtract." The comparison with Thucydides, considered in light of what we have said, would seem to clarify a passage in Demosthenes' *On the Crown* 227, which is given in manuscript S as ὅταν οἰόμενοι περιεῖναι χρήματα τῷ λογίζησθε, ἂν καθαίρωσι αἱ ψῆφοι καὶ μηδὲν περιῇ συγχωρεῖτε, "whenever, thinking that someone has surplus money, you do an audit, if the counters [on the abacus] remove [?] and no money is left, you agree with it"; for καθαίρωσι the vulgate has καθαραὶ ὦσιν ("are empty"), and Rauchenstein proposed καθαιρεθῶσιν ("are removed"), a conjecture that Weil called "excellent, if there were any example of the verb used in the sense of ἀναιρεῖν or ἀντιαναιρεῖν" ("subtract"). It seems to me that here too there is an elimination of corresponding elements throughout, and that a form of the verb καθαιρεῖν in its place is therefore very strong.

In Phormio's response we find an identical element, when he discusses, quite rightly, the famous Peloponnesian courage (2.89.3): "But this advantage will in all justice now belong to us (μᾶλλον νῦν περιέσται), if to them in the other area; as they are not superior to us in natural courage (εὐψυχίᾳ γε οὐδὲν προφέρουσι), but each of us is more confident, according to our experience in our particular department."

That, at its subtlest and most emphatic, is the same calculus that we have seen in Antiphon, when he wrote, in the last speech of the third *Tetralogy* (4.4.3): κοινοῦ δὲ τοῦ τεκμηρίου ἡμῖν ὄντος <καὶ> τούτῳ, τῷ παντὶ προέχομεν, "Since this line of reasoning is equal for us and for this man [our opponent], we are ahead in the total."

Moreover, even when such an elaborate arithmetical operation is absent we often find that Thucydides expresses the idea of measurement and comparison in a very simple form. In that case, the arguments are evaluated as if they were quantities. This is what happens, for example, in the speech of the Plataeans, where we find the notion of elements exposed to view, but this time of different importance (3.56.5): "It is just that our actual failure now, if it really is a failure, should be compared (ἀντιθεῖναι) to our loyalty; you will find in the comparison that the latter outweighs the former (καὶ μείζω τε πρὸς ἐλάσσω εὑρήσετε)."

The same idea of comparison between quantities recurs constantly with less distinctive expressions. For example, when Pericles envisions the effort of each of two peoples in unfamiliar fields, he says: "For our experience on the sea nevertheless is a greater (πλέον) advantage on land than their military experience is on the sea" (1.142.5). Also, when he describes Athenian superiority in one passage he says: "Our situation seems to me to be exempt from the elements that I have criticized in them, and has other advantages besides[54] that they cannot equal (οὐκ ἀπὸ τοῦ ἴσου), and which are significant" (1.143.3). And then, alluding to the Athenian chances, he explains: "And so the desolation of all of Attica will no longer be the same thing (οὐκέτι ἐκ τοῦ ὁμοίου ἔσται) as the pillaging of one part of the Peloponnese" (1.143.4).

---

54. In the two steps indicated by the phrase and referring, successively, first to the negative and then the positive aspect of the question, we recognize as well the two steps of the operation described above: elimination and then emergence of the positive advantage. Here, quite simply, the elimination always implies the advantage.

In addition, does not the very principle of an inversion consist of exposing an adversary's greater inferiority, greater mistakes, and greater problems? Thus we have found in the antilogy at Camarina the use of the comparative with πολύ: the Syracusans deserved much more mistrust (6.86.2); there was "much more" truth in the safety offered by the Athenians (6.86.5). This is an element that recurs in almost all the debates. At Naupactus, Phormio says to his men: "So do not fear their boldness; rather, it is you who inspire them with a much greater and more valid fear" (2.89.5: πολὺ δὲ ὑμεῖς ἐκείνοις πλείω φόβον παρέχετε καὶ πιστότερον). At Plataea the same feature turns up several times: it is the Plataeans who wronged the Greeks more and who deserve to be punished (3.63.1: ὡς δὲ ὑμεῖς μᾶλλόν τε ἠδικήκατε τοὺς ῞Ελληνας καὶ ἀξιώτεροί ἐστε πάσης ζημίας); it is they who acted in a "much more" shameful and guilty fashion (3.63.3: πολὺ δέ γε αἴσχιον καὶ ἀδικώτερον); and lastly, in recent events, they are "at least as" guilty as the Thebans (3.65.1: οὐ νομίζομεν οὐδ᾽ ἐν τούτοις ὑμῶν μᾶλλον ἁμαρτεῖν, "We do not think we are more at fault than you even in these things"). They even compared claims to deserving greater pity (3.67.3: καὶ γὰρ ἡμεῖς ἀνταποφαίνομεν πολλῷ δεινότερα παθοῦσαν, "For we declare that [our generation] has suffered much more terrible things").

The principle on which the antilogic method rests thus seems clear. And although it is in the Greek tradition to assimilate the two meanings of the verb λογίζεσθαι ("calculate/reason") and the noun λογισμός ("calculation/reasoning") in defining calculation and reflection, this feature is shown in a particularly noticeable way in the methodology in question, at least as practiced by Thucydides.

It actually seems that Thucydides, with his well-known preference for abstraction and rigor, should have been particularly pleased to shape his ideas as mathematical quantities. These easily add up and multiply in his work. The Syracusans, before the final battle, declare (7.67.1): "With us it is different. The original estimate of ourselves, which gave us courage in the days of our unskillfulness, has been strengthened, while the conviction added to it (προσγεγενημένης) that we must be the best seamen of the time, if we have conquered the best, has given a double measure (διπλασία) of hope to every man among us." Similar qualities are brought out by the neuter adjectives, which are forcefully opposed (3.44.4: καὶ οὐκ ἀξιῶ ὑμᾶς τῷ εὐπρεπεῖ τοῦ ἐκείνου λόγου τὸ χρήσιμον τοῦ ἐμοῦ ἀπώσασθαι, "And I insist that you not reject [subtract] my useful advice because of his specious argument"). The various aspects of a situation are joined in mathematical propositions (3.37.3: ἀμαθία τε μετὰ σωφροσύνης ὠφελιμώτερον ἢ δεξιότης μετὰ ἀκολασίας, "Lack of learning combined with moderation is more useful than cleverness combined with lack of restraint"). The formulas and even the forms of thought seem to indicate this tendency. In this feature we recognize not only the harmony that seems to exist between a form of expression then fashionable and Thucydides' own intellectual inclinations, but also the reworking that he has imposed on this form of expression. One might even say that it was Thucydides who pushed the form as far as it could go in the way of precision and scientific order; there is no doubt that it is for that reason that his antilogies leave readers with the impression of such analytical rigor.

The Place of the Method in Intellectual History and in the Work of Thucydides

This rigor, obviously, is not without rigidity. And perhaps that is what explains why this mode of analysis should have had a very brief popularity. Moreover, along with Antiphon's *Tetralogies* (which, without pretending to the same richness or subtlety, are nevertheless the most closely related rhetorical form), Thucydides' antilogies—at least the more technical of them—retain a rigidity that one is tempted to call archaic. Like those statues with feet together and arms vertical, their beauty seems constrained by invisible ties, locked into a fixed position, that will be cast off later.

One might wonder if the reasons for this rejection, and the explicit or implicit criticism behind them, could with any justification be used against Thucydides.

It was a double rejection.

In rhetoric the change is accomplished without controversy. Here the antilogy method had served only to provide a framework, or for particular arguments; we notice only that the frameworks become more and more flexible. The part devoted to refutation no longer constitutes an independent element. Perhaps under the influence of Socrates, Isocrates introduces freer habits of composition, adding the content of thought itself with greater facility.[55] Demosthenes initially stays more faithful to the prior tradition; his speech *For the Megalopolitans* shows that at the beginning of his career, he follows the tenets of tradition even into the area of political speech;[56] but his great political defense speeches, with their variations of tempo, soon renounce these methods:[57] his debating gained in flexibility what it risked losing in formal rigor.

On the other hand, in the area of philosophy, Plato denounces the dangers of the antilogy method from an intellectual point of view. He thinks that the method leads only to a fallacious rigor, lacking any constructive value.

The best criticism is contained in the text of the *Republic* itself quoted previously. It was based on the idea that the proper use of this method always needs a third person as auditor and judge. Following that method, says Socrates, we will have to have judges to settle a debate. If, on the other hand, we examine things as just now, by coming to an agreement, we will be our own judges and advocates.[58] Moreover, if the point is to seek the truth, the person whose agreement is most desirable is not the audience, but the interlocutor himself. It is only through persuasion rather than defeat that one can hope to move beyond the world of conflict and uncertainty. Hence, instead of two people who are both more or less wrong, and from a final judgment that is reached by approximation, one may move to a method that allows both to move forward together, and by elimination to distinguish the true from the false with assurance. So dialogue will then

---

55. On these points, see Navarre 1900, 271–73.

56. The speech takes the form of a series of responses to the objections of those in contradiction: 6: ἀλλὰ νὴ Δία . . . φήσομεν, "But by Zeus we Athenians will object"; 11: ἔστι τοίνυν τοιοῦτός τις λόγος παρὰ τῶν ἀντιλεγόντων, "Well, there is an argument like this from the opponents"; 14: θαυμάζω τοίνυν καὶ τῶν λεγόντων τοῦτον τὸν λόγον, "Well, I am amazed at those who argue this argument"; 19: ἀλλὰ μήν, ἅ γέ φασιν, "And yet listen, they say that." And in almost every case, there occurs an almost complete reversal: Surely we should not ally ourselves with the Thebans πρὸς οὓς παρεταττόμεθ', "*against whom* we stood in battle"? Yes, we should, since that will preserve the peace ὑπὲρ ἧς . . . παρετάξασθε, "*for which* you stood in battle" (10). Must we not cultivate friendship with the Lacedaemonians in order to regain Oropus? No, because making that assumption is simply to assume the worst about the Lacedaemonians (11–13). Would Athens appear to be changeable? No, it is the ambition of other states that causes changes (14–15).

57. Even Demosthenes remarks that political reasoning is not mere bean counting: οὐ τιθεὶς ψήφους· οὐ γὰρ ἐστιν ὁ τῶν πραγμάτων οὗτος λογισμός, "not by counting tokens; for this is not a way to calculate events" (*On the Crown* 229).

58. *Republic* 348b.

take the place of dialectical jousting.[59] Instead of a series of arguments on one side and then on the other, presented without any controls, each is weighed, adopted, or rejected by agreement; there is no more room for the fallacious argument: corresponding to the adoption of dialogue is the rejection of the sophistic.

This evolution from antilogy to dialogue was not alien to the eristic;[60] and it is perceptible at the very core of Thucydides' work; once he desires to push his analysis further and higher than he has been accustomed, he is led to set against each other no longer just two speeches, but every argument, toe to toe; and so he wrote the Melian Dialogue.

Nevertheless, the Melian Dialogue is not a Platonic dialogue, and for a reason. The purposes Plato had in mind could not in fact have had either meaning or relevance within history.

Given as a start that its subject is political reality, no one could expect agreement about the facts from the dialogue's speakers: even between the real Euphemus and the real Hermocrates no Platonic dialogue was appropriate. Furthermore, they are there to uphold different positions, not to come to an agreement. So too for Thucydides: as a historian, his job is not to give us a reflection on the different points of view, but to put us in the best possible position from which to judge objectively for ourselves. Thucydides' history addresses that same third party, that arbiter, whom, according to Plato, antilogy requires. And if this method, which no one else ever practiced in a more systematic way, was to any degree justified, it turns out to be that it was precisely in his work.

This form of expression and this form alone allows him to satisfy at the same time two demands that seem to govern his work—the need for objectivity and the need for rationality.

By presenting successively the two antithetical speeches without intervening in his own words at any point, Thucydides respects the rules of accuracy and impartiality that the historian must observe. But, in addition, this self-effacement is balanced by the very structure that he gave the two speeches. Measuring them one against the other, opposing argument

---

59. Of course, Plato's dialogues themselves also address a "third person," the reader: and they usually leave him to go some of the way on his own. Yet they provide a certain number of givens that he is obliged to accept, and that he must then organize for himself.

60. In fact, Aristotle's *Topics* deals with dialogue, not antithetical discourse.

to argument, using, in favor of each, all the resources of an expert dialectician, emphasizing, by the form itself, anything incomplete or ambivalent in either speech, allowing us to follow step by step, through parallelisms, echoes, repetitions, the progress of the refutations or inversions, he facilitates to the greatest degree the task of those arbiters who are his readers, and clearly shows them the points in dispute as well as the implications of the different justifications. Before the plans of the orators have been tested by the facts, they are tested by reasoning. Before their arguments attain a verdict, they clash in the minds of the readers. That testing and that confrontation are all the more rigorous for having been pushed into the background and seeming, from the outside, quite artificial. This explains the extreme subtlety that Thucydides brings to his antilogies: grounded in logic, they allow him to shrink further the gap separating raw facts from the realm of reasoning. If he was able to make more of his adopted style than anyone else, it was because that style served his deeper ambitions.

While these are, on the whole, the characteristics of antilogies in Thucydides, it is perhaps not imprudent to venture some conclusions about their authenticity.

First, not all the speeches are organized as antilogies, and not all the antilogies are equally as rich in dialectical procedures as those we have viewed. Thus the demands of historical fidelity, the need for precise analysis, consistent with the facts, take priority in Thucydides' work over the taste for dialectic.

Yet he used these procedures, to the extent that it seems to have been possible.[61] It is true that they were meaningful only when applied to the true intentions of individuals and according to the precise way in which they regarded the facts; but we can also say that such a rational measurement could not have been set out perfectly by any of the speakers; it could be done only by someone who was in a position to organize one speech in relation to another, to eliminate every random element, and to reconstruct the whole according to the best dialectical rules. And so when we read the excuse Thucydides gives in 1.22.1, where he states that it was "difficult to reproduce exactly the contents of the speeches, both when he had heard

---

61. In the course of this chapter I have examined particularly characteristic examples; however, in the debates in Thucydides' work there is always at least some parallelism, repetition, reversal, and so forth in a passage.

them in person, or for someone reporting to him about them from some source or other," we must conclude that such accuracy, even had it been easier to attain, was not his only ideal.[62] No doubt he did not reconstruct the speeches by inserting into them the arguments that seemed in his eyes the best ones, as scholars who are partial to free composition say. But neither can one say that he merely altered their literary qualities, as those partial to authenticity demand.[63] Style, in the antilogies, is inseparable from the construction of the arguments. And the best construction possible represents ὡς δ' ἂν ἐδόκουν ἐμοὶ ἕκαστοι περὶ τῶν αἰεὶ παρόντων τὰ δέοντα μάλιστ' εἰπεῖν, "with the closest approximation of how I judged the individuals would have said what [they thought] needed to be said about the respective situations." It is possible to implement this without discarding, for the general thought, the words really spoken: ἐχομένῳ ὅτι ἐγγύτατα τῆς ξυμπάσης γνώμης τῶν ἀληθῶς λεχθέντων, "keeping as close as possible to the overall policy recommendation of their actual words." But it is his optimal ordering that is also what, by juxtaposing the theses in the subtlest, most rigorous, and most systematic way, establishes, in the readers' eyes, their true and reasoned relationship.

Owing to this marginal license, which appears nothing but formal, Thucydides can in the final analysis carry his rational transposition a little further still; so all this dialectical cunning is not simply for effect; it serves a specific function in his history: it allows Thucydides, without ever abandoning his habitual objectivity, to introduce a more concentrated analysis, at a cost to his historical speakers but to the profit of his narrative's clarity. That is how the same practice that permitted the historian to demonstrate in the midst of an unpretentious narrative clear relationships between facts (chapter 1), and then in more complex accounts to elucidate a palpable link between calculation and action (chapter 2), produces, with this seemingly minor technique of antithetical speeches, his crowning achievement.

---

62. He might at the very least wish to know the whole text in order to reconstruct on the basis of it the antilogies most in keeping with the ξυμπάσης γνώμης τῶν ἀληθῶς λεχθέντων, "the overall policy recommendation of their actual words."

63. See Gomme 1945, ad loc.: "If he was to give a speech as such at all, the *words*, the style, that is the *literary* quality (as opposed to the historical content) must be his own" (italics are Gomme's).

4

Investigating the Past

The "Archaeology"

The three preceding studies have attempted to show the methods by which Thucydides, in describing the facts, makes a sequence of logical relationships appear that, while not jeopardizing the demands of historical accuracy, give to those facts greater intelligibility and reveal implicit elements of his judgment on them. Such an outcome obviously has no value unless the facts have been firmly established beforehand. Thucydides states in 1.22 that he has been zealous about confirming the validity of his information for all the events of the war. There has never been any reason to doubt his claim. It must be said that he was, in this respect, a very privileged historian, since the potential documentation available to him was limitless.

Thucydides did not, however, restrict himself to the role of historian of the present. Quite specifically, there is in the work a historical account relating to facts from a much earlier time that were more difficult to confirm. That account, usually termed the "Archaeology," treats the whole period from the origins of Greece to Thucydides' own era. His aim was to show that the Peloponnesian War was more important than anything that had preceded it: in the earlier periods "there was nothing on a greater scale, either in war or in other matters" (1.1.3).

A thesis such as that needed to be demonstrated. To do that, one needed to know about those periods. How could Thucydides have known? Where would he look? His method of zealous inquiry was no help; there was no documentation. He did have some sources: besides epic, he would likely consult the logographers and local records, the works entitled κτίσεις πόλεων ("foundations of cities") and genealogies. Beside the fact that these sources were incomplete and their reliability more or less suspect, their subject was hardly the same as that of Thucydides.

The first of the text's innovations—and not the least—was to redefine historical material itself. Before Thucydides, names of heroes and memorable exploits had been the subjects of history; Herodotus was still writing "in order to ensure that what men had done not be erased from memory by time, and so that the great and marvelous exploits of both Greeks and barbarians never cease to be extolled" (1.1). But in his Archaeology, Thucydides was interested in the state of civilization, in commerce, lifestyle, habitat, the sea.

For that there was little that contemporary sources could provide, at least not in any systematic or descriptive way. The thesis implied that the history of the past would be treated in a new and positive light; for this, Thucydides' only tool would be his capacity to reason.

He himself was very conscious that this was both difficult and original. He refers to both at the beginning and at the end of his narrative. At the beginning he writes (1.1.3): "It was impossible to determine clearly after so much time . . . but my belief is based on my study as far back as possible, and the deductions I concluded were convincing." He repeats this in closing (1.20.1): "I grant that there will be difficulty in believing every particular detail." And (1.21.1): "On the whole, however, the conclusions I have drawn from the proofs quoted may, I believe, safely be relied on."

The body of the narrative itself is no less characteristic. The words constantly remind us that this is a *personal* thesis (δοκεῖ, "it seems," in 1.3.2, 1.3.3, 1.9.1, 1.9.3, 1.10.4), based on what was most probable (εἰκός in 1.4, 1.9.5, 1.10.3 bis, 1.10.4), and scattered throughout a system of argument and proof (τεκμήριον, "evidence," in 1.3.3 and 1.9.3; δηλοῦν, "make clear," in

1.3.1, 1.5.2, 1.11.3; σημεῖον, "sign," in 1.6.2 and 1.10.1; παράδειγμα, "example," 1.2.5; and then all the γάρ, "for," γοῦν and γ' οὖν, "at any rate," and other particles of logic that appear in abundance).

These chapters of the work offer the favored quality of showing the constructive rationalism of Thucydides grappling now not with the problems of historical description but with a search for the truth itself.

By that I do not mean to say we can separate one from the other. Rather, the intellectual methods that distinguish the entire work are identical to the methods we find in these chapters. It is just that they are pressed much farther than in the other parts of the work. They penetrate to its substance; they give it its existence. We might say that the exposition suffers doubly under the burden of this reasoning effort. It presents peculiarities of a logical and even philological sort that have sometimes earned him criticism from scholars; their presence can be explained by the intense work of elaboration that pervades the text.

These are impossible to miss when we attempt to draw out the different arguments that are the basis of the work. For this, the very nature of the material Thucydides treated allows us to proceed to this study in two successive ways: first by considering the arguments themselves directly, then by considering them in terms of their conclusions and in light of what modern scholarship thinks it possible to establish. In fact, these arguments tend to reconstitute facts, and, either by comparison or through archaeological discoveries, it is possible today to evaluate, to some extent, the results of Thucydides' endeavor. By doing so, we have some chance of measuring with still greater precision the merits and risks of the method Thucydides followed, or at least its originality.

Method

The methods by which Thucydides intended to establish the truth involved at every level the working of his mind. This is so clear, so consistent, so strongly conveyed, in the expression itself that in some respects his text, coming at the end of the fifth century, stands out like a true manifesto.

The Sciences of History

Above all it must be recognized that, to a great extent, the text introduces certain methods on which history today continues to rely: this is at least what results from the first stage in the reasoning developed by Thucydides—that is, in his use of sources and documents.

It is true that occasionally he refers simply and without commentary to some specific fact; but that generally occurs when he is describing facts after the Trojan War.[1] For the time before the war, he is forced to turn to the poets; and toward them he felt a legitimate mistrust. Even credulous Herodotus had his scruples about them as sources, and when reporting particularly surprising events, he would gently add (2.120): "If we may say something on the authority of the poets." Thucydides' circumspection went beyond this. He was suspicious of poets *per se*, and his account is partly directed against them; the interpretation he gives of the Trojan War, in any case, contrasts with the idealism of Homer;[2] in the same passage he even says (1.10.3): "Being a great poet, he probably embellished to make it seem greater"; and in the conclusion he repeats that (1.21.1): "We are less willing to believe the poets who celebrated certain facts by making them more attractive by exaggerating." Given those conditions, how was he to use these sources? Thucydides takes multiple precautions and also founds a critical method that could not be faulted even today.

Basically, he only used the poets when they provided information in an almost involuntary way. This might involve general facts, those that for the poet and his contemporaries seemed quite obvious. For example, the use of a name, for which the work gave evidence; thus in 1.3.3: "Homer gave the best proof: he who lived at a time long after the Trojan War never gave the name Hellene to that group; he used it only for the companions of Achilles from Phthiotis, who were the first true Hellenes; and in his poems he uses

---

1. He seems to accept as a given the date of the Trojan War and a number of other dates that followed it. He knows the Corinthian Ameinocles (1.13.3) and the development of various fleets. He is even willing to make statements in cases that seem to contradict traditions known to us, such as the late development of the fleets of Aegina and Athens (1.14.30). For the earlier period, he refers to the difficulty in finding reliable sources; and he could be selective about them; cf. 1.9.2: "Indeed, the account given by those Peloponnesians who have been the recipients of the most credible tradition is this."

2. 1.9.3: οὐ χάριτι τὸ πλέον ἢ φόβῳ, cf. *Odyssey* 5.306–7: χάριν Ἀτρείδῃσι φέροντες.

the terms Danaans, Argives, Achaeans. He also did not use the term barbarian." In this case, Thucydides' interpretation, applied to a fixed piece
of data, exposes a very deep condition of political life, the lack of unity.
Sometimes the evidence in poetry involved an issue of morality, such as
piracy, the existence of which is implied not in the entire work but at least
in a number of passages (1.5.2):[3] "We find ancient poets putting to incom-
ing travelers everywhere alike the question of whether they are pirates—
implying that those being asked would not disavow the profession, and
those concerned to know would not condemn it." So Thucydides' interpretation deduces a custom from a mundane detail. The evidence might
concern a characteristic of power, a characteristic for which there is ample
evidence. To show Agamemnon's maritime strength, Thucydides uses two
sources of this type; one is a simple indication of fact, so he adds a caveat
(1.9.4): "The strength of his navy is shown by the fact that his own was
the largest contingent, and that of the Arcadians was furnished by him;
this at least is what Homer says, if his testimony is deemed sufficient"; but
this evidence is confirmed by a different passage that in itself provides information only indirectly, through a process of pure deduction: the text of
Homer speaks of islands in a general way, and Thucydides concludes (οὖν,
"therefore") from the presence of islands the existence of a fleet (1.9.4).

The same principle is applied several times in the work: Thucydides
thinks about the facts in the epic in order to draw from them information
that the epic did not aim to provide and that was not on the mind of the
poet. The example that in its clarity and certainty is the most admirable is
the reasoning that allows Thucydides to shed light on the role played by the
problem of supplies, according to the attitude of the Greeks who "turned
to cultivation of the Chersonese and to piracy from want of supplies"
(1.11.1). If they had been free of this worry, they might have been stronger
in victory.[4] Yet another example, even more elaborate, is one bearing on

---

3. The issue mentioned by Thucydides appears only twice in the *Odyssey* (3.72, 253) and once
in the *Hymn to Apollo* (452). To that we might add 14.230, in which Odysseus describes himself as
a pirate; and above all, Thucydides read other "Homeric" poems no longer known to us.

4. In the same chapter, a victory was confirmed by reasoning on the basis of a reference to the
construction of a fortification. But in that case we are troubled by our ignorance about what this
fortification was, one that was probably mentioned in poems that are lost today. Nevertheless, we
note the organization of multiple examples of his reasoning; cf. below, p. 155.

the number of men sent against Troy, in chapter 10. Thucydides is able to make an informed calculation from two isolated indicators that seemed (ὡς ἐμοὶ δοκεῖ) reasonably (γοῦν) to mark the two extremes, and he averaged the two, after determining the likelihood (εἰκός) that there were no other elements to include in the accounting.[5] Moreover, most surprising in this bit of logic is that he seems so little justified in it. Thucydides gives all the steps in his calculation, but not the result: he concludes simply that it gives a somewhat high number. Now, his calculation, when we actually carry it out, would mean, for the Greek army about 102,000 men, in other words a large number, larger than the site of Troy would allow us to believe, larger than the number in the pharaonic armies invading Syria. Even if there is no contradiction between this number and the assessment given by Thucydides,[6] we can at least say then that it is inconclusive, and here it is the method that is original rather than the result.

Thucydides appears to have been aware of this quality of originality. In a number of cases his innovations are the source of actual historical methods still in existence today.

The first of his innovations has made him the founder of archaeology. He did not of course conduct excavations, but he did use the data that had come to light in the purification of Delos. Here again, however, in his reasoning he was clearly emphatic about the method itself. In 1.8.1 he wrote: "All the graves on the island were taken up, and it was found that above half their inmates were Carians: they were identified by the fashion of the arms buried with them, and by the method of interment, which was the same as the Carians still follow." This explains the principle behind his reasoning. These explanations were hardly necessary: it was perhaps useful to prove the existence of piracy; it was perhaps good to specify that this was normally practiced by islanders; but the fact that they

---

5. His reasoning, although never more methodical, has never been more reckless: not only does he permit himself to hypothesize; he uses numbers. But Thucydides also takes care to specify that the result is relative, as valid as the opinion of Homer (i.e., mostly embellished) can be: "even so" (1.10.3), the number obtained was a lower one.

6. This is my belief, despite Gomme (1945, ad loc.). Herodotus (9.30) spoke of 110,000 men at Plataea; and Thucydides' indication (1.10.5: ὡς ἀπὸ πάσης τῆς Ἑλλάδος "considering it was sent in common from all of Greece") rules out any comparison with the expeditions of isolated cities, including Athens. In order to compare, we would need to add all the forces involved on the two sides during the Peloponnesian War.

were Carians changed nothing; and this was not even a novelty.[7] Moreover, while Thucydides insists on furnishing his evidence, even when none is needed, we should note that he does so as a general principle: he does not say what those "arms" were, nor what the "method of interment" was.[8]

So it is impossible for readers to grasp the meaning of his words. Once again, the method of verification is shown to be more important than what is verified.

When verification depends not on archaeological documentation but rather on facts observed elsewhere, then it finds a basis in a method of comparison; and there again Thucydides has been assiduous about that innovation. Of course the work was not entirely original, in this aspect or others: Herodotus would, on occasion, draw conclusions about the present from the past; he did so regarding the language spoken by the Pelasgians (1.57): "If we may make a conjecture (τεκμαιρόμενον) based on what remains today from the Pelasgians . . ."; but there the issue involved only an isolated fact and a case with obvious continuity. Thucydides, however, frequently resorts to the same method, not hesitating to compare Greeks of the past with the barbarians of his own day; thus in two chapters we read the following about piracy (1.5.2): "An illustration of this is furnished by the honor with which some of the inhabitants of the continent still regard a successful marauder"; about pillaging on land (1.5.3): "The same pillaging prevailed also on land. And even at the present day many parts of Hellas still follow the old fashion, among the Ozolian Locrians and the Aetolians, for instance, and the Acarnanians and that region of the continent"; about the custom of carrying weapons (1.6.2): "And the fact that the people in these parts of Hellas are still living in the old way points to a time when the same mode of life was once equally common to all"; and finally, about the

---

7. Herodotus has Carians coming from islands (1.171) and describes them as pirates (2.152). Thucydides disagrees with him only about the date of their departure, which he places much earlier; here his argument has no bearing on the date.

8. For the σκευῇ τῶν ὅπλων ("weapons gear"), he could not be referring to the particularities described by Herodotus (1.171), because those soon extended to all Greeks; so we are forced to hypothesize about them (cf., for example, Meyer 1928, 216; Poulsen 1909, 31–32). Concerning τρόπος ("manner"), are we to understand it to mean simply the orientation (cf. Plutarch, *Solon* 10)? It is difficult to see how that would permit such a precise identification: so we must choose among various modes of pre-Hellenic burial (cf., among others, Tsountas 1899 for certain tombs with weapons and jewelry).

custom of participating in sports without being nude (1.6.5): "It is but a few years since that the practice ceased. To this day among some of the barbarians . . .". In every one of these cases, the evidence is of slight importance and the facts quite secondary. Thucydides seems above all to have wished to show how reasoning might apply in this area. This is so true that he does not hesitate to add, in a rather revealing aside, a commentary that applied generally becomes something of a rule (1.6.6): "Indeed, many other points would show that the ancient Greek world lived in a manner analogous to the barbarian world of today." Henceforth the truth was crystal clear.

It is a rationalist manifesto in every sense of the word, for the diverse methods it introduces suggest critical rigor, deductive logic, and even, to some extent, the establishment of broad general principles open to comparison and analogy.[9]

The Web of Reasoning

In history as Thucydides conceives it, intellectual activity and rationalist zeal do not end there. These diverse methods, of a truly scientific quality, supply in each detailed instance one argument or another; but this argument itself is an organized proof. By itself, it would often be inconclusive: it is valid only within the system provided by Thucydides.

Within that system, it joins others and is confirmed, corroborated, verified.

Thucydides seems to have been driven by the sheer pleasure he took in verifying. The verification swells gradually. The judgment on the Trojan War, offered in 1.3.5, is thus differentiated by a series of parentheses containing his evidence. The longest of these fills chapters 4–8, but it is not alone; just as he returns to the Trojan War in 1.8.4, there is a new parenthesis about Agamemnon's power; then, just when he is finally ready to judge the expedition (1.9.4), Thucydides stops again to dispel not simply

---

9. We might add that in establishing logical relationships between fertility and instability (1.2), between piracy and the bearing of arms (1.6), between commerce and the location of cities (1.7), he was laying the foundation of several other modern sciences, from political geography to sociology. At any rate, although rational reflection on these relationships led him to pave the way for these sciences, he was not so imprudent as to apply his conclusions to the establishment of the facts.

a faulty doctrine, but a poor justification of something he nevertheless acknowledged as true (1.10.1): "While it is true that Mycenae was small . . . , we cannot use that as a clear indication that casts doubt . . ."; thus it is the argumentation itself he wishes to correct; for him, that is what mattered.

The gathering of so much evidence and reasoning[10] does not happen without difficulty. The system begins to get complicated; and in the end clarity, which had been the goal of all these considerations, suffers.

From this come certain initial and obvious difficulties of the format. The long parenthesis in chapters 4–8 offers a clear example.

It is, however, carefully framed. Thucydides says, in chapter 4, that *Minos* routed *the Carians from the islands* and worked to suppress *piracy*. First he proves the existence of *piracy* (1.5–8), then its having been practiced by the *Carians who inhabited islands at that time* (1.8.1). Finally, he returns to *Minos* (1.8.2). So the proof is made in a chiasmus, and he returns to the exact point from which he started.

Yet the substance of this demonstration of the proof is oddly inflated. The existence of piracy is established first by two examples, one borrowed from the comparative method, the other from the interpretation of the poets. To this proof are added two signs of corroboration, both well known for quite a long time: bearing of arms (1.6) and the location of cities (1.7). Now, the bearing of arms was not a fact relating only to piracy, but to brigandage in general. Is Thucydides going to fail to make this supplementary argument? Certainly not: he chooses to expand the idea, and by a kind of parenthesis, to incorporate into his proof this additional fact; hence the extension noted at 1.5.3: "The same pillaging prevailed also on land." After that, the narrative resumes, because the most important case is about piracy and specifically about piracy practiced by island people (1.8.1: "The islanders too were great pirates . . . Carians and Phoenicians"). In order best to group together all the convergent signs, Thucydides does not hesitate to wander off on various detours and starts to float, sometimes beyond the bounds of the theses being demonstrated. This floating produces oddities in the phrasing, which led some editors mistakenly, and a bit naively, to restore order in places where the desire to strengthen the demonstration

---

10. This aspect of the text is clearly shown by Hammond 1952.

seemed to have sown disorder: for Steup, it was all the points from 1.5.3 to 1.8 that were out of place,[11] and that "von dem Herausgeber des Werkes sehr ungeschickt eingefugt worden ist (has been ineptly inserted by an editor of the work)"!

The detail in certain sentences often imitates a comparable thought process. As a result, where concision combines with emphasis, we sometimes notice awkwardness in phrasing.

An early example of this is provided by the remarks in chapter 3 about the name of the Greeks. These comments are, in themselves, parenthetical:[12] they belong to a corollary, or a demonstration *a fortiori*, proving that the Greeks did nothing of importance in common before the Trojan War: they did not even have a name that was common to them all. In articulating this idea, Thucydides expresses himself in a singularly abrupt manner. The sentence begins with δοκεῖ δέ μοι (1.3.2: "and it seems to me"), which is without effect on the first verb of the sentence (εἶχεν, "[Greece] had") but then in the second functions as a personal rather than impersonal verb (with εἶναι, "to exist," and παρέχεσθαι, "to provide") and ends by having no effect on the last verb (ἐδύνατο, "was able"). The grammatical oscillation is so abnormal that here again many editors have wished to absolve Thucydides with their own corrections.[13] Actually, however, we should note that the demonstration itself is inflected by that same pattern of movement. First there is an idea easily set forth: the name "Greeks" did not apply to all of them. But Thucydides immediately adds a whole theory, more hypothetical, about the fact that in the beginning this name did not exist at all and about the way it developed. It is not until the end of the phrase that he returns to the more solid ground of the beginning, with the extension of the name to all Greeks. The longest demonstration, the middle part, is thus devoted to the boldest hypothesis, and the one that is least essential to his thesis, and δοκεῖ weighs most heavily on this part of the sentence. So the irregularity of his style reflects the mental detour in

---

11. Steup regards these chapters as added later and poorly integrated into the context, but intended to be better integrated later; but they actually constitute an intellectual addition by Thucydides himself, in which the desire to provide proof pushes aside the desire for formal regularity.

12. See 3.4: δ' οὖν (resumptive), "Well, then . . .".

13. εἶχεν: ἔχειν Reiske; ἐδύνατο om. M, dell. Van der Mey, Jones.

which, in the very middle of his sentence, Thucydides sets off far afield to find a vague but supporting confirmation.[14]

Like the comments about the name of the Greeks, those concerning Agamemnon's inherited power in chapter 9 are, to some extent, a parenthesis:[15] they actually do little except to confirm, *a fortiori*, the idea that some increase in power occurred between the time of Minos and that of the Trojan War. And these remarks result in one of Thucydides' most troublesome phrases: "Eurystheus was killed in Attica by the Heraclids; Atreus was his mother's brother; and Eurystheus did not . . .". Circumstances and explanations grow to the detriment of formal regularity. First there are genitive absolutes (whose subject is sometimes Atreus and sometimes Eurystheus), then a parenthetical clause (whose subject is again Atreus), and explanations of that (in one of which the subject is the Mycenaeans): he needs all this, this whole maze, in order to account for the role played by each one— first of Atreus's regency and then of the transformation of that regency into royalty. But by this accumulation of accessory explanations, leaving them as accessory and subordinating them to the rest, we are left with a sentence so awkward as to be obscure; it is useless to try to fix it.[16] Moreover, the desire to explain everything is all the more remarkable here in that it involves, on Thucydides' part, an unusual process: he, normally so attentive to avoid details of fact, especially uncertain ones, suddenly multiplies proper names and geographic details; he adopts a version unknown to Homer, making Eurystheus the king of Mycenae, and uses incidental traditions like the battle against the Heraclids or the murder of Chrysippus. One could say that the need for a strong demonstration has got the better not only of the coherence of the sentence but also of his caution regarding traditions.

Everything yields to these demands: chapters 3 and 9 have shown this as far as the structure of the sentences is concerned; the same could be said of that which, better than anything else, conveys movement in the

---

14. We might take this nuance into account by means of a slightly forced translation on the order of "And, it seems to me, even this name was not used to designate the whole; rather, before Hellen, the son of Deucalion, such a name would not even have existed at all."

15. The idea that adheres most directly to what precedes is that of his navy. The heritage of the Pelopids is both less original and less important for his thesis. I have already discussed chapters 9–11 in Romilly 1954.

16. However, a number of corrections have been proposed, from the most acceptable (Ἀτρεῖ deleted by Gomme) to the ridiculous (βουλομένων καὶ τῶν Μυκηναίων φόβῳ τῶν Ἡρακλειδῶν damn. Steup).

sentences: the particles. Chapter 11 provides a good example. This chapter responds to chapter 9. Neither one judges the expedition; both add to the judgment a fairly loose commentary; just as the first explained the possibility of the Trojan War by Agamemnon's power, the second explains by the lack of financial resources the limited nature of the war despite that power. This new personal thesis is based on one proof, drawn from his reasoning about Homer and linked with a hypothetical counterproof. Yet this appeal to Homer already raises a problem here,[17] one that some editors have wanted to "correct" in order to make the text consistent with what we know today.[18] It is, however, clear that in this case we are dealing with evidence that has not come down to us: Thucydides is willing to include it because it serves his point, but mentions it in passing because it is only a secondary confirmation; he alludes to it rather than sacrifice another piece of evidence; he is emphatically brief.

So it should not be surprising that the sentence itself suffers for that brevity. What happens in the chapter is what happened in chapters 4–8. The idea to demonstrate is actually that the minor importance of the number of troops is explained by the lack of money. But Thucydides immediately adds to that a related and supporting idea: that same lack of money also meant that not even all of those troops could be used in the war; some were sent out to find provisions by pillage or farming. This is the related idea that the chapter is intended to show, but it takes a bounce and comes to replace the initial idea and to deepen its impact. The deviation is indicated by particles. To introduce this corresponding idea, Thucydides uses an irregular connector: τε, implying two parallel elements, is answered not with τε or καί, as the connection would suggest, but δέ, more suitable for a different, independent, element. Moreover, since the distinction between the two ideas should be clearly indicated, even when only to underline their very coexistence, and since, moreover, every detail needing to be proven, the subordinate clause becomes separated from the principal clause by a parenthetical explanation, Thucydides repeats that δέ at the beginning of the principal clause in a twist that, while correct, is very rare: he uses it nowhere else. For both the first δέ and for the second, corrections

---

17. See above, p. 148 n. 4.

18. ἐκράτησαν: ἐκρατήθησαν Cobet, Thiersch, Humphreys, Earle, etc. ‖ ἐτειχίσαντο: ἔτει ι' ἐτειχίσαντο Robertson // δῆλον δέ . . . ἐτειχίσαντο post χρησάμενοι transp. Lucas.

have been proposed:[19] both correspond to the movement of the thought itself, always looking for corroborating proof and willing to make a diversion in order to find it.

We could cite other similarly rough passages.[20] Those that can be translated only by using one particle in place of another may be the mistakes of a copyist; but, in general, the movement that breaks the regularity of the sentence parts is the same as the one that interrupts the normal flow between chapters: it is the movement of a mind engaged in demonstrating, indulging the pleasure of bringing in new evidence drawn from a corresponding fact and establishing a sort of system in which each element remains distinct but becomes part of a whole that is both fuller and more convincing.

Interpretation of the Whole

Yet if this is so, this very quality attests to the presence, in these pages, of another way of reasoning, one that may express itself in the work less directly, but no less perceptibly. This reasoning arises from a general likelihood, residing in the agreement of the facts between themselves and in their coherence—in other words, in their conformity with the interpretation of the whole as presented by Thucydides.

On this level internal probability comes before the proofs; and the truth of each fact is no longer established only by one argument or another, but by its potential to be part of the whole.

This whole is much more precise and much more remarkable than the simple thesis posed at the beginning, according to which, in past epics, "nothing was on a large scale, war no more than anything else." The chapters that back up this statement are rare indeed. Of the three that relate to the Trojan War, we have seen that only the end of chapter 10 tries to calculate scale. What is more, this thesis is not really original to Thucydides.[21] Additionally, if he had been motivated only by a desire to show

---

19. Bekker suggested changing the first δέ to τε; Earle, removing the second δέ.

20. For particles, I could cite the use of καί . . . τε, which I included in my edition, in 1.9.3, where it is included in all the manuscripts. There, this incorrect linkage corresponds to the introduction of the newest and most important idea: Agamemnon also had a fleet. It would mark the transition to a different but corresponding idea.

21. Herodotus clearly says that in the past "the Greek nation generally was weak" (1.143).

this, it is not clear why he needed to delay describing and even proving, sometimes despite the prevailing opinion,[22] the importance of Minos's empire, or the wealth and maritime power of Agamemnon. The fact is that the thesis counts for little in the theory: the point is not to show that earlier epochs were less important than the present, but to show why. And for that, Thucydides needed to explain all of Greek history, from the beginnings to the Peloponnesian War, by emphasizing what in his view made war, like anything else, important: in other words, financial and maritime resources. Every chapter of the narrative contributes directly to showing that the importance of these enterprises is linked to that of resources, and to the successive advancements seen in each domain.

The basis for such a construction is, for Thucydides, an elaborate theory of power. That Athens should have provided him the model is hardly in doubt, since the two poles on which all power in the Greek world sits squarely are the same ones on which Athens built its empire: a fleet and a treasury. Around these two poles, the whole Athenian system soon turns; and the analysis explaining the process of all this is shown forcefully.

A *fleet* allows *commerce*. Commerce brings *revenue*. Revenue creates a *treasury*. The treasury, for its part, is tied to *stability*, which leads to the existence of *walls*. And these three terms, fleet-treasury-walls, make it possible for a state to *group* numerous other states under its domination, and to acquire a *force*.

Of course Thucydides never gives any such sweeping and absolute analysis; he proceeds as he always does, making his thinking clear by means of comparisons, repetitions, analogies; and these linkages are strengthened by seeming to be inevitable. Built on certain key words, always the same ones, the text seems to establish the basis for a systematically realistic interpretation of history.

At the same time, we understand that everything that goes into this system is thereby taken as a probability, and therefore as significant.

In the beginning, everything is absent. The first two sentences of chapter 2 bring together in a negative statement all the key words without exception. The weakness of the earlier periods was essentially owing to an insufficiency in two key areas, maritime and financial; there was neither

---

22. See below, p. 165.

commerce nor fixed relationships (1.2.2: τῆς γὰρ ἐμπορίας οὐκ οὔσης, οὐδ'ἐπιμειγνύντες ἀδεῶς ἀλλήλοις οὔτε κατὰ γῆν οὔτε διὰ θαλάσσης, "There was no trade, nor even safe communication with each other, by land or along the sea"), and there were no *financial reserves* (περιουσίαν χρημάτων). To this latter point is added the lack of *walls* (ἀτειχίστων). Together they explain the general *instability* in which early Greeks lived (οὐ πάλαι βεβαίως οἰκουμένη, "long ago did not have a stable population"), and, consequently, *the lack of alliances and the lack of strength* (καὶ δι' αὐτὸ οὔτε μεγέθει πόλεων ἴσχυον οὔτε τῇ ἄλλῃ παρασκευῇ, "That is why neither large cities nor other preparedness provided power").

This thoroughly negative tableau will serve as both the point of departure and the basis for comparison.

The progress announced at the end of chapter 3 is exclusively maritime (1.3.4: "And even this expedition brought them together only *when use of the sea was much more developed* [θαλάσσῃ ἤδη πλείω χρώμενοι]"); and yet, the different terms stay tightly linked, as the subsequent chapters will show.

With chapter 4, we see the first of these advances. Here the text, which is very short, is perfectly framed by two decisive words evoking the sea and money (1.4): "And the first person known to us by tradition as having established a navy is Minos. He made himself master of what is now called the Hellenic sea"; and he cleared the sea of pirates in order to "assure the return of his *revenues*."

As we have shown, the following chapters form a parenthesis. During the course of his demonstration, however, Thucydides is led to comment on, relative to the location of cities, the difference between ancient and modern conditions: the way in which he does so introduces once more the same fleet-money combination, to which now he adds walls: "With respect to cities, later on, in an era of increased facilities of *navigation* and a greater *supply of wealth* (περιουσίας ... χρημάτων), we find the shores becoming the site of *walled* cities" (1.7.1).

The same advances are finally expressed directly when, following this digression, the narrative returns to Minos and the consequences of his action. The set of two major concepts is now joined, not only by walls, but by stability (1.8.3): "The coast populations now began to apply themselves more closely to the acquisition of *wealth*, and their life became more *settled*; some even began to build themselves *walls* on the strength of their newly acquired riches." An important conclusion is drawn on the basis of this set: power is concentrated in the hands of those who are richest. With a subtle emphasis, Thucydides shows in this passage just how the economic factor worked in a double way in this case, furnishing both the motive of weakness and a means of strength (1.8.3):[23] "For the love of gain would reconcile the weaker to the domination of the stronger, and the possession of reserves of wealth enabled the more powerful to reduce the smaller cities to subjection."

So we should not be surprised then, by the attraction of the section relating to the Trojan War. The two chapters 9 and 11, in which the emphasis is clear, both relate to this system of explanation. The first explains how the concentration of forces drawn into the Trojan War was possible because of the double nature of Agamemnon's power: the legacy of descent from two lines from Pelops with, first, *money* (πλήθει χρημάτων), and *maritime strength* (καὶ ναυτικῷ τε ἅμα ἐπὶ πλέον τῶν ἄλλων ἰσχύσας, "also powerful beyond others in his navy"); this realist and original interpretation[24] not only merited a digression for the purpose of demonstration, but was almost indispensable to Thucydides' system of interpretation. The same is true for the digression in chapter 11, a counterpoint to it; in the positive analysis, Thucydides emphasizes especially the maritime element; in the negative analysis, he stresses particularly the financial aspect; in fact, while the concentration of forces could not have been very large, the reason, he writes, is "not due so much to scarcity of men as of *money*" (1.11.1).

Following this description of the negatives, Thucydides takes up the period after the Trojan War, and the reader can again realize the advances yet to be made: it took a long time before Greece had *stability* (1.12.4: βεβαίως, "securely"). The progress by which this was won is described beginning in chapter 13, and naturally the progress was twofold (1.13.1): "As the acquisition of *wealth* (τῶν χρημάτων τὴν κτῆσιν) became more of an objective, the *revenues* (τῶν προσόδων) of the states increasing, tyrannies were established almost everywhere." In addition, Greece "began to fit out *fleets* and apply itself more closely to the sea" (1.13.1).

---

23. See below, p. 161. Moreover, the hierarchical state born of wealth will tend to be more and more elaborate and will lead to a new development of wealth.

24. See above, p. 147 and n. 2.

The latter theme introduces a long expansion about the history of successive thalassocracies; here the theory has so far surpassed the original thesis that the wars then intervene only when they can show something about the sea.[25] This history of the thalassocracies ends with further advances in wealth and a new concentration of power (1.15.1): "All their insignificance did not prevent their being an element of the greatest power to those who cultivated them, alike in revenue and in dominion." The power of Athens was already on the horizon, born of its navy (1.18.2) and accomplished, as we learn at the very end of the account, by tribute (1.19).

Interpreted in this way, the rest of the history becomes an intelligible system, and every argument that will take its place in it acquires increased prominence.

There is no doubt that this system represents Thucydides' greatest originality. Moreover, with it he has given history a foundation not only critical and reasoned, but also positive and realist in the most modern sense of the term: it is in fact based on an analysis and puts economic factors front and center, in an area and at a time when to do so required some audacity.

It is equally clear that Thucydides himself is fully aware of this originality: the pains he takes to show the framework of his doctrine are very revealing in this regard.

We should not, however, be exactly surprised to find that this effort burdens the prose style to the point of introducing some peculiarities of its own as well. Moreover, if Thucydides marks the characteristics of his method with such pride, and if he multiplies proofs and confirmations to the detriment of structural clarity and balanced phrasing, he must do so because the theory behind his method is precious to him. And we can understand that, when it comes to showing the framework itself, he may be less willing than ever to sacrifice clarity to the requirements of stylistic form.

The readers' vexation in the face of seemingly superfluous or unwelcome elements makes their presence stand out. It is typical that, over a sequence of six chapters, the harshest criticism has been brought, in at least five cases, against those words we have called key words, which correspond to the very essence of the doctrine.

In 1.8.3, concerning the early clusters of powers and the authority that the powerful had over the smaller cities, the words used are περιουσίας

---

25. As in 1.13.4, on the naval battle between Corinthians and Corcyraeans.

ἔχοντες ("possessing surpluses"), which seemed to some a superfluous addition. "περιουσίας ἔχοντες ist nicht zu erklären (cannot be explained)," in the Classen-Steup edition; according to the commentary given in that edition, the simple δυνατώτεροι ("more powerful") sufficed to explain the basis for domination, and, if one wanted to give meaning to περιουσίας, it would be necessary to imagine dropping a word like χώρας ("land"); otherwise, the financial element, which had earlier served as a goal for weak states, appeared, awkwardly, to mean two things at once. Yet we should not be surprised either by Thucydides' inconsistency or by the dual nature of the financial element. The emphasis here is simply precision; it corresponds to a clear doctrine: that all enterprises depend on financial reserves. Pericles described it clearly: "Reserves (περιουσίαι), it must be remembered," he said, "maintain a war rather than forced contributions" (1.141.5); and further (2.13.3): "In war, it is primarily judgment and financial reserves (χρημάτων περιουσίᾳ) that bring success." In the Archaeology itself, the word is repeated often enough that the importance of the point cannot be doubted.[26] Establishing a double rapport, in which money is shown to be both motive and means, is not at all alien to Thucydides' way of thinking. When he speaks of the creation of the Athenian Empire he shows in the same way, that by agreeing to pay tribute in lieu of going on a campaign, Athens' allies were preparing for an inequality of condition that explained both the defections and the ease with which Athens was able to crush them:[27] we perceive here a snowball effect, Athenian domination causing the defections that, ultimately, come to reinforce that domination. The rational principle is the same; and that is understandable, since, in both cases, the fundamental idea is the same: it consists in showing the role played by economic superiority in the process of domination.[28] As a result, the use of the words περιουσίας ἔχοντες in 1.8.3 is legitimate in

---

26. See also the placement of the word in 1.11.2.

27. 1.99.1–3. The first section is meant to explain the defections. The two following sections explain the weakness of the allies at the time of these defections.

28. In a less obvious way, but still clear, the end of chapter 2, in the Archaeology itself, also establishes a double connection: in it we see that owing to its aridity Attica was not devastated by revolts; but, in a complementary way, it actually gained inhabitants from cities that were prey to revolts, which contributed to its growth (μείζω ἔτι, "still greater"). Steup also found this duplication so disconcerting that he concluded that all of section 2.6 "has been added later to the beginning of our chapter (zu dem Hauptteil unseres Kap. Nachträglich hinzugefügt worden ist)!"

every respect: if the words appear somewhat superfluous, that is precisely because Thucydides wanted to make a point; and if they establish a dual relationship, that gives only more weight to the importance he attaches to this economic factor.

It is also to this factor that the words τῆς τροφῆς ἀπορίᾳ ("because of lack of provisions") in chapter 11 refer. The concept of the lack of reserves for provisions dominates the entire passage, one that has the stamp of a dominating logic. Thucydides first sets forth his thesis: the *lack of money* explains the relative weakness of the expedition against Troy; then he gives the (double) proof: the troop numbers were limited by *lack of provisions*, and their ineffectiveness was also due to *lack of provisions*. The counterargument held that if the army had had the *reserves for provisions*, it would have easily defeated Troy. The conclusion reached is that the *lack of money*, in Troy as elsewhere, hindered the Greeks. This chapter is framed by ἡ ἀχρηματία ("lack of money") and δι' ἀχρηματίαν ("because of the lack of money"): at each point in the demonstration, we find "lack of provisions" (τῆς γὰρ τροφῆς ἀπορίᾳ—τῆς τροφῆς ἀπορίᾳ.—περιουσίαν δὲ . . . τροφῆς). The second mention of this *lack of provisions* appeared to some editors (Van Herwerden, Stahl, Croiset) as needing to be removed. Actually, the first time the word was used, at the beginning, should have, given the position of the particle, sufficed for the whole: so the words are superfluous, not only in terms of the thought, but also for the proper balance in the sentence. We have shown, however, that any such balance had already been undermined by the pressure of the arguments, and particularly by the use of the particles.[29] If the second part of the proof is given as more or less independent of the first, constituting an addition, a detour, why should we find it surprising that Thucydides yields to the temptation to repeat the words that are the most important element in his idea? Formal regularity is never his way, and he is always willing to repeat certain terms. In any case, the importance of the economic factor emerges all the more forcefully thanks to the break and the repetition.[30]

A little later, at the beginning of chapter 13, there are two groups of words that Krüger and Van Herwerden wished to remove from a single

---

29. See above, p. 155.
30. The position of the words has also been well defended by Hammond (1952).

sentence: "Since Greece . . . was occupied (even more than before)[31] with acquiring wealth, we see tyrannies becoming established in cities (with the growth of revenues)."[32] It would be useless to go into detail; once again, Thucydides, usually so concise, is reproached for being too emphatic: once again, the points he emphasizes are, on the one hand, developmental (meaning wealth), and on the other, the importance of the economic factor used here, with some originality,[33] to explain political situations.

What is surprising about the fact that he specifies both the level of development,[34] and the shape it takes, in this case the economic factor?

Reserves allows for major undertakings, but revenues lift an individual and allow him to ascend to power.[35]

Moreover, in the same chapter, recalling the rise of Corinth's power, Thucydides is equally emphatic about what he finds to be identical conditions. He has described an earlier period when, owing to their privileged location for commerce by land, the Corinthians were "powerful with money" (χρήμασί τε δυνατοὶ ἦσαν). Then he comes to the period of navigation and shows that Corinth became a center of maritime commerce: henceforth it was "a city powerful with revenues of money" (δυνατὴν ἔσχον χρημάτων προσόδῳ τὴν πόλιν). There is little difference in the expressions between one period and the other. But does that call for a correction, writing with Steup δυνατωτάτην ("most powerful") or with Maddalena δυνατὴν μᾶλλον ("more powerful")? No one would dare to agree who thought about the precision that the notion of revenues or treasure conveys in other passages; the acquisition of a new market, more developed, gives to the wealth of Corinth a more stable and, in some way, more active quality.

Be that as it may, and even if there is a place for correcting this or that in these chapters, it is possible to say that even there the similarity in the cases

---

31. ἔτι: τι or ἤδη Krüger, Earle ‖ ἢ πρότερον dell. Krüger, Van Herwerden.

32. Τῶν προσόδων μειζόνων γιγνομένων dell. Krüger, van Herwerden, post Ἑλλάς transp. Müller, προσόδων <τισὶ τῶν εὐδαιμόνων> conj. Steup.

33. Compare this, for example, with what Plato (*Republic* 562a) and Aristotle (*Politics* 5.3.1305a) will say about the origins of tyranny.

34. ἔτι μᾶλλον ἢ πρότερον ("still more than before") recalls 8.3: μᾶλλον ἤδη τὴν κτῆσιν τῶν χρημάτων ποιούμενοι ("acquiring wealth still more").

35. It is accurate to say the establishment of tyranny corresponds to the enormous economic development of the seventh and sixth centuries; about that process, see Ure 1922, 374; and on the importance of money for the tyrant, see *Oedipus the King* 542.

constitutes in itself an argument: it cannot be by chance that those words that draw our attention are so often of the same order; and it is clearly Thucydides' interpretation that imposes its presence and weight on every detail of the expression.

This interpretation is the third and final step achieved by reasoning in the pursuit of truth. After the critical work that formed the basis for the scientific methods, and after the logical work constructing the system of proofs, it represents the organizing principle, which reassembles a coherent whole. It is clearly at the very beginning of each of the hypotheses Thucydides infers; it reinforces by its probabilities each of the separate demonstrations; and lastly, it allows us to attribute to each fact a meaning beyond its evidentiary one.

There is little doubt that Thucydides had teachers and allies in the deployment of the intense rationality in these pages. The sophists, in their logic and positivism; the doctors, in their diagnostic research; the Athenians of the fifth century generally, in their faith in human possibility—all comprise a propitious and stimulating context for this undertaking. But in no other text does the triumph of reasoning in all its aspects appear so absolute. This explains the masterful appeal that the narrative can justly claim.

Results

Success and Failure

The unknown has been mastered. To the extent that our role, as modern readers, is that of arbiters, we are obliged to attest that on all essential points Thucydides' reconstruction has been verified and is not only valid, but brilliant.

We cannot repeat enough the extent to which his reconstruction is freed from anything mythological, or even simply suspect. Along with the "sons of Zeus," such fictional characters as Pelasgus and Lycurgus have departed from history, and Thucydides is able to draw his own conclusions without any hazardous details about the "Pelasgic race" or the "return of the Heraclids."

Having removed all of that to start with a clean slate, he reconstructs, with uncanny felicitousness, the principal stages. That there was first a nomadic period, followed by a period of great migrations, is not questioned today: without going into the many examples of indirect evidence for this, it suffices to cite the regular desert raids in the delta known from the Tell el-Amarna tablets. Nor is there any longer any doubt about the two great moments that Thucydides identifies in the sequence of historical advancements, namely the two thalassocracies of Crete and Mycenae. It is possible that the very recent study of Mycenaean records will shed valuable light on this still poorly understood epoch; but enough is already known to describe the existence of these two thalassocracies. Cycladic excavations have so clearly confirmed the importance of the first of these that today there is no need to emphasize the point further. While archaeological excavations are more indicative of the extent of Mycenaean civilization than of King Agamemnon's powers, at least the non-Greek texts that invite us to see his empire in the Ahhiyawa, and on the tablets of Bogaz Köy the name of Atarissiyas, attest well the existence of an important power, maintaining relations with various Hittite kings and exercising real influence overseas.

In both cases, Thucydides' exceptional insight is all the more remarkable in denoting his disagreement with Herodotus. The only historical thalassocracy Herodotus recognized was that of Polycrates. There was Minos's kingdom, but it belonged to the era of legend; as for Agamemnon, he was not taken into consideration (3.122): "Polycrates is the first Hellene we know of who ever attempted to control the sea, except, of course, for Minos of Knossos and anyone who might have ruled the sea before Minos. But in what is told about the human race, Polycrates was the first." Clearly, Thucydides did not have any more factual data than Herodotus had. He too knew of Minos from tradition and gives even fewer details than Herodotus (1.173) about the man and his ancestry. As for Mycenae, Thucydides thought that it was a small city (1.10.1). But the different interpretation he gives to the same sources accurately indicates the contrast between their points of view and their methods: based on his own research, Thucydides was able to extract from the tradition what was important; and it was also his research that, in every case, allowed him, with good reason, to be more assertive than his predecessors.

It does not detract from this remarkable achievement to point out certain details that reveal some of the limits, or risks, in this method. These were beyond Thucydides' control. He was as prudent or as bold as the difficulties facing him and the tools at his disposal entailed. If we, after the fact, sometimes charge him with being inexact, it is because reason alone in the end could not carry such an undertaking to a perfect result. To criticize the affirmations of Thucydides' Archaeology in light of the facts is thus to apply, to some extent, the method of reasoning to history.

Thucydides never lapsed into serious error. We can say, however, that in his exposition of the facts he is almost too rational, to the extent that he carries out a type of historical unification.

Minos and Agamemnon

Even in the description of the two thalassocracies, Crete and Mycenae, Thucydides' categorizations are somewhat clouded.

Minos did indeed have a fleet; he achieved mastery in the Aegean. Did he rule over (ἦρξε) the Cyclades and establish the first colonies there (οἰκιστής, "colonizer")? Certainly the Cretan economy, to which the Cyclades submitted, could not have functioned had Crete not been assured of its pledges and benefits; the legend of the Minotaur seems to reflect the memory of some harsh conscription, and the innumerable storage jars at Knossos suggest in-kind offerings. Yet it is difficult not to feel that the very words used by Thucydides are more applicable to Athenian reality than to that of Crete. We do not know if Crete was an empire; at any rate, nowhere are Minoan remains found in such numbers as in the country undoubtedly most independent, that is, Egypt. We might say that Thucydides could not help explaining, completing, projecting an image of the present onto the past.

We see this in a curious little detail: Steup, observing that the beginning of the sentence concerning Minos (παλαίτατος ὧν ἀκοῇ ἴσμεν, "the oldest of those in oral tradition") does not fit with the last part, which, regarding the Cyclades, is too specific, concludes that the last part is an awkward later addition.[36] Rather, we might conclude that Thucydides' thinking was meticulous and led him to see the first thalassocracy beneath the outlines of an early empire. It is even possible that, despite what Herodotus says,[37] we

---

36. Steup adds another argument: the absence of any explanation (given later) of the piracy practiced by the Carians. It is especially characteristic that Thucydides would take care to specify right away the forms of this domination without giving even the most relevant details.

37. Herodotus specifically says that his research showed no trace of tribute by the Carians (1.171). In fact, according to Thucydides (perhaps because they were no longer to be found there in Homer) they were no longer in the islands; and as for Herodotus, he does not claim that no tribute was paid to Minos, and he acknowledges that Minos had vast territories under his rule (*ibid.*: κατεστραμμένου γῆν πολλήν, "having subjected much territory").

should understand the προσόδους at the end of the chapter to mean actual tribute.[38] In any case, the "modern" aspect of the description is undeniable.

In the description of the power exercised by Agamemnon this quality is even clearer. The set of legends Thucydides preserves are arranged according to formulae with fresh appeal: Atreus, as a democrat, flattered (τεθεραπευκότα) the people; Agamemnon, when he controls others by means of fear, according to Thucydides' very new and realistic interpretation, acts just like a fifth-century head of state, like a man essentially equal to others, in a world in which people had minds open to everything except when it came to self-interest. Since Agamemnon's power was obviously established,[39] one has to wonder whether, in addition to this increase in power, there was not some special and particularly solemn authority making him, as he said, more kingly (βασιλεύτερος) than Achilles.[40] Nilsson (1932, 135) and Meyer (1928, 249) thought that this aspect, already disappearing in the epic, made it possible to rediscover the memory of an earlier system, comparable to that of the Teutonic kingdoms. If that is so, then Thucydides risks being almost overly realist, and too rigidly projecting current models on past ones.

The same tendency could likewise be found in every chapter of the Archaeology; and to the extent that Thucydides' account lends itself to criticism, it generally could be charged with being too centered on Athens alone and too ready to accept progress in the direction of a single goal.

The Unity of the Presentation

It is not that, in the first of these charges, he risks being mistaken; it is that it allows for omissions; or rather, since Thucydides is far too thorough to leave out anything important, it is notable in the relative importance that he attributes to different elements of his account.

First, he is concerned only with Greece. If we compare the list of thalassocracies that are treated in Eusebius (*Chronicle*, pp. 225ff.) with the summary given by Thucydides in chapter 13, we notice that unlike

---

38. This could also mean commerce; Thucydides does not explain. But commerce would not require installing his own sons as sovereigns.

39. See in the *Iliad* itself, in addition to the inequality lamented by Achilles in book 1, evidence like 1.185, 281; 2.577, 580; 9.97; 16.54.

40. *Iliad* 9.160; see Allen 1921, 65ff.

Eusebius, Thucydides begins with Corinth but neglects all the thalassocracies included by tradition prior to the seventh century: Lydians, Pelasgians, Thracians, Rhodians, Phrygians, Cypriots, Phoenicians, Egyptians, Carians. Of course it was not necessary to include all of these, and much of the evidence seems to have come secondhand from a later time. But the fact that Thucydides deliberately omitted everything that was not Greek is characteristic.

Even within the Greek world, he was interested in little besides the peninsula and the group of countries sharing a common history. Naturally, he did not ignore Sicily; but every mention he makes of it is offered with some regret and somewhat awkwardly.

We see this in chapter 17 when, speaking of the tyranny, Thucydides gives the reasons why the tyrants never undertook major actions: "Nothing very notable was accomplished under their direction, beyond actions directed at their neighbors." He added: "Those from Sicily attained the highest level of power" (οἱ γὰρ ἐν Σικελίᾳ ἐπὶ πλεῖστον ἐχώρησαν δυνάμεως). This awkwardly added part of the sentence seems aimed at an exception.[41] This is a sizable one, if all the power of the tyrants of Sicily is really reduced to the level of minor expeditions against its neighbors. Modern discomfort has been so strong that some have wished to correct the text in various ways, and most felt obliged, quite simply, to eliminate that whole part of the sentence:[42] in that case, the objection relative to Sicily would have presented itself not to Thucydides' mind, but to that of an ancient reader who was quick to add an interpolation.[43] It seems, however, reasonable to attribute this to Thucydides and to consider this minor discrepancy in the text as revealing his frame of mind. Likewise, an analogous

41. This is sometimes read: "I am not speaking of the ones from Sicily, for they at least . . .". This translation would lessen the gravity of the omission but seems hard to allow: the γάρ of omission is common but should normally introduce a reason for the omission ("I am not speaking of the ones from Sicily, for they are too distant, their power ephemeral, their case is different"; not "for I should mention them"!). I take this as "I qualify this, for those from Sicily, obviously, . . .".

42. In place of οἱ γάρ Cobet suggests μόνοι γὰρ οἱ. On the side of those who would suppress, there are Wex, Krüger, Böhme-Widmann, Van Herwerden, Stahl, Hude, Classen, Steup, Delachaux, and Maddalena.

43. This interpolator is supposed to have taken it from Herodotus 3.125: "Among the tyrants who reigned at Syracuse, no other Hellenic tyrant deserves to be compared to Polycrates from the point of view of magnificence." But Herodotus was referring simply to facts known to everyone, and of course most especially to Thucydides.

regret appears in the following chapter, when, referring to the expulsion of the tyrants, Thucydides writes that most—"the last, with the exception of those from Sicily" (1.18.1)—were expelled by Sparta. So the Sicilian territory is set apart, and for this reason it seems possible to establish general rules to which Sicily constitutes an exception, a major exception, and yet for Thucydides' purposes a negligible one.

Thucydides' attempt at simplification does not end there: even within Greece itself, he seems at times to leave in the shadows anything that would instead concern Sparta and continental power.

Already in chapter 15, in the way that he plays down the importance of wars and conquests on land ("No war was fought that resulted in power; all those that took place were directed against neighboring countries") we note that he omits Pheidon's domination in the Peloponnese as well as the Lacedaemonian wars, out of which the Peloponnesian League will suddenly emerge in 1.18.1.[44] The omission might seem surprising at first, but to understand it we must imagine that Thucydides is thinking of the importance of wars like the Peloponnesian War; to make that war completely comprehensible we must imagine that the paradigm of a great power is, for him, Athenian power. As a result, the existence of Sparta is suddenly revealed in a parenthesis (1.18.1: ἡ γὰρ Λακεδαίμων). In that parenthesis, Thucydides must go back to the Dorian invasion and show his readers a type of power that is new for them, since it is based not on a fleet and on money, but on internal order: "As far as anyone can tell, between the end of the present war and the time when Lacedaemonians began to live under the same regime, there are more than four hundred years; that is the reason for the power that allowed them to rule the affairs of other cities." One might say that, at the last moment, Sparta has suddenly been attached to the account, as a surprise and as though by accident, with no preparation or explanation of its predominance.

From this point on, that predominance seems to be considered a fact. We soon learn that, at the time of the Persian Wars, the Lacedaemonians in fact "prevailed in power" (1.18.2: δυνάμει προύχοντες), and then, against the Athenians, they were shown to be most powerful, "one the first naval, the other the first military power in Hellas" (1.18.2). This account, then,

---

44. See Gomme 1945, ad loc. For similar omissions, see Täubler 1927, 83.

can end with a contrasting image of two sides soon to be at war with each other. Still it is not certain that in this conclusion the roles of both are equal. It is not actually clear to whom the entire final sentence refers (1.19): καὶ ἐγένετο αὐτοῖς ἐς τόνδε τὸν πόλεμον ἡ ἰδία παρασκευὴ μείζων ἢ ὡς τὰ κράτιστά ποτε μετὰ ἀκραιφνοῦς τῆς ξυμμαχίας ἤνθησαν. According to some scholars, the pronoun designates both Athenians and Lacedaemonians, and the meaning is "Both found their resources for this war separately to exceed the sum of their strength when the alliance flourished intact" (1.19). According to others the reference is to the Athenians alone, they by themselves being stronger than they had ever been during the full high point of the alliance.[45] Actually, only the first interpretation agrees with the context: it matches the general idea expressed at the beginning of the Archaeology, that the Peloponnesian War is more important than any that preceded it, because the "the preparations of both the combatants were in every department in the last state of perfection" (1.1). The last sentence is an echo of the first, and the rigor that Thucydides shows in this entire account is recognizable in this new feature. Any hesitation, on the other hand, stems from the fact that the sentence, from a historical point of view, would apply more aptly to Athens alone. It was Athens that had evolved before the war; and Thucydides knows that well: in another passage later, referring more directly to Athens, he compares its progress with Spartan inertia (1.118.2). This is so true that even when he is speaking of the two cities in the Archaeology, it is clear that he is thinking primarily of Athens: at the end of chapter 18 he credits both with advances, but he explains that they achieved these "whether during treaties or at war, either with each other or with their own allies in revolt," an explanation that, from all appearances, is more suitable in the case of Athens than of Sparta. Perhaps the same is true in this case. Regardless of the interpretation one adopts, it is certainly analysis of Athens that prevails in the sentence: either Thucydides means to speak about Athens alone, or, if he means both cities, that

---

45. On the side of the first interpretation, see Classen, Grote, Herbst, Croiset, Delachaux, Täubler, Gomme, and Maddalena; on the other side are Stahl, Steup, Forbes, Hauvette, and Marchant. Within both of these interpretations there can be variation in the interpretation of τῆς ξυμμαχίας (alliance between Sparta and Athens / group of allies of Athens) and even about the interpretation of μετά (with the contribution of / in the time when they had): as many as six different meanings have been proposed.

equilibrium is merely superficial and what is meant to be a very general reflection has shifted, involuntarily, toward Athens.

To review this very coherent and systematic development, it seems that Thucydides has, in the end, more or less consciously edited out and dropped anything that might fall outside the system. It is not an accident when, in chapter 12, he presents a simplified view of colonization in Asia, omitting everything except Ionian colonization and, within Ionian colonization, anything that was not initiated by Athens: this is clearly the process by which he sacrifices everything that does not relate to his primary focus of attention. Except for whatever leads to Athenian thalassocracy he does not concern himself with the Lacedaemonian system, or with the states located around the edges of the Greek world, or with non-Greek states; everything takes place as if, deeply penetrated by doctrines of thalassocracy that the Athenian democracy had just developed, Thucydides, in turning to the past to research the formation of power, is conforming to a schema and limits himself to a framework, both of which are defined by his own views.

This simplification and unification recur in the contempt in which he holds barbarians. The comparative method on which he is so insistent consists of defining Greeks of old as like modern barbarians, as if barbarians are, by definition, backward in relation to Greeks; and certain remarks can hardly apply to countries like Egypt or Persia, as noted by A. W. Gomme (1945) on 1.6.1: "Living under arms was customary always, as it was for barbarians."

This point of view may explain certain perhaps doubtful opinions about details. So in his view, the χιτών ("tunic") went from Athens to Ionia; to Herodotus (5.87–88), that garment came from Ionia and was originally Carian. This hypothesis accords with the Semitic origin of the word, and also with the fact that linen was cultivated in Asia.[46] Thucydides, however, is not a curious enough traveler that he would have conceived such an idea regarding the question, and his reasoning, not motivated to imagine Asiatic influences, rather leads him to see in whatever was Greek, and especially Athenian, the principle of what is seen elsewhere.

---

46. Ultimately, moreover, whatever the situation in Athens, it is certainly in Asia Minor where we first hear about Ἰάονες ἑλκεχίτωνες, "Ionians with trailing tunics" (*Iliad* 13.685). It is, however, the latter evidence that could have been guiding Thucydides.

Only one history interests him: the one leading from barbarism to the Athenian Empire.

Continuity

In this way, because it is overly centered and overly unified, the account is also simplified in its lines. Not only does Thucydides leave in the shadows the fact that other civilizations coexisted; he neglects equally that to some extent they form a sequence. And, by omitting external influences, he also omits even more the high points and the low, the ends and the new beginnings.

In particular, he offers no scope for imagining what excavations have revealed regarding, for example, the heights attained by Cretan civilization and the decline following the end of the Mycenaean period.

In his presentation of the facts, instability and piracy came first, followed by the advances of Minos. But could he have suspected what those advances were? If he had known, as we do, about the splendors of Crete, would he have said in chapter 6 that the Athenians were the first to lay aside the weapons that the prevalence of piracy had made necessary? If he had known, as we do, about the ports of Crete,[47] could he have stated so confidently that coastal cities were a later development than cities in the interior? These two errors—if that is not too strong a word—are the result of the manner in which Thucydides presents a theory of progress. In reality, archaeological discoveries have shown that during the Minoan era commerce was flourishing in the Aegean Sea, and inversely that the end of the Mycenaean period and the era of the Dorian invasion, though poorly understood, were marked by upheavals that were certainly the result of renewed piracy. A. W. Gomme (1945, 119) wrote of 1.12.3: "The eleventh and tenth centuries were, to judge from their material remains, a time of poverty and disorder, far less civilized than the preceding centuries, with scarcely any of that free communication between the different districts that is a characteristic

---

47. Even in Greece itself there is evidence of very old settlements on the coast; although these were not great centers, there are several examples, including Brauron, Eleusis, Epidaurus, and Nauplion. Particularly in Crete, there were numerous ports: Mochlos, Pseira, Zakro, Palaikastro; while Knossos is about five kilometers from the sea, Mallia, which was inhabited during the Minoan period, is separated by only a thin strip of land, and Gournia is in a small valley mostly open to the sea.

of the later Bronze Age." But how would Thucydides have known about successive modifications? Does he not use, as proof of the existence of piracy before Minos, Homeric texts? His account suggests a fairly constant evolution, leading from piracy to commerce; in that evolution, a series of advances, though they are not immediately widely adopted, at least pave the way for what follows and are not completely different from it.

One even wonders to what extent Thucydides does adopt such an evolution from start to finish. Clearly, it is present in each of the two groups of chapters covering, in one (1.2–11), the origins of the Trojan War and, in the other (1.12–19), the time since the Trojan War. Between these two groups the sequence is more in doubt. The structure of the account, and also that of the history, appear in a very different light, according to whether one sees in that continuity or a new beginning.

There is no doubt, obviously, that the Trojan War marked the end of an epoch and the beginning of another. It is very likely that the passage in 1.2, in which are juxtaposed "the period before and the still older epochs" (τὰ γὰρ πρὸ αὐτῶν καὶ τὰ ἔτι παλαίτερα), refers to the distinction between these two periods. In any case, the period leading up to the Trojan War belongs to the realm of legend, and Thucydides relies on evidence drawn from the poets; the period following belongs to history, and those facts are dated with precision.[48] That break is even more marked in the narrative itself, since, beginning with chapter 3, Thucydides specifically says that his words will be valid throughout the period preceding the Trojan War (πρὸ γὰρ τῶν Τρωικῶν); he repeats this "terminus" at the end of that chapter and at the end of 8, and he continues to emphasize the expedition against Troy until the end of 11; after that, a clear transition marks the beginning of a new period (ἐπεὶ καὶ μετὰ τὰ Τρωϊκά . . . , "since also after the Trojan War . . .".[49] In fact it would not be surprising to find in that a distinction very natural to historians and one often used by them.[50]

---

48. The migration of the Boeotians in Boeotia and the Dorian invasion (1.12.3) are the first two dated events, and also the first two events mentioned that occur after the Trojan War.

49. This break appears in analyses, though in different ways, offered by the scholia on 1.4 and 1.12. The importance of the break has been contested by Classen and Steup but upheld by Schadewaldt (1929) and Täubler (1927).

50. See Diodorus 4.1: "Ephorus of Cumae, a disciple of Isocrates, having chosen to write a universal history, was silent on anything that was drawn from ancient mythology, and his work began with the return of the Heraclids. Also, Callisthenes and Theopompus."

In striking contrast, some have wished to give even greater contrast to this break: E. Täubler has tried to establish that the entire second part was a reproduction of the first, and that chapter 12 in particular reproduced chapter 2 exactly.

In fact, the parallels are remarkable. Like chapter 2, chapter 12 is about instability: τὸ μεταναστάσεις ("migrations") in one corresponds μετανίσταντο ("they migrated") in the other; and οὐ πάλαι βεβαίως ("not securely in ancient times") of the first to μόλις τε . . . ἐν πολλῷ χρόνῳ . . . βεβαίως ("at last . . . after a long time securely") in the second. As in chapter 2, this instability poses an obstacle to development in Greece: τὸ μὴ ὁμοίως αὐξηθῆναι ("increased by migrations unlike the rest") in one there is a corresponding μὴ ἡσυχάσασα αὐξηθῆναι ("without security and an increase in population") in the other. And lastly, as in chapter 2, the idea of this instability leads Thucydides to an insight regarding colonization: corresponding very rigorously to ἀποικίας ἐξέπεμψε ("sent colonies") is ἀποικίας ἐξέπεμψε in the other.

Are we then to believe that Thucydides, far from being unaware of the decline that marked the end of the Mycenaean period, is so strongly aware of it that he makes his history begin again with that decline, thus introducing all of what some have called the "Greek Middle Ages" between the end of chapter 11 and the beginning of chapter 12?

A deeper study of the text suggests a different explanation.

First, we should not find the parallels in the text too arresting. The fact that there are recurring themes is not surprising, and I have tried to show how this is in fact a systematic rule in the entire Archaeology. Moreover, when we look even more closely, we see, for example, that the colonization found in chapter 2 echoes that of chapter 12 only because it is the same: it appears in the beginning only in an allusion, in anticipation, in a remark about the development of Athens. Thus the parallelisms seen here are not very different from others,[51] and we should not rush to infer from the dialectical repetition of a theme a retrograde repetition of history itself.

Such an explanation is actually difficult to reconcile with the text as a whole. There is nothing in it that suggests starting over, while everything suggests continuity: in the following chapter, speaking of the acquisition

---

51. Likewise the two developments that Täubler considers parallel in the following coincide only slightly.

of wealth, Thucydides does not say that Greece was again engaged in the acquisition of wealth, but that it was "more engaged than ever before." And in chapter 12 itself, we need only look at the words of introduction: these are only look at the words of introduction: these are ἐπεί ("since") and καί ("and");[52] ἐπεί unarguably gives it a causal meaning, and καί just as unarguably implies an idea of continuity. Had Thucydides wished to suggest an idea of a new beginning, he would not have written ἐπεί, and in place of καί, he would have written αὖθις or πάλιν; or at least we would find one or the other of these words somewhere in the account.

Instead, the words he does use become perfectly clear when we study closely the mode of argumentation that governs the composition of the whole.

The text is not in fact a narrative; besides all the instances of reasoning whose presence has been noted in the account, there is still one, one of the boldest, that governs the exposition in general.

This reasoning consists in proving in every case the inferiority of an epoch using the advances that were made subsequently. Of course in the beginning Thucydides provides some direct assertions of the weakness of Greece in the most ancient periods; but starting with the end of chapter 3, he mentions the advances that continue to be made up until the Trojan War, and the following chapters prove their existence: "Even that expedition did not unite them until maritime activity was more advanced. For Minos . . .". That function of the account is repeated twice: when we reach the period of the Trojan War (1.8.4: "And these conditions were even more noticeable later when the expedition against Troy took place"), and when he prepares to assess its importance (1.9.5: "So this expedition ought to give us some idea about what had preceded it").

So the characteristics specific to ancient Greece are deduced from the advances made between the earliest times and the Trojan War. But the same was true after that. The Trojan War was really just one stop along a journey. Thucydides says that it was more important than anything before it, but less important than events today (1.10.3); and, to prove this, he first shows its limits in a direct analysis (1.10–11), and then, just as before, he

---

52. See also the words of the conclusion: πάντα δὲ ταῦτα ὕστερον τῶν Τρωικῶν ἐκτίσθη ("All these foundations occurred later than the Trojan War"); these seem to show that at the time of the Trojan War (before, during, and just after) such installations would have been impossible.

joins to it a *proof* drawn from the advances remaining to be made (1.12: ἐπεὶ καὶ μετὰ τὰ Τρωικά . . . , "Since even after the Trojan War . . ."), the formulation of which begins in chapter 13.

Moreover, this account will not reach modern times, since it too, at the end of chapter 17, ends in the idea of further progress to be made: "Thus for a long time all sorts of reasons restrained Greece . . .".

Thus the reasoning consists in describing what went before by a contrast with what followed, and thereby alternating, for each successive period, a positive point of view with a negative one. Ancient times are judged by the work of Minos and Agamemnon—the weaknesses of the Trojan War and the subsequent years are made apparent by comparison with the maritime advances that follow them—and even that progress is put in perspective by comparison with the most recent advances of modern times.

Moreover, this type of reasoning is so natural for Thucydides that we find it reflected even within the argument. In particular the history of maritime progress is twice interrupted by a restrictive conclusion, showing that we have not yet reached modern times: in 1.14.1 we see that this progress still (ἔτι) includes few triremes;[53] this leads to the history of the development of the trireme; and, once again, in 1.14.3 we see that Greek fleets are characteristically both late and delayed (οὔπω, "not yet"), beginning with the Athenian.[54]

This sense of historical progress explains a variety of characteristics in the text and may explain the direction that the account takes here. It is surprising, in fact, that the Archaeology looks so far back in time.

Thucydides recalls, in both the introduction and the conclusion, the difficulty that he had in investigating little-known facts; even if we alter the first sentence,[55] we still need to explain how Thucydides can combine, in

---

53. Thucydides, as in the entire first part, takes special care to remind us, when the first progress is achieved, that its role is to shed more light on the inadequacies of the previous period; and in the same way, the introduction of the developments leading to colonization ended with a caution: πάντα δὲ ταῦτα ὕστερον τῶν Τρωικῶν ἐκτίσθη ("All these foundations were made after the Trojan War"), just as that of maritime advances is accompanied by a cautionary note: πολλαῖς γενεαῖς ὕστερα γενόμενα τῶν Τρωικῶν ("These things happened many generations later than the Trojan War").

54. ὄψε τε ("and late") in 1.14.3 plays the same role with respect to the argument as the information in 1.3.4, 1.12.4, and 1.14.3.

55. On the suggested corrections for τὰ γὰρ πρὸ αὐτῶν ("the things before them"), see the corresponding note in my edition; I agreed that one could preserve the text, considering that the part of the sentence relative to the difficulty about information referred primarily to τὰ ἔτι παλαίτερα, which followed it.

the conclusion in which he treats "ancient facts" (1.20.1: τὰ παλαιά) and the caution about information (1.21), an account that actually goes all the way to the present time. Even acknowledging that he is thinking especially of the heroic period and the Trojan War, the disjuncture is nevertheless rather large. Steup felt this and concluded that chapters 18 and 19 are out of place.[56]

That might be true if these chapters occurred in the text as directly relating to the subject, to the thesis. When we observe, however, the way the text is constructed, it becomes obvious that their role is somewhat indirect. They serve as proof of the epoch of tyranny, which itself in turn serves as proof for the preceding period, and so on. They belong to the argument, but not to the thesis being argued. Likewise, the real judgment about the period to which they relate will be given later, in a direct manner; it is found in chapter 23. These chapters are simply the evidence of a different period.

The final example of an apparent oddity in the Archaeology serves therefore in its turn to draw our attention to the last of the reasonings that form its framework. This is possibly the most natural one of all, but it is also the most risky. It suggests that, in the absence of evidence to the contrary, we can attribute to history a progression that always moves in the same direction. That progress may fluctuate between high moments, stagnation, and even regression; Minos had eradicated piracy once; the Corinthians did so in their turn. But overall, and viewed very broadly, it develops in a single direction.

Certainly such a representation is the most normal; and, when there are not many reference points to keep in mind, it is legitimate to trace the simplest line between those known. Yet the less firmly established the facts involved, the less prudent that approach is seen to be; the mind-set that encourages this lack of prudence is that of rationalism. Herodotus, who was not very interested in tracking major paths of development, being guided only by his curiosity and having only his own inquiries as a source of information, came up with a quite different theory of history; indeed, the preamble of his work concludes with these words (1.3–4): "I shall . . . proceed

---

56. "From this it necessarily results that 20–21 cannot have always been separated from 17 by 18 and 19." (Hieraus ergiebt sich mit Notwendigkeit, dass die c. 20 und 21 nicht immer durch c. 18 und 19 von c. 17 getrennt gewesen sein können.)

with the rest of my story recounting alike human cities both small and great, since many of those that were great long ago have become small, and some that are great in my own time were small before. And so, persuaded that human prosperity never remains fixed in the same place, I shall make mention of both without discrimination." Thucydides obviously would argue no differently; he knows that history shows, for every city, both high and low points; he knows that the Mycenaeans were once powerful, and can well imagine the end of both Lacedaemonian and Athenian power. Nevertheless, whereas Herodotus's history opens with the reflection on this unpredictable fluctuation, that of Thucydides situates itself right from the start on a broad enough basis to allow for continuity: by looking at Greece generally, rather than this or that city, at material conditions of existence and power, not at this or that historical event, from the outset, he removes variation in favor of unity. How could he have been able, by reason alone, to find his way back to something that, by nature, eludes it?

The Method in General

The criticisms that can be brought against Thucydides' reconstruction come down to a single one: it is precisely his reasoning that gives to a certain term in a passage a modern glint, his selecting, orienting, casting light wherever he likes, his holding back and channeling. He plays down the barbarian civilizations and the difference between the glory of Crete and the obscurity of the post-Mycenaean age.

In general, however, the sum of all these critiques amounts to little. The only real objection concerns just this absence of differentiation between successive moments in development. Although it is true that Thucydides was free not to mention—or leave open to surmise—a continuity about which he was uninformed, it would have been impossible for him to have foreseen a diversity about which he had no information either. The worst criticism is thus a negative one. It bears on what is missing; it exposes an impossibility. With a little more information, Thucydides would have been protected against it.

In other words, the very nature of the criticisms shows that, if Thucydides' method alone did not allow him to construct a reality about which he lacked sufficient evidence, inversely, that method must have been entirely adequate to do so, once the research had been completed and particularly in all the rest of the work where research had been carried out with a rigor that is well known (1.22.2): ὅσον δυνατὸν ἀκριβείᾳ περὶ ἑκάστου ἐπεξελθών, "after examining as exactly as possible in detail."

Because it acts alone, and without a great deal of information, reason runs risks here that it does not encounter elsewhere. That is why it is presented here in such an intense form. Because it is working alone, and daring to do something new and rare, it unleashes all its possibilities, all its resources; it is not afraid openly to proclaim their existence. The text compiles reasonings and methodological research; that is what gives it its value, what makes it, in one sense, such a noble testament. That is also, at least as it seems to me, what explains its oddities and its difficulties.

If, however, owing to this dual trait, the Archaeology differs from the rest of the work, it should be remembered that the difference is, ultimately, only one of degree. The reasoning is more original, more frequent; but the principle is found elsewhere. We have shown in fact in preceding chapters that in order to construct his account Thucydides chooses to bring out connections, lines of explanation, linkages. The relationship of the narrative to the speeches and of the speeches to each other only reinforces those lines of explanation and draws them together more closely. But in his very choice of these lines, how could Thucydides have proceeded in any way other than that of the Archaeology? When he describes the causes of the war, he deals with factors whose origins, lying in a past of which little is known, the Archaeology broadly examines. The presence of numerous details helps to make the method more certain but does not change its principle; their presence clarifies the selection but does not render it unnecessary. And the account, while stopping along its journey at all the stages of exactitude, nevertheless remains the construction, the hypothesis, and the argument of Thucydides.

Thus the Archaeology shows with exceptional power and intensity the qualities that characterize Thucydides' own method and cast of mind. It also in turn displays with exceptional power those qualities that characterize his entire work. In that case, this short text, with all its peculiarities, its audacities, and its gaps, may stand as the farthest point reached by the historical genre in this direction, at the moment when, straining to reduce the subject entirely to its own laws, reasoning manages at last with a supreme effort to project the single clearest and sharpest image of all, an image of itself.

Conclusion

The more closely one studies Thucydides' work, the more its structure reveals a subtle organization. Not a word is randomly chosen, and actions are organized throughout it in coherent groups; the lines become clear; goals are contrasted to outcomes. The arguments are sharpened and recur, gradually revealing an uncompromising judgment. Reasonings are woven together to seek a truth—whether they discover it or invent it, we can no longer say for certain. All these different procedures are always intended to ease a transposition through which, gradually, everything is meaningful, each element fitting into a clear system of intelligible relationships in which the how and the why are registered with equal precision.

This predominant characteristic notwithstanding, we should not lose sight of the fact that Thucydides' work remains, above all, a history. And the great value of the transposition he effects is that it does so in the form of a narrative, in which nothing is forced or falsified. Rigor is not in fact incompatible with animation or flexibility. In Thucydides' account there are people, facts, and deeds, each clearly distinctive. Circumstances determine how each part is framed. One battle is not described exactly like another, nor is one speech composed like the one next to it. Most importantly, we never shift from a narrative into a demonstration, or from an isolated fact into a general rule. The account may draw evidence from the demonstration; an isolated fact implies the potential repetition; but Thucydides never confirms anything himself; as a result, he never risks saying too much. In his eyes history should always reach toward absolute intelligibility, though it never claims for all that to be able to attain it.

And this dual character of historical work, of the *historia rerum gestarum*, "the story of things done," may also define his attitude toward historical development, the *res gestae*, "things done."

Clearly the entire work of Thucydides implies its rational character. There is no doubt that the connections that his narrative establishes exist in his eyes between the facts themselves, independently of the thought that grasps them. When he rigorously presents an extensive system of cause and effect, he obviously supposes that reality was shaped by those links. One can say even more. For the elements that he strives to organize do not appear as if unexpectedly to play roles of which we can merely take note. As much as possible, Thucydides gives these elements a place in a dialectical whole. He indicates to what extent one might account for them in advance, predict their action, make use of them, or alter their intervention. As a result, he supposes that there may be a certain number of laws, or constants, that events must ordinarily obey.

To answer the question of the extent to which history, as Thucydides conceives it, is capable of discovering these laws would require a separate study. Nevertheless there are two comments that can be made here.

First, it is obvious that Thucydides tends to recognize these laws wherever he can. His speeches are all laden with generalizations, from the most banal maxims to the most sweeping political analyses. The narrative is supported by these analyses; the narrative also contributes, by its very contents, to exposing general relationships, since, their main lines being retraced and related to their deepest causes, events themselves take on an exemplary quality, and their sequences become capable of recurrence. A single political necessity gives unity to a large series of facts; a single strategic difficulty explains a whole series of military events—not to speak of the fact that a single characteristic is found constantly through the entire development of Greece in ancient times. There are laws for human endeavors; and it is possible to find, amid its diverse crises, affiliations that lend themselves to classification and provide the best basis for action.

But if, because of such qualities, Thucydides' account sometimes seems to tend toward a kind of sociology, it is quite clear that none of these rules ever claims universality. The sequences that he exposes may correspond to a probability—and even this he does not formulate plainly; they could not claim in any case to be anything more. They do not allow the least degree of speculation about either the near or distant future, nor even the outcome of any situation that might perhaps recall conditions combined in his account. The chance of randomness and individual freedom always retain their role. Even the most enduring conditions (such as those that the Archaeology brings to light) have no reason not to change some day.

We should not conclude from this that reasoning, as sovereign as it may be regarding the past, is useless with regard to the future. Reasoning cannot know or predict the future, but it can collaborate on it. Even if it is unsure of a result, reasoning must, it seems, strive to use all its powers to clarify an action. This, at least, is what emerges brilliantly in Thucydides' work. By engaging in such thorough analyses after the fact, he most certainly teaches us how to engage in them before acting. The whole history is really nothing but a series of experiments by which a distinction is made between more correct calculations and less correct ones. It supposes the existence of an intelligence both political and military, one capable of greatly minimizing uncertainty. And this is also the meaning of Pericles' fine statements in the Funeral Oration when he affirms the value of the debate (2.40.2): "Speech is not in our eyes an obstacle to action: what *is* rather an obstacle is not to be informed in advance by speech before going to do what one must." And Diodotus later takes up the same notion (3.42.2): "Whoever claims that words do not clarify deeds is a fool, or biased; it is foolish to believe that there is any other way of explaining the uncertainty of what will happen." But even these reasonings, which have undergone debate, can always be taken by surprise; Pericles, who is throughout the work the most admirable example of a man who knows how to think rationally about policy and calculate every step, ends by failing; and that is not surprising ultimately, for it is also he who reminds us (1.140.1): "Events that occur can sometimes proceed with less sense than human intentions; that is why for things that happen contrary to reasoning we usually blame chance."

In his manner of envisioning the action, as in his historical methodology, Thucydides shows the same conjoined leanings: he puts the claims of reasoning above all else, and he uses every means possible, to the greatest extent possible, to support them. But the very faith he brings to that effort is all the more worthy of our admiration in that nonetheless, at no instant and in no area, does he ever forget their limitations.

WORKS CITED

Abbott, G. F. 1925. *Thucydides, a Study in Historical Reality*. London: Routledge.

Allen, T. W. 1921. *The Homeric Catalogue of Ships*. Oxford: Clarendon Press.

Beloch, Karl Julius. 1914. *Griechische Geschichte*. Vol. 2, pts. 1–2. Strasbourg: Karl Trüber.

Bodin, Louis. 1914. "La bataille de Naupacte." *Revue des études grecques* 27: xlix–l. Abstract of a communication delivered at a meeting of the Association des Études Grecques, February 14, 1914.

——. 1935. "Thucydide et la campagne de Brasidas en Thrace: Remarques sur la composition de l'exposé." In *Mélanges offerts à Octave Navarre par ses élèves et ses amis*, 47–55. Toulouse: E. Privat.

——. 1939. "Alcibiade interprète à Sparte de l'appel des Syracusains au Péloponnèse." In *Actes du Congrès de Strasbourg, 20–22 avril 1938, Association G. Budé*, 89–90. Paris: Les Belles Lettres.

——. 1940. "Diodote contre Cléon: Quelques aperçus sur la dialectique de Thucydides." *Revue des études anciennes* 42: 36–52.

——. 1975. *Lire le Protagoras: Introduction à la méthode dialectique de Protagoras*. Edited by Paul Demont. Paris: Les Belles Lettres.

Bourguet, E. 1919. "Sur la composition du Phèdre." *Revue de métaphysique et de morale* 26: 335–51.

Bousquet, Jean, and Youry Fomine. 1952. *Le trésor de Cyrène*. Fouilles de Delphes, vol. 2, Topographie et architecture. Paris: E. de Boccard.

Classen, Johannes, and Julius Steup. 1892–1922. *Thukydides, erklärt von J. Classen, bearbeitet von Julius Steup*. 8 vols. Berlin: Weidmann.

Cornford, F. 1907. *Thucydides Mythistoricus*. London: Edward Arnold.

Croiset, Alfred. 1886. *La poésie de Pindare et les lois du lyrisme grec*. Paris: Hachette.

Dain, Alphonse, and Paul Mazon. 1950. *Sophocle*. Vol. 1, *Les trachiniennes, Antigone*. Collection des Universités de France. Paris: Les Belles Lettres.

Diels, Hermann, and Walther Kranz. 1951. *Die Fragmente der Vorsokratiker, griechisch und deutsch*. 6th ed. Berlin: Weidmann.

Duchemin, Jacqueline. 1968. *L'agon dans la tragédie grecque*. 2nd ed. Paris: Les Belles Lettres. First published in 1948.

Dupréel, Eugène. 1948. *Les sophistes: Protagoras, Gorgias, Prodicus, Hippias*. Bibliothèque Scientifique, vol. 14, Philosophie et histoire. Neuchâtel: Éditions du Griffon.

Ehrenberg, Victor. 1954. *Sophocles and Pericles*. Oxford: Blackwell.

Festugière, A. J. 1936. *Contemplation et vie contemplative selon Platon*. Paris: J. Vrin.

Finley, John Huston. 1940. "The Unity of Thucydides' History." In *Harvard Studies in Classical Philology* Suppl. 1, 255–97. Republished in 1967 in J. H. Finley, *Three Essays on Thucydides* (Cambridge, MA: Harvard University Press), 118–70.

———. 1942. *Thucydides*. Cambridge, MA: Harvard University Press.

Glotz, Gustave, and Robert Cohen. 1931. *Histoire grecque*. Vol. 2, *La Grèce au Ve siècle*. Paris: Presses Universitaires de France.

Gomme, A. W. 1945. *Historical Commentary on Thucydides*. Vol. 1, *Introduction and Commentary on Book I*. Oxford: Oxford University Press.

———. 1954. *The Greek Attitude to Poetry and History*. Sather Classical Lectures 27. Berkeley: University of California Press.

Hammond, N. G. L. 1952. "The Arrangement of Thought in the Proem and in Other Parts of Thucydides I." *Classical Quarterly* 2: 127–41.

Kannicht, Richard. 2004. *Tragicorum graecorum fragmenta (TrGF)*. Vol. 5, *Euripides*. 2 pts. Göttingen: Vandenhoeck & Ruprecht.

Koyré, Alexandre. 1945. *Introduction à la lecture de Platon*. New York: Brentano's.

Lamb, W. R. M. 1914. *Clio Enthroned, a Study in Prose-Form in Thucydides*. Cambridge: Cambridge University Press.

Legrand, Ph.-E. 1932. *Herodote, Histoires*. Collection des Universités de France. Paris: Les Belles Lettres.

Luschnat, Otto. 1942. *Die Feldherrnreden im Geschichtswerk des Thucydides*. Philologus Suppl. 34.2. Leipzig: Dieterich'sche Verlagsbuchhandlung.

Marbot, Jean-Baptiste. 1988. *The Memoirs of Baron de Marbot*. Translated by Arthur John Butler. London: Greenhill Books, Lionel Leventhal Limited.

Mazon, Paul. 1948. *Introduction à l'Iliade*. Collection des Universités de France. Paris: Les Belles Lettres.

Meyer, Eduard. 1928. *Geschichte des Altertums*. Vol. 2, *Die Zeit der ägyptischen Grossmacht*. Stuttgart and Berlin: J. G. Cotta'sche Buchhandlung Nachfolger.

Münch, H. 1935. *Studien zu den Exkursen des Thukydides*. Heidelberg: Bilabel.

Navarre, Octave. 1900. *Essai sur la rhétorique grecque avant Aristote*. Paris: Hachette.

Nilsson, Martin P. 1932. *The Mycenaean Origin of Greek Mythology*. Sather Classical Lectures 8. Berkeley: University of California Press.

Norwood, Gilbert. 1945. *Pindar*. Sather Classical Lectures 19. Berkeley: University of California Press.

Pearson, Lionel. 1939. "Thucydides and the Geographical Tradition." *Classical Quarterly* 33: 48–54.

Poulsen, Frederik. 1909. "Fragment d'un grand vase funéraire découvert à Delos." *Monuments et mémoires de la Fondation Eugène Piot* 16: 25–37.

Robert, Fernand. 1950. *Homère*. Paris: Presses Universitaires de France.

Robin, L. 1933. *Platon, Phèdre*. Collection des Universités de France. Paris: Les Belles Lettres.

Romilly, Jacqueline de. 1954. "À propos des commentaires de Thucydide sur la guerre de Troie." *Revue du nord* 36 (142): 105–9.

———. 1955. Review of *The Greek Attitude to Poetry and History*, by A. W. Gomme. *Revue de philologie, de littérature et d'histoire anciennes* 29: 252–53.

———. 1963. *Thucydides and Athenian Imperialism*. Translated by Philip Thody. Oxford: Basil Blackwell.

Romilly, Jacqueline de, Raymond Weil, and Louis Bodin. 1953–72. *Thucydide, La guerre du Péloponnèse*. Collection Guillaume Budé. Paris: Les Belles Lettres.

Schadewaldt, Wolfgang. 1929. *Die Geschichtschreibung des Thukydides und die thukydidesische Frage*. Berlin: Weidmann.

Schaerer, René. 1938. *La question platonicienne: Étude sur les rapports de la pensée et de l'expression dans les Dialogues*. Mémoires de l'Université de Neuchâtel 10. Neuchâtel: Secrétariat de l'Université.

Schmid, Wilhelm, and Wilhelm von Christ. 1929. "Thukydides." In *Geschichte der griechischen Literatur*, 5:3–223. Handbuch der Altertumswissenschaft, founded by Iwan von Müller; new ed. by Walter Otto, sect. 7, pt. 1. Munich: C. H. Beck.

Steup, Julius. See Classen and Steup 1892–1922.

Täubler, Eugen. 1927. *Die Archäologie des Thukydides*. Leipzig: Teubner.

Thibaudet, Albert. 1990. "La campagne avec Thucydide." In *Thucydide: Histoire de la guerre du Peloponnèse, traduction, introduction, notes*, edited by J. de Romilly, 3–140. Paris: Robert Laffont. Originally published in 1922.

Tsountas, Christos. 1899. "Κυκλαδικά II." Ἀρχαιολογική Ἐφημερίς: 74–134.

Ure, P. N. 1922. *The Origin of Tyranny*. Cambridge: Cambridge University Press.

Voilquin, Jean, trans. 1948. *Thucydide, Histoire de la guerre du Péloponnèse*. 2 vols. Paris: Garnier Frères. Translation and introduction by Jean Voilquin; notes by Jean Capelle.

Wassermann, F. M. 1947. "The Melian Dialogue." *Transactions of the American Philological Association* 78: 18–36.

Weidauer, Klaus. 1954. *Thukydides und die Hippokratischen Schriften: Der Einfluss der Medizin auf Zielsetzung und Darstellungsweise des Geschichtswerks*. Heidelberger Forschungen. Heidelberg: C. Winter.

Weil, Éric. 1951. "La place de la logique dans la pensée Aristotelicienne." *Revue de métaphysique et de morale* 56: 283–315. Reprinted in E. Weil, *Essais et Conférences*, vol. 1, *Philosophie* (Paris: Vrin, 1991), 43–80.

Zuntz, Günther. 1955. *The Political Plays of Euripides*. Manchester: Manchester University Press.

Index of Thucydidean Passages Discussed

Bold indicates a full study of the passage; * indicates passages which are the primary object of analysis in chapters 1 or 4, and which are not indexed more precisely.

General Index